SHADOW *and* ACT

SHADOW *and* ACT

by Ralph Ellison

VINTAGE BOOKS
A Division of Random House / New York

FIRST VINTAGE BOOKS EDITION, February 1972

ISBN: 0-394-71716-3

Library of Congress Catalog Card Number: 64-18928

MANUFACTURED IN THE UNITED STATES OF AMERICA

The author wishes to thank the following for permission to reprint material:

"That Same Pain, That Same Pleasure: An Interview." Reprinted with permission from *December* Magazine, vol. III, no. 2, Winter 1961. Copyright © 1961 by December Corporation.

"Twentieth-Century Fiction and the Black Mask of Humanity." Copyright 1953 by the President and Fellows of Harvard College.

"Change the Joke and Slip the Yoke." *Partisan Review,* vol. XXV, no. 2, Spring 1958.

"Stephen Crane and the Mainstream of American Fiction," an Introduction to *The Red Badge of Courage and Four Great Stories by Stephen Crane.* Copyright © 1960 by Ralph Ellison. Reprinted by permission of Dell Publishing Co., Inc.

"Richard Wright's Blues." Reprinted with permission from the *Antioch Review,* vol. 3, no. 2. Copyright 1945 by The Antioch Press. Material from *Black Boy* by Richard Wright (Harper & Brothers, 1945) appears by permission of Harper & Row, Publishers, Incorporated; material quoted from "Black Boys and Native Sons" (*Dissent,* Autumn 1963) appears by permission of the author, Irving Howe.

"Beating That Boy." Reprinted by permission of *The New Republic.*

"The World and the Jug." Reprinted by permission from *The New Leader* of December 9, 1963. "A Rejoinder" (published originally as "People Are Living Under Here"), by permission from *The New Leader* of February 3, 1964. Material from Irving Howe's "Black Boys and Native Sons" appearing in these articles is quoted by permission of the author.

"The Art of Fiction: An Interview." *Paris Review,* Spring 1955, and *Writers At Work: The Paris Review Interviews,* Second Series. Reprinted by permission of The Viking Press, Inc.

"Living with Music." *High Fidelity,* December 1955.

"The Golden Age, Time Past." First published in *Esquire* Magazine © 1958 by Esquire, Inc.

"As the Spirit Moves Mahalia," "On Bird, Bird-Watching, and Jazz," "The Charlie Christian Story," and "Remembering Jimmy." By permission of the author and *Saturday Review.*

"Blues People" appeared originally as "The Blues" in *The New York Review,* vol. 1, no. 12.

"Some Questions and Some Answers." *Preuves,* May 1958. By permission.

"The Shadow and The Act." By permission of *The Reporter.* Copyright 1949 by Fortnightly Publishing Company.

"The Way It Is," from *The Negro and Victory,* vol. XLV, *New Masses.* By permission of Dialogue Publications.

FOR

Morteza Sprague

A DEDICATED DREAMER IN A

LAND MOST STRANGE

Contents

Contents /

Introduction

When the first of these essays was published I regarded myself—in my most secret heart at least—a musician. This was the result, in part, of a complicated, semiconscious strategy of self-deception, a refusal by my right hand to recognize where my left hand was headed. Actually I had been devoting as much time and energy to reading and writing as to music, and was passionately engaged, night and noon, in acquiring the basic knowledge and skills of the novelist. Thus the earliest, most agonizingly written pieces presented here (none has been retouched) were the results of a crucial conflict raging deep within me, the products of an activity, dreamlike yet intense, which was waxing on the dark side of my mind and assuming even then a major importance in shaping my life. In this sense, writing was an acting-out, symbolically, of a choice which I dared not acknowledge. Indeed, I repressed it beneath my old concern with music and my current involvement in the intense social and political activity which claimed so many of us who came of age during the thirties.

One might say that with these thin essays for wings I was launched full flight into the dark.

At stake here, beyond the veil of consciousness, was the question of what seemed possible for me in terms of self-achievement, and linked to this was the question of what was the most desirable agency for defining myself. Writing provided me a growing satisfaction and required, unlike music, no formal study—but the designation "writer" seemed to me most unreal. Not only this, for despite the naïveté of my involvement with literature—and ignoring the crucial question of talent—my standards were impossibly high. Therefore, the chances of my producing anything of quality seemed nonexistent. Besides, I still believed that my real self was destined to be fulfilled in music, that art which had focused my ambitions from the age of eight and the only art, given my background, that seemed to offer some possibility for self-definition. Obviously I was still quite young and, fortunately, still given to play and adventure.

For in the beginning writing was far from a serious matter, it was playing with the secret lore of a fascinating but less glorious art to which I owed, I believed, no prior dedication. (It would be many years before I was to learn of my father's hope that I would become a poet.) Nor had I invested in writing any long hours of practice and study. Rather it was a reflex of reading, an extension of a source of pleasure, escape and instruction. In fact, I had become curious about writing by way of seeking to understand the aesthetic nature of literary power, the devices through which literature could command my mind and emotions. It was not, then, the *process* of writing which initially claimed my attention, but the finished creations, the artifacts—poems, plays, novels. The act of learning writing technique was, therefore, an amusing investigation of what seemed at best a secondary talent, an exploration, like dabbling in sculpture, of one's potentialities as a "renaissance man." This, surely, would seem a most unlikely and even comic concept to introduce here; and yet it is precisely because I come from where I do (the Oklahoma of the years between World War I and the Great Depression) that I must introduce it, and with a straight face.

Anything and everything was to be found in the chaos of

Oklahoma; thus the concept of the Renaissance Man has lurked long within the shadow of my past, and I shared it with at least a half dozen of my Negro friends. How we actually acquired it I have never learned, and since there is no true sociology of the dispersion of ideas within the American democracy, I doubt if I ever shall. Perhaps we breathed it in with the air of the Negro community of Oklahoma City, the capital of that state whose Negroes were often charged by exasperated white Texans with not knowing their "place." Perhaps we took it defiantly from one of them. Or perhaps I myself picked it up from some transplanted New Englander whose shoes I had shined of a Saturday afternoon. After all, the most meaningful tips do not always come in the form of money, nor are they intentionally extended. Most likely, however, my friends and I acquired the idea from some book or from some idealistic Negro teacher, some dreamer seeking to function responsibly in an environment which at its most normal took on some of the mixed character of nightmare and of dream.

One thing is certain, ours was a chaotic community, still characterized by frontier attitudes and by that strange mixture of the naïve and sophisticated, the benign and malignant, which makes the American past so puzzling and its present so confusing; that mixture which often affords the minds of the young who grow up in the far provinces such wide and unstructured latitude, and which encourages the individual's imagination—up to the moment "reality" closes in upon him—to range widely and, sometimes, even to soar.

We hear the effects of this in the southwestern jazz of the thirties, that joint creation of artistically free and exuberantly creative adventurers, of artists who had stumbled upon the freedom lying within the restrictions of their musical tradition as within the limitations of their social background, and who in their own unconscious way have set an example for any Americans, Negro or white, who would find themselves in the arts. They accepted themselves and the complexity of life as they knew it, they loved their art and through it they celebrated American experience definitively in sound. Whatever others thought or felt, this was their own powerful statement, and only nonmusical assaults upon their artistic integrity—mainly economically inspired changes of fashion—were able to compromise their vision.

Several of the essays deal with jazz, and it is perhaps pardonable if I recall that much of so-called Kansas City jazz was actually brought to perfection in Oklahoma by Oklahomans. It is an important circumstance for me as a writer to remember, because while these musicians and their fellows were busy creating out of tradition, imagination and the sounds and emotions around them a freer, more complex and driving form of jazz, my friends and I were exploring an idea of human versatility and possibility which went against the barbs or over the palings of almost every fence which those who controlled social and political power had erected to restrict our roles in the life of the country. Looking back, one might say that the jazzmen, some of whom we idolized, were in their own way better examples for youth to follow than were most judges and ministers, legislators and governors (we were stuck with the notorious Alfalfa Bill Murray). For as we viewed these pillars of society from the confines of our segregated community we almost always saw crooks, clowns or hypocrites. Even the best were revealed by their attitudes toward us as lacking the respectable qualities to which they pretended and for which they were accepted outside by others, while despite the outlaw nature of their art, the jazzmen were less torn and damaged by the moral compromises and insincerities which have so sickened the life of our country.

Be that as it may, our youthful sense of life, like that of many Negro children (though no one bothers to note it—especially the specialists and "friends of the Negro" who view our Negro American life as essentially nonhuman) was very much like that of Huckleberry Finn, who is universally so praised and enjoyed for the clarity and courage of his moral vision. Like Huck we observed, we judged, we imitated and evaded as we could the dullness, corruption and blindness of "civilization." We were undoubtedly comic because, as the saying goes, we weren't supposed to know what it was all about. But to ourselves we were "boys," members of a wild, free outlaw tribe which transcended the category of race. Rather we were Americans born into the forty-sixth state, and thus, into the context of Negro-American post-Civil War history, "frontiersmen." And isn't one of the implicit functions of the American frontier to encourage the individual to a kind of dreamy wakefulness, a state in which he makes—in all ignorance of the accepted limitations of the possible—rash efforts, quixotic gestures, hopeful testings of the complexity of the known and the given?

Spurring us on in our controlled and benign madness, was the voracious reading of which most of us were guilty and the vicarious identification and empathic adventuring which it encouraged. This was due, in part, perhaps to the fact that some of us were fatherless—my own father had died when I was three—but most likely it was because boys are natural romantics. We were seeking examples, patterns to live by, out of a freedom which for all its being ignored by the sociologists and subtle thinkers was implicit in the Negro situation. Father and mother substitutes also have a role to play in aiding the child to help create himself. Thus we fabricated our own heroes and ideals catch-as-catch can, and with an outrageous and irreverent sense of freedom. Yes, and in complete disregard for ideas of respectability or the surreal incongruity of some of our projections. Gamblers and scholars, jazz musicians and scientists, Negro cowboys and soldiers from the Spanish-American and First World Wars, movie stars and stunt men, figures from the Italian Renaissance and literature, both classical and popular, were combined with the special virtues of some local bootlegger, the eloquence of some Negro preacher, the strength and grace of some local athlete, the ruthlessness of some businessman-physician, the elegance in dress and manners of some head-waiter or hotel doorman.

Looking back through the shadows upon this absurd activity I realize now that we were projecting archetypes, re-creating folk figures, legendary heroes, monsters even, most of which violated all ideas of social hierarchy and order and all accepted conceptions of the hero handed down by cultural, religious and racist tradition. But we, remember, were under the intense spell of the early movies, the silents as well as the talkies; and in our community, life was not so tightly structured as it would have been in the traditional South—or even in deceptively "free" Harlem. And our imaginations processed reality and dream, natural man and traditional hero, literature and folklore, like maniacal editors turned loose in some frantic film-cutting room. Remember, too, that being boys, yet in the play-stage of our development, we were dream-serious in our efforts. But serious, nevertheless, for *culturally* play is a preparation, and we felt that somehow the human ideal lay in the vague and constantly shifting figures—sometimes comic but always versatile, picaresque and self-effacingly heroic—which evolved from our wildly improvisionary projections—figures neither white nor black, Christian nor Jewish, but representative of certain desirable essences, of skills and powers physical, aesthetic and moral.

The proper response to these figures was, we felt, to develop ourselves for the performance of many and diverse roles, and the fact that certain definite limitations had been imposed upon our freedom did not lessen our sense of obligation. Not only were we to prepare but we were to perform—not with mere competence but with an almost reckless verve;

with, may we say (without evoking the quaint and questionable notion of *negritude*), Negro American style? Behind each artist there stands a traditional sense of style, a sense of the felt tension indicative of expressive completeness; a mode of humanizing reality and of evoking a feeling of being at home in the world. It is something which the artist shares with the group, and part of our boyish activity expressed a yearning to make any- and everything of quality *Negro American;* to appropriate it, possess it, re-create it in our own group and individual images.

And we recognized and were proud of our group's own style wherever we discerned it—in jazzmen and prize fighters, ballplayers and tap dancers; in gesture, inflection, intonation, timbre and phrasing. Indeed, in all those nuances of expression and attitude which reveal a culture. We did not fully understand the cost of that style but we recognized within it an affirmation of life beyond all question of our difficulties as Negroes.

Contrary to the notion currently projected by certain specialists in the "Negro problem" which characterizes the Negro American as self-hating and defensive, we did not so regard ourselves. We felt, among ourselves at least, that we were supposed to be whoever we would and could be and do anything and everything which other boys did, and do it better. Not defensively, because we were ordered to do so; nor because it was held in the society at large that we were naturally, as Negroes, limited—but because we demanded it of ourselves. Because to measure up to our own standards was the only way of affirming our notion of manhood.

Hence it was no more incongruous, as seen from our own particular perspective in this land of incongruities, for young Negro Oklahomans to project themselves as Renaissance Men than for white Mississippians to see themselves as ancient Greeks or noblemen out of Sir Walter Scott. Surely our fantasies have caused far less damage to the nation's sense of reality, if for no other reason than that ours were expressive of a more democratic ideal. Remember, too, as William Faulkner made us so vividly aware, that the slaves often took the essence of the aristocratic ideal (as they took Christianity) with far more seriousness than their masters, and that we, thanks to the tight telescoping of American history, were but two generations from that previous condition. Renaissance Men, indeed!

I managed, by keeping quiet about it, to cling to our boyish ideal during three years in Alabama, and I brought it with me to New York, where it not only gave silent support to my explorations of what was then an unknown territory, but served to mock and caution me when I became interested in the communist ideal. And when it was suggested that I try my hand at writing, it was still with me; thus I went about writing rashly unaware that my ambitions as a composer had been fatally diverted.

But once involved, however, I soon became consciously concerned with craft, with technique. And through my discipline of consciousness acquired from the study of music theory I was gradually led, often reluctantly, to become consciously concerned with the nature of the culture and the society out of which American fiction is fabricated. The pieces collected here are one of the results, and their basic significance, whatever their value as information or speculation, is autobiographical.

They are concerned with three general themes: with literature and folklore, with Negro musical expression—especially jazz and the blues—and with the complex relationship between the Negro American subculture and North American culture as a whole. Most are occasional pieces, written for magazines whose editors provided opportunities for me to reduce my thinking—indeed, often to discover what I *did* think—to publishable form. Nevertheless, they are a by-product of that effort, basic to the fiction-writer's confrontation of the world, of converting experience into symbolic action. Good fiction is made of that which is real, and reality is difficult to come by. So much of it depends upon the individual's willingness to discover his true self, upon his defining himself—for the time being at least—against his background.

Thus these essays represent, in all their modesty, some of the necessary effort which a writer of my background must make in order to possess the meaning of his experience. They are an attempt to transform some of the themes, the problems, the enigmas, the contradictions of character and culture native to my predicament, into what André Malraux has described as "conscious thought." For me some such effort was necessary before I could discover the true subject matter of my fiction; before I could identify the areas of life and personality which claimed my mind beyond any limitations *apparently* imposed by my racial identity.

The act of writing requires a constant plunging back into the shadow of the past where time hovers ghostlike. When I began writing in earnest I was forced, thus, to relate myself consciously and imaginatively to my mixed background as American, as Negro American, and as a Negro from what in its own belated way was a pioneer background. More important and inseparable from this particular effort, was the necessity of determining my true relationship to that body of American literature to which I was most attracted and through which, aided by what I could learn from the literatures of Europe, I would find my own voice, and to which I was challenged, by way of achieving myself, to make some small contribution, and to whose composite picture of reality I was obligated to offer some necessary modifications.

This was no matter of sudden insight but of slow and blundering discovery, of a struggle to stare down the deadly and hypnotic temptation to interpret the world and all its devices in terms of race. To avoid this was very important to me, and in light of my background far from simple. Indeed, it was quite complex, involving as it does a ceaseless questioning of those formulas through which historians, politicians, sociologists, and an older generation of Negro leaders and writers—those of the so-called "Negro Renaissance"—had evolved to describe my group's identity, its predicament, its fate and its relation to the larger society and the culture which we share.

Here the question of reality and personal identity merge. Yes, and the question of the nature of the reality which underlies American fiction and thus the human truth which gives fiction viability. In this quest, for such it soon became, I learned that nothing could go unchallenged; especially that feverish industry dedicated to telling Negroes who and what they are, and which can usually be counted upon to deprive both humanity and culture of their complexity. I had undergone, not too many months before taking the path which led to writing, the humiliation of being taught in a class in sociology at a Negro college (from Park and Burgess, the leading textbook in the field) that Negroes represented the "lady of the races." This contention the Negro instructor passed blandly along to us without even bothering to wash his hands, much less his teeth. Well, I had no intention of being bound by any such humiliating definition of my relationship to American literature. Not even to those works which depicted Negroes negatively. Negro Americans have a highly developed ability to abstract desirable qualities from those around them, even from their enemies, and my sense of reality could reject bias while appreciating the truth revealed by achieved art. The pleasure which I derived from reading had long been a necessity, and in the *act* of reading, that marvelous collaboration between the writer's artful vision and the reader's sense of life, I had become acquainted with other possible selves—freer, more courageous and ingenuous and, during the course of the narrative at least, even wise.

At the time I was under the influence of Ernest Hemingway, and his description, in *Death in the Afternoon,* of his thinking when he first went to Spain became very important as translated in my own naïve fashion. He was trying to write, he tells us . . .

> and found the greatest difficulty aside from knowing truly what you really felt, rather than what you were supposed to feel, and had been taught to feel, was to put down what really happened in action; what the actual things were which produced the emotion that you experienced . . .

His statement of moral and aesthetic purpose which followed focused my own search to relate myself to American life through literature. For I found the greatest difficulty for a Negro writer was the problem of revealing what he truly felt, rather than serving up what Negroes were supposed to feel, and were encouraged to feel. And linked to this was the difficulty, based upon our long habit of deception and evasion, of depicting what really happened within our areas of American life, and putting down with honesty and without bowing to ideological expediencies the attitudes and values which give Negro American life its sense of wholeness and which render it bearable and human and, when measured by our own terms, desirable.

I was forced to this awareness through my struggles with the craft of fiction; yes, and by my attraction (soon rejected) to Marxist political theory, which was my response to the inferior status which society sought to impose upon me (I did not then, now, or ever *consider* myself inferior). I did not know my true relationship to America—what citizen of the United States really does?—but I did know and accept how I felt inside. And I also knew, thanks to the old Renaissance Man, what I expected of myself in the matter of personal discipline and creative quality. Since, by the grace of the past and the examples of manhood picked willy-nilly from the continuing-present of my background, I rejected all negative definitions imposed upon me by others, there was nothing to do but search for those relationships which were fundamental.

In this sense fiction became the agency of my efforts to answer the questions: Who am I, what am I, how did I come to be? What shall I make of the life around me, what celebrate, what reject, how confront the snarl of good and evil which is inevitable? What does American society *mean* when regarded out of my *own* eyes, when informed by my *own* sense of the past and viewed by my *own* complex sense of the present? How, in other words, should I think of myself and my pluralistic sense of the world, how express my vision of the human predicament, without reducing it to a point which would render it sterile before that necessary and tragic —though enhancing—reduction which must occur before the fictive vision can come alive? It is quite possible that much potential fiction by Negro Americans fails precisely at this point: through the writers' refusal (often through provincialism or lack of courage or opportunism) to achieve a vision of life and a resourcefulness of craft commensurate with the complexity of their actual situation. Too often they fear to leave the uneasy sanctuary of race to take their chances in the world of art.

Be that as it may, these essays are a witness of that which I have known and that which I have tried and am still trying to confront. They mark a change of role, a course, and a slow precarious growth of consciousness. They were written in New York and in Rome, and the last were composed during my time as Writer-in-Residence at Rutgers University. The very least I can say about their value is that they performed the grateful function of making it unnecessary to clutter up my fiction with half-formed or outrageously wrong-headed ideas. At best they are an embodiment of a conscious attempt to confront, to peer into, the shadow of my past and to remind myself of the complex resources for imaginative creation which are my heritage. Consciousness and conscience are burdens imposed upon us by the American experiment. They are the American's agony, but when he tries to live up to their stern demands they become his justification. What more is there to say? What more need be said? Beyond expressing my thanks to those publishers, editors and magazines which granted me an audience.

Over the years many people have encouraged me in my writing, both by example, by confidence in my talent, and by helpful criticism. Indeed, there are far too many, considering that the essays collected here go back almost to the beginning of my writing, to be mentioned. Nevertheless, I wish to acknowledge my special indebtedness to Stanley Edgar Hyman, with whom I've shared a community of ideas and critical standards for two decades, and to Kenneth Burke, the stimulating source of many of these; to Albert L. Murray, who has insisted upon the importance of the over-all point of view developed here since we were students at Tuskegee Institute, and whose memory, files, and criticism have been invaluable; to Jimmy Rushing, who through his friendship and through our many hour-long telephone conversations has helped to keep my sense of my Oklahoma background— especially the jazz—so vividly alive; to Irving Kolodin, at whose requests most of the essays on music came to be written; and to Albert R. Erskine and James H. Silberman of Random House, without whom this book would be most formless indeed. Finally, there has been the help of my beloved wife, Fanny McConnell, who has shown, again and again, through her sacrifices, encouragement and love, more faith in the writer and his talent than the writer has shown in himself.

—RALPH ELLISON
May, 1964

The SEER
and the SEEN

That Same Pain, That Same Pleasure: *An Interview*

RICHARD G. STERN: Last night we were talking about the way in which your literary situation has been special, the way in which you as a Negro writer have vaulted the parochial limitations of most Negro fiction. Accepting this, not debating it, would you want to talk a bit about the sources of the strength by which you escaped them?

RALPH ELLISON: Well, to the extent that one cannot ever escape what is given I suppose it had less to do with writing per se than with my desire, beginning at a very early age, to be more fully a part of that larger world which surrounded the Negro world into which I was born. It was a matter of attitude. Then there were the accidents through which so much of that world beyond the Negro community became available to me. Ironically, I would have to start with some of the features of American life which it has become quite fashionable to criticize in a most unthinking way—the mass media. Like so many kids of the twenties, I played around with radio—building crystal sets and circuits consisting of a few tubes, which I found published in the radio magazines. At the time we were living in a white middle-class neighborhood, where my mother was custodian for some apartments, and it was while searching the trash for cylindrical ice-cream cartons which were used by amateurs for winding tuning coils that I met a white boy who was looking for the same thing. I gave him some of those I'd found and we became friends. Oddly enough, I don't remember his family name even though his father was pastor of the leading Episcopal church in Oklahoma City at that time, but his nickname was Hoolie and for kids of eight or nine that was enough.[1] Due to a rheumatic heart Hoolie was tutored at home and spent a great deal of time playing by himself and in taking his parents' elaborate radio apart and putting it back together again, and in building circuits of his own. For all of his delicate health, he was a very intelligent and very alive boy. It didn't take much encouragement from his mother, who was glad to have someone around to keep him company, for me to spend much of my free time helping with his experiments. By the time I left the community, he had become interested in short-wave communication and was applying for a ham license. I moved back into the Negro community and began to concentrate on music, and

---

[1] Thanks to the Reverend Kenneth R. Coleman, Chaplain of the Episcopal Church at Yale University, to whom (in 1963) I related the circumstances of this old friendship, I was put in touch with the Reverend R. A. Laud Humphreys, Historiographer of the Episcopal Diocese of Oklahoma, who in turn kindly interested himself in the mystery of my childhood friend. Thus I now know not only that "Hoolie" is the son of the Reverend Franklin Davis and Mrs. Davis, but that his real name is Henry Bowman Otto Davis. He is now an electronics expert connected with the Air Force.

was never to see him again, but knowing this white boy was a very meaningful experience. It had little to do with the race question as such, but with our mutual loneliness (I had no other playmates in that community) and a great curiosity about the growing science of radio. It was important for me to know a boy who could approach the intricacies of electronics with such daring and whose mind was intellectually aggressive. Knowing him led me to expect much more of myself and of the world.

The other accident from that period lay in my mother's bringing home copies of such magazines as *Vanity Fair* and of opera recordings which had been discarded by a family for whom she worked. You might say that my environment was extended by these slender threads into the worlds of white families whom personally I knew not at all. These magazines and recordings and the discarded books my mother brought home to my brother and me spoke to me of a life which was broader and more interesting, and although it was not really a part of my own life, I never thought they were not for me simply because I happened to be a Negro. They were things which spoke of a world which I could some day make my own.

STERN: Were you conscious at this time of peculiar limitations upon your freedom of action, perhaps even your freedom of feeling?

ELLISON: Well, now, remember that this was in Oklahoma, which is a border state and as the forty-sixth state was one of the last of our territories to achieve statehood. Although opened to American settlers in 1889, at the time of my birth it had been a state only seven years. Thus it had no tradition of slavery, and while it was segregated, relationships between the races were more fluid and thus more human than in the old slave states. My parents, like most of the other Negroes, had come to the new state looking for a broader freedom and had never stopped pushing against the barriers. Having arrived at the same time that most of the whites had, they felt that the restriction of Negro freedom was imposed unjustly through the force of numbers and that they had the right and obligation to fight against it. This was all to the good. It made for a tradition of aggressiveness and it gave us a group social goal which was not as limited as that imposed by the old slave states. I recognized limitations, yes; but I thought these limitations were unjust and I felt no innate sense of inferiority which would keep me from getting those things I desired out of life. There were those who stood in the way but you just had to keep moving toward whatever you wanted.

As a kid I remember working it out this way: there was a world in which you wore your everyday clothes on Sunday, and there was a world in which you wore your Sunday clothes every day—*I* wanted the world in which you wore your Sunday clothes every day. I wanted it because it represented something better, a more exciting and civilized and human way of living; a world which came to me through certain scenes of felicity which I encountered in fiction, in the movies, and which I glimpsed sometimes through the windows of great houses on Sunday afternoons when my mother took my brother and me for walks through the wealthy white sections of the city. I know it now for a boy's vague dream of possibility. Hoolie was part of it, and shop-window displays of elegant clothing, furniture, automobiles—those Lincolns and Marmons!—and of course music and books. And for me none of this was hopelessly beyond the reach of my Negro world, really; because if you worked and you fought for your rights, and so on, you could finally achieve it. This involved our American Negro faith in education, of course, and the idea of self-cultivation—although I couldn't have put it that way back during the days when the idea first seized me. Interestingly enough, by early adolescence the idea of Renaissance Man had drifted down to about six of us, and we discussed mastering ourselves and everything in sight as though no such thing as racial discrimination existed. As you can see, quite a lot of our living was done in the imagination.

STERN: At one part of your life you became conscious that there was something precious in being a Negro in this country at this time. Can you remember when you discovered this?

ELLISON: Well, part of it came from the affirmation of those things in the Negro environment which I found warm and meaningful. For instance, I had none of the agricultural experience of my mother, who had grown up on a farm in Georgia, and although in twenty minutes you could move from Oklahoma City into deep farm country, I shared none of the agricultural experience of many of my classmates. I was of the city, you see. But during the fall cotton-picking season certain kids left school and went with their parents to work in the cotton fields. Now, most parents wished their children to have no contact with the cotton patch, it was part of an experience which they wanted to put behind them. It was part of the Old South which they had come west to forget. Just the same, those trips to the cotton patch seemed to me an enviable experience because the kids came back with such wonderful stories. And it wasn't the hard work which they stressed, but the communion, the playing, the eating, the dancing and the singing. And they brought back jokes, *our* Negro jokes—not those told about Negroes by whites —and they always returned with Negro folk stories which I'd never heard before and which couldn't be found in any books I knew about. This was something to affirm and I felt there was a richness in it. I didn't think too much about it, but what my schoolmates shared in the country and what I felt in their accounts of it—it seemed much more real than the Negro middle-class values which were taught in school.

Or again: I grew up in a school in which music was emphasized and where we were taught harmony from the ninth through the twelfth grades, and where much time was given to music appreciation and the study of the shorter classical forms but where jazz was considered disreputable. Of course, this is part of the story of jazz even today. So much of the modern experimentation in jazz springs—as far as Negro jazz modernists are concerned—from a misplaced shame over the so-called low-class origins of jazz. These are usually men of Negro middle-class background who have some formal training in music and who would like for jazz to be a "respectable" form of expression tied up with other forms of revolt. They'd like to dry up the deep, rowdy stream of jazz until it becomes a very thin trickle of respectable sound indeed. Be that as it may, despite my teachers, the preachers and other leaders of the community, I was with those who found jazz attractive, an important part of life. I hung around the old Blue Devils Orchestra out of which the famous Basie band was formed. I knew these people and admired them. I knew Jimmy Rushing, the blues singer, who then was not quite the hero of the middle-class people whom I knew, that he is today after years of popular success. But for us, even when he was a very young man, a singer who came home to the city once in a while, Jimmy represented, gave voice to, something which was very affirming of Negro life, feelings which you couldn't really put into words. Of course, beyond jazz there was all the boasting, the bragging that went on when no one but ourselves was supposed to be listening, when you weren't really being judged by the white world. At least when you *thought* you weren't being judged and didn't care if you were. For instance, there is no place like a Negro barbershop for hearing what Negroes really think. There is more unself-conscious affirmation to be found here on a Saturday than you can find in a Negro college in a month, or so it seems to me.

Getting back to your question, I suppose my attitude toward these elements of Negro life became a discipline toward affirming that which felt desirable to me over and beyond anything which we were taught in school. It was more a matter of the heart than of the mind.

STERN: You found something precious, special, and associated it with jazz. Now, between finding that jazz was a vehicle for special qualities which you admired in Negroes and finding that literature was a vehicle, you yourself wanted to employ—

ELLISON: I wanted to be a composer but not a jazz composer, interestingly enough. I wanted to be a symphonist.

STERN: How about that then?

ELLISON: Well, I had always listened to music and as far back as I can remember I had the desire to create. I can't remember when I first wanted to play jazz or to create classical music. I can't remember a time when I didn't want to make something, whether it was a small one-tube radio or a crystal set, or my own toys. This was a part of the neighborhood where I spent most of my childhood. There were a number of us who were that way.

STERN: Did your desire to be a symphony composer rather than a jazz instrumentalist stand for a sort of denial of your own cultural situation as a Negro?

ELLISON: No, no. You see, what is often misunderstood nowadays is that there wasn't always this division between the ambitions of jazz musicians and the standards of classical music; the idea was to master both traditions. In school the classics were pushed at us on all sides, and if you danced, if you shared any of the social life of the young people, jazz was inescapable; it was all around you. And if you were a *musician* you were challenged by its sounds and by the techniques required to produce them. In fact, we admired such jazzmen as the late bassist Walter Page and the trumpeter Icky Lawrence over all other local musicians, because although they usually played in jazz bands, they could go into any theater pit and play the scores placed before them. They played the arrangements for the silent movies at sight and we found this very impressive. Such men as Lawrence and Page— and there were several others—had conservatory training as well as a rich jazz experience and thus felt no need to draw a line between the two traditions. Following them, our ideal was to master both. It wasn't a matter of wanting to do the classics because they denied or were felt to deny jazz, and I suppose my own desire to write symphonies grew out of an attraction to the bigger forms and my awareness that they moved many people as they did me in a different way. The range of mood was much broader.

STERN: Can you describe the difference in your own feelings about the two forms?

ELLISON: I can try, but since I shall be trying to recall emotions having to do with the non-verbal medium of music, and at a time when I was a very young and inarticulate boy, I can only give you vague impressions. You see, jazz was so much a part of our total way of life that it got not only into our attempts at playing classical music but into forms of activities usually not associated with it: into marching and into football games, where it has since become a familiar fixture. A lot has been written about the role of jazz in a certain type of Negro funeral marching, but in Oklahoma City it got into military drill. There were many Negro veterans from the Spanish-American War who delighted in teaching the younger boys complicated drill patterns, and on hot summer evenings we spent hours on the Bryant School grounds (now covered with oil wells) learning to execute the commands barked at us by our enthusiastic drillmasters. And as we mastered the patterns, the jazz feeling would come into it and no one was satisfied until we were swinging. These men who taught us had raised a military discipline to the level of a low art form, almost a dance, and its spirit was jazz.

On the other hand, I became a member of the school band while in the eighth grade and we played military music, the classical marches, arrangements of symphonic music, overtures, snatches of opera, and so on, and we sang classical sacred music and the Negro spirituals. So all this was a part of it, and not only did we have classes in music appreciation right through school, on May Day we filled the Western League Ball Park wrapping maypoles and dancing European folk dances. You really should see a field of little Negro kids dancing an Irish jig or a Scottish fling. There must have been something incongruous about it for the few whites who came to see us, but there we were and for us the dance was the thing. Culturally everything was mixed, you see, and beyond all question of conscious choices there was a level where you were claimed by emotion and movement and moods which you couldn't put into words. Often we wanted to share both: the classics and jazz, the Charleston and the Irish reel, spirituals and the blues, the sacred and the profane. I remember the breakfast dances, the matinée dances along with the tent meetings, and the more formal Afro-Methodist Episcopal Christmas services which took place in our church; they all had their special quality. During adolescence I remember attending sunrise services, which took place before Christmas morning. It was a very sacred service, but I remember my mother permitting me to leave after the services were over to attend a breakfast dance.

She didn't attend dances herself and was quite pious by that time, but there was no necessary clash between these quite different celebrations of Christmas, and for me the two forms added quite a bit to my sense of the unity of the life I lived. Just the same, there were certain yearnings which I felt, certain emotions, certain needs for other forms of transcendence and identification which I could only associate with classical music. I heard it in Beethoven, I heard it in Schumann. I used to hear it in Wagner—he is really a young man's composer; especially a young bandsman with plenty of brass. I was always a trumpeter, so I was always listening for those composers who made the most use, the loudest use, of the brass choir. Seriously though, you got glimpses, very vague glimpses, of a far different world than that assigned by segregation laws, and I was taken very early with a passion to link together all I loved within the Negro community and all those things I felt in the world which lay beyond.

STERN: So pretty early you had a sense of being part of a larger social or cultural complex?

ELLISON: Put it this way: I learned very early that in the realm of the imagination all people and their ambitions and interests could meet. This was inescapable, given my reading and my daydreaming. But this notion, this vague awareness, was helped along by the people I came to know. On the level of race relations, my father had many white friends who came to the house when I was quite small, so that any feelings of distrust I was to develop toward whites later on were modified by those with whom I had warm relations. Oklahoma offered many opportunities for such friendships. I remember also an English actress named Emma Bunting—I wonder what happened to her? Anyway, when I was a child, Emma Bunting used to bring over a repertory company each summer, and when she performed in Oklahoma City, her maid, a very handsome Negro woman named Miss Clark, used to stay with us. There was no segregation in the downtown theatres during that period—although it came later—and my mother went frequently to plays and was very proud of a lace bag which Emma Bunting had given her. You see, there is always some connection. Miss Clark brought not only the theatre into our house but England as well. I guess it's the breaks in the pattern of segregation which count, the accidents. When I reached high school I knew Dr. Ludwig Hebestreit, a conductor who formed the nucleus of what became the Oklahoma Symphony—a German for whom I used to cut the grass in exchange for trumpet lessons. But these lessons were about everything else. He'd talk to me about all that lay behind music, and after I'd performed my trumpet lesson and been corrected he'd say, "You like such and such a composition, don't you?" And I'd say, "Yes," and he'd sit down at the piano with a piece of scoring paper and in a few minutes he would have written out passages of the orchestration and show me bar by bar how the sounds were blended.

"The strings are doing this," he'd say, "and the trumpets are playing this figure against the woodwinds," and so on.

Most of it was over my head, but he made it all so logical and, better still, he taught me how to attack those things I desired so that I could pierce the mystery and possess them. I came to feel, yes, that if you want these things and master the technique, you could get with it. You could make it yours. I came to understand, in other words, that all that stood between me and writing symphonies was not simply a matter of civil rights—even though the civil rights struggle was all too real. At that time my mother was being thrown into jail every other day for violating a zoning ordinance by moving into a building in a section where Governor Alfalfa Bill Murray had decided Negroes shouldn't live . . .

STERN: You went on then to Tuskegee, and you studied music seriously, and came up to New York more or less intending to . . .

ELLISON: To go back to Tuskegee. I came up during my junior year hoping to work and learn a little about sculpture. And although I did study a bit, I didn't get the job through which I hoped to earn enough money for my school expenses, so I remained in New York, where I soon realized that although I had a certain facility with three-dimensional form I wasn't really interested in sculpture. So after a while I blundered into writing.

STERN: The music you had given up by this time?

ELLISON: No, no, I was still trying to be a musician. I was doing some exercises in composition under Wallingford Riegger, and although I was much behind his advanced students I stayed there and studied with him until I had to have a tonsillectomy. It turned out to be a pretty chronic case and caused a lot of trouble, and by the time I tried to go back to my classes my mother died out in Ohio and I left New York for a good while. It was during the period in Dayton, I started trying seriously to write and that was the breaking point.

STERN: Can you remember why you started to write or how?

ELLISON: I can remember very vividly. Richard Wright had just come to New York and was editing a little magazine. I had read a poem of his which I liked, and when we were introduced by a mutual friend he suggested that I try to review a novel for his magazine. My review was accepted and published and so I was hooked.

STERN: You were launched . . .

ELLISON: Oh no, not really launched.

STERN: You were conscious that such a thing was possible. Was Wright famous at that time?

ELLISON: No, Wright hadn't written *Native Son*. He had

published *Uncle Tom's Children*, which was the real beginning of his fame, and he was already working on *Native
Son*. I remember the first scene that he showed me, it was
the poolroom scene—it isn't the first scene but it was one
of the first written and I was to read the rest of the book
as it came out of the typewriter.

STERN: At that time were you dissatisfied with the sort of
work Wright was doing?

ELLISON: Dissatisfied? I was too amazed with watching the
process of creation. I didn't understand quite what was
going on, but by this time I had talked with Wright a lot
and he was very conscious of technique. He talked about
it not in terms of mystification but as writing know-how.
"You must read so-and-so," he'd say. "You have to go
about learning to write *consciously*. People have talked
about such and such a problem and have written about it.
You must learn how Conrad, Joyce, Dostoievsky get their
effects . . ." He guided me to Henry James and to Conrad's prefaces, that type of thing. Of course, I knew that
my own feelings about the world, about life, were different, but this was not even a matter to question. Wright
knew what he was about, what he wanted to do, while I
hadn't even discovered myself. I knew only that what I
would want to express would not be an imitation of his
kind of a thing.

STERN: So what sort of thing did you feel Wright was not
doing that you wanted to do?

ELLISON: Well, I don't suppose I judged. I am certain I did
not judge in quite so conscious a way, but I think I felt
more complexity in life, and my background made me
aware of a larger area of possibility. Knowing Wright himself and something of what he was doing increased that
sense of the possible. Also, I think I was less interested
in an ideological interpretation of Negro experience. For
all my interest in music, I had been in love with literature

for years and years—if a writer may make such a confession. I read everything. I must have read fairy tales until I was thirteen, and I was always taken with the magical quality of writing, with the poetry of it. When I came to discover a little more about what I wanted to express I felt that Wright was overcommitted to ideology— even though I, too, wanted many of the same things for our people. You might say that I was much less a social determinist. But I suppose that basically it comes down to a difference in our concepts of the individual. I, for instance, found it disturbing that Bigger Thomas had none of the finer qualities of Richard Wright, none of the imagination, none of the sense of poetry, none of the gaiety. And I preferred Richard Wright to Bigger Thomas. Do you see? Which gets you in on the—directs you back to the difference between what Wright was himself and how he conceived of the individual; back to his conception of the quality of Negro humanity.

STERN: Did you think you might write stories in which Negroes did not appear?

ELLISON: No, there was never a time when I thought of writing fiction in which only Negroes appeared, or in which only whites appeared. And yet, from the very beginning I wanted to write about American Negro experience and I suspected that what was important, what made the difference, lay in the perspective from which it was viewed. When I learned more and started thinking about this consciously, I realized that it was a source of creative strength as well as a source of wonder. It's also a relatively unexplored area of American experience simply because our knowledge of it has been distorted through the overemphasis of the sociological approach. Unfortunately many Negroes have been trying to define their own predicament in exclusively sociological terms, a situation I consider quite short-sighted. Too many of us have accepted a statistical interpretation of our lives and thus much of that which makes us a source of moral strength to America goes unappreciated and undefined. Now, when you try to trace American values as they find expression in the Negro community, where do you begin? To what books do you go? How do you account for Little Rock and the sit-ins? How do you account for the strength of those kids? You can find sociological descriptions of the conditions under which they live but few indications of their morale.

STERN: You felt as you were starting to get serious about writing that you had a special subject to write about?

ELLISON: Yes, I think so. Well, let's put it this way: Sometimes you get a sense of mission even before you are aware of it. An act is demanded of you but you're like a sleepwalker searching for some important object, and when you find it you wake up to discover that it is the agency through which that mission, assigned you long ago, at a time you barely understood the command, could be accomplished. Thus while there appeared to be no connection between my wanting to write fiction and my mother's insistence, from the time I was a small boy, that the hope of our group depended not upon the older Negroes but upon the young, upon me, as it were, this sense of obligation got into my work immediately. Of course, these are very complicated matters, because I have no desire to write propaganda. Instead I felt it important to explore the full range of American Negro humanity and to affirm those qualities which are of value beyond any question of segregation, economics or previous condition of servitude. The obligation was always there and there is much to affirm. In fact, all Negroes affirm certain feelings of identity, certain foods, certain types of dancing, music, religious experiences, certain tragic attitudes toward experience and toward our situation as Americans. You see, we do this all within the community, but when it is questioned from without—that's when things start going apart. Like most Americans we are not yet fully conscious of our identity either as Negroes or Americans. This affirmation of which I speak, this insistence upon achieving our social goal, has been our great strength and also our great weakness because the terms with which we have tried to define ourselves have been inadequate. We know we're not the creatures which our enemies in the white South would have us be and we know too that neither color nor our civil predicament explain us adequately. Our strength is that with the total society saying to us, *"No, No, No, No,"* we continue to move toward our goal. So when I came to write I felt moved to affirm and to explore all this—not as a social mission but as the stuff of literature and as an expression of the better part of my own sense of life.

STERN: Somebody has described a literary situation as one which commemorates what a man feels is passing or threatened. Did you feel that your work might be a commemoration of values which were disappearing as you wrote about them?

ELLISON: How shall I say? Yes, I do feel this. Now just how consciously I was concerned with it at the time I wrote I don't know. When I started writing *Invisible Man* I was reading Lord Raglan's *The Hero,* in which he goes into figures of history and myth to account for the features which make for the mythic hero and at the same time I got to thinking about the ambiguity of Negro leadership during that period. This was the late forties and I kept trying to account for the fact that when the chips were down, Negro leaders did not represent the Negro community.

Beyond their own special interests they represented white philanthropy, white politicians, business interests, and so on. This was an unfair way of looking at it, perhaps, but there was something missing, something which is only now being corrected. It seemed to me that they acknowledged no final responsibility to the Negro community for their acts and implicit in their roles were constant acts of betrayal. This made for a sad, chronic division between their values and the values of those they were supposed to represent. And the fairest thing to say about it is that the predicament of Negroes in the United States rendered these leaders automatically impotent, until they recognized their true source of power—which lies, as Martin Luther King perceived, in the Negro's ability to suffer even death for the attainment of our beliefs. Back in the forties only preachers had real power through which to effect their wills but most of these operated strictly within the Negro community. Only Adam Powell was using the power of the Negro church to assert the Negro's political will. So at that time a thick fog of unreality separated the Negro group from its leaders— But let me tell you a story: At Tuskegee during graduation week countless high-powered word artists, black and white, descended upon us and gathered in the gym and the chapel to tell us in high-flown words what the Negro thought, what our lives were and what our goals should be. The buildings would be packed with visitors and relatives and many guardians of race relations—Northern and Southern. Well, the Negro farm people from the surrounding countryside would also come to the campus at the same time. Graduation week was a festival time for the surrounding Negro community, and very often these people would have children and relatives taking part in the ceremonies in progress in the chapel and the gym. But do you know that while the big-shot word artists were making their most impressive speeches, the farm people would be out on the old athletic field dancing square dances, having picnics, playing baseball and visiting among themselves as though the ceremonies across the wide lawns did not exist; or at best had no connection with the lives they led. Well, I found their celebrations much more attractive than the official ceremonies and I would leave my seat in the orchestra and sneak out to watch them; and while my city background had cut me off from the lives they led and I had no desire to live the life of a share-cropper, I found their unrhetorical activities on the old football field the more meaningful.

STERN: The familiar liberal hope is that any specialized form of social life which makes for invidious distinctions should disappear. Your view seems to be that anything that counts is the result of such specialization.

ELLISON: Yes.

STERN: Now, a good many people, millions, are damaged permanently, viciously, unfairly by such distinctions. At the same time, they contribute, as you more than perhaps any writer in the world have seen, to something marvelous. Some sort of decision probably has to be made by an individual who is sensitive to this paradox—I wonder what yours is. Do you want the preservation of that which results in both the marvelous and the terrible, or do you feel that the marvelous should not endure while the terrible endures along with it?

ELLISON: I am going to say something very odd. In the first place, I think that the mixture of the marvelous and the terrible is a basic condition of human life and that the persistence of human ideals represents the marvelous pulling itself up out of the chaos of the universe. In the fairy tale, beauty must be awakened by the beast, the beastly man can only regain his humanity through love. There are other terms for this but they come to much the same thing. Here the terrible represents all that hinders, all that opposes human aspiration, and the marvelous represents the triumph of the human spirit over chaos. While the terms and the conditions are different and often change, our triumphs are few and thus must be recognized for what they are and preserved. Besides, I would be hard put to say where the terrible could be localized in our national experience, for I see in so much of American life which lies beyond the Negro community the very essence of the terrible.

STERN: Yes, but the last few days we have been talking about some of the particular meannesses which are characteristic of the Negro situation . . . Just the fact that there are four Negro congressmen, when adequate representation would mean that there'd be twenty . . .

ELLISON: Yes.

STERN: And hundreds of things of this sort, many of which result in crippling injustices and meannesses. Now, can this go on? And if it doesn't go on, will this mean the elimination of that which you have commemorated in fiction?

ELLISON: Well, what I have tried to commemorate in fiction is that which I believe to be enduring and abiding in our situation, especially those human qualities which the American Negro has developed despite and in rejection of the obstacles and meannesses imposed upon us. If the writer exists for any social good, his role is that of preserving in art those human values which can endure by confronting change. Our Negro situation is changing rapidly, but so much which we've gleaned through the harsh discipline of Negro American life is simply too precious to be lost. I speak of the faith, the patience, the humor, the sense of timing, rugged sense of life and the manner of expressing it which all go to define the American Negro. These are some of the things through which we've confronted the obstacles and meannesses of which you speak and which we dare not fail to adapt to changed conditions lest we destroy ourselves. Times change but these possessions must endure forever—not simply because they define us as a group, but because they represent a further instance of man's triumph over chaos. You know, the skins of those thin-legged little girls who faced the mob in Little Rock marked them as Negro but the spirit which directed their feet is the old universal urge toward freedom. For better or worse, whatever there is of value in Negro life is an American heritage and as such it must be preserved. Besides, I am unwilling to see those values which I would celebrate in fiction as existing sheerly through terror; they are a result of a tragicomic confrontation of life.

I think that art is a celebration of life even when life extends into death and that the sociological conditions which have made for so much misery in Negro life are not necessarily the only factors which make for the values which I feel should endure and shall endure. I see a period when Negroes are going to be wandering around because, you see, we have had this thing thrown at us for so long that we haven't had a chance to discover what in our own background is really worth preserving. For the first time we are given a choice, we are making a choice. And this is where the real trouble is going to start. The South could help. If it had a sense of humor, you know, the South could say, "All right, we will set aside six months and there will be complete integration—all right, you don't have to integrate the women—but there will be complete integration as far as anything else is concerned. Negroes may go anywhere, they may see how we entertain, how we spend our leisure, how we worship, and so on," and that would be the end of the whole problem. Because most Negroes could not be nourished by the life white Southerners live. It is too hag-ridden, it is too obsessed, it is too concerned with attitudes which could change everything that Negroes have been conditioned to expect of life. No,

I believe in diversity, and I think that the real death of the United States will come when everyone is just alike.

As for my writer's necessity of cashing in on the pain undergone by my people (and remember I write of the humor as well), writing is my way of confronting, often for the hundredth time, that same pain and that same pleasure. It is my way of seeing that it be not in vain.

—From *December*, Winter 1961.

Twentieth-Century Fiction
and the Black Mask
of Humanity

When this essay was published in 1953, it was prefaced with the
following note:

"When I started rewriting this essay it occurred to me that its
value might be somewhat increased if it remained very much as
I wrote it during 1946. For in that form it is what a young member of a minority felt about much of our writing. Thus I've left
in much of the bias and short-sightedness, for it says perhaps as
much about me as a member of a minority as it does about literature. I hope you still find the essay useful, and I'd like to see
an editorial note stating that this is an unpublished piece written not long after the Second World War."

Perhaps the most insidious and least understood form of
segregation is that of the word. And by this I mean the word
in all its complex formulations, from the proverb to the novel
and stage play, the word with all its subtle power to suggest
and foreshadow overt action while magically disguising the
moral consequences of that action and providing it with symbolic and psychological justification. For if the word has the
potency to revive and make us free, it has also the power to
blind, imprison and destroy.

The essence of the word is its ambivalence, and in fiction it is never so effective and revealing as when both potentials are operating simultaneously, as when it mirrors both good and bad, as when it blows both hot and cold in the same breath. Thus it is unfortunate for the Negro that the most powerful formulations of modern American fictional words have been so slanted against him that when he approaches for a glimpse of himself he discovers an image drained of humanity.

Obviously the experiences of Negroes—slavery, the grueling and continuing fight for full citizenship since Emancipation, the stigma of color, the enforced alienation which constantly knifes into our natural identification with our country —have not been that of white Americans. And though as passionate believers in democracy Negroes identify themselves with the broader American ideals, their sense of reality springs, in part, from an American experience which most white men not only have not had, but one with which they are reluctant to identify themselves even when presented in forms of the imagination. Thus when the white American, holding up most twentieth-century fiction, says, "This is American reality," the Negro tends to answer (not at all concerned that Americans tend generally to fight against any but the most flattering imaginative depictions of their lives), "Perhaps, but you've left out this, and this, and this. And most of all, what you'd have the world accept as *me* isn't even human."

Nor does he refer only to second-rate works but to those of our most representative authors. Either like Hemingway and Steinbeck (in whose joint works I recall not more than five American Negroes) they tend to ignore them, or like the early Faulkner, who distorted Negro humanity to fit his personal versions of Southern myth, they seldom conceive Negro characters possessing the full, complex ambiguity of the human. Too often what is presented as the American Negro (a most complex example of Western man) emerges an oversimplified clown, a beast or an angel. Seldom is he drawn as that sensitively focused process of opposites, of good and evil, of instinct and intellect, of passion and spirituality, which great literary art has projected as the image of man. Naturally, the attitude of Negroes toward this writing is one of great reservation. Which, indeed, bears out Richard Wright's remark that there is in progress between black and white Americans a struggle over the nature of reality.

Historically this is but a part of that larger conflict between older, dominant groups of white Americans, especially the Anglo-Saxons, on the one hand, and the newer white and non-white groups on the other, over the major group's attempt to impose its ideals upon the rest, insisting that its exclusive image be accepted as *the* image of the American. This conflict should not, however, be misunderstood. For despite the impact of the American idea upon the world, the "American" himself has not (fortunately for the United States, its minorities, and perhaps for the world) been finally defined. So that far from being socially undesirable this struggle between Americans as to what the American is to be is part of that democratic process through which the nation works to achieve itself. Out of this conflict the ideal American character—a type truly great enough to possess the greatness of the land, a delicately poised unity of divergencies—is slowly being born.

But we are concerned here with fiction, not history. How is it then that our naturalistic prose—one of the most vital bodies of twentieth-century fiction, perhaps the brightest instrument for recording sociological fact, physical action, the nuance of speech, yet achieved—becomes suddenly dull when confronting the Negro?

Obviously there is more in this than the mere verbal counterpart of lynching or segregation. Indeed, it represents a projection of processes lying at the very root of American culture and certainly at the central core of its twentieth-century literary forms, a matter having less to do with the mere "reflection" of white racial theories than with processes molding the attitudes, the habits of mind, the cultural atmosphere and the artistic and intellectual traditions that condition men dedicated to democracy to practice, accept and, most crucial of all, often blind themselves to the essentially undemocratic treatment of their fellow citizens.

It should be noted here that the moment criticism approaches Negro-white relationships it is plunged into problems of psychology and symbolic ritual. Psychology, because the distance between Americans, Negroes and whites, is not so much spatial as psychological; while they might dress and often look alike, seldom on deeper levels do they think alike. Ritual, because the Negroes of fiction are so consistently false to human life that we must question just what they truly represent, both in the literary work and in the inner world of the white American.[1]

Despite their billings as images of reality, these Negroes of fiction are counterfeits. They are projected aspects of an internal symbolic process through which, like a primitive tribesman dancing himself into the group frenzy necessary

---

[1] Perhaps the ideal approach to the work of literature would be one allowing for insight into the deepest psychological motives of the writer at the same time that it examined all external sociological factors operating within a given milieu. For while objectively a social reality, the work of art is, in its genesis, a projection of a deeply personal process, and any approach that ignores the personal as at the expense of the social is necessarily incomplete. Thus when we approach contemporary writing from the perspective of segregation, as is commonly done by sociology-minded thinkers, we automatically limit ourselves to one external aspect of a complex whole, which leaves us little to say concerning its personal, internal elements. On the other hand, American writing has been one of the most important twentieth-century literatures, and though negative as a social force it is technically brilliant and emotionally powerful. Hence were we to examine it for its embodiment of these positive values, there would be other more admiring things to be said.

for battle, the white American prepares himself emotionally to perform a social role. These fictive Negroes are not, as sometimes interpreted, simple racial clichés introduced into society by a ruling class to control political and economic realities. For although they are manipulated to that end, such an externally one-sided interpretation relieves the individual of personal responsibility for the health of democracy. Not only does it forget that a democracy is a collectivity of *individuals,* but it never suspects that the tenacity of the stereotype springs exactly from the fact that its function is no less personal than political. Color prejudice springs not from the stereotype alone, but from an internal psychological state; not from misinformation alone, but from an inner need to believe. It thrives not only on the obscene witch-doctoring of men like Jimmy Byrnes and Malan, but upon an inner craving for symbolic magic. The prejudiced individual creates his own stereotypes, very often unconsciously, by reading into situations involving Negroes those stock meanings which justify his emotional and economic needs.

Hence whatever else the Negro stereotype might be as a social instrumentality, it is also a key figure in a magic rite by which the white American seeks to resolve the dilemma arising between his democratic beliefs and certain antidemocratic practices, between his acceptance of the sacred democratic belief that all men are created equal and his treatment of every tenth man as though he were not.

Thus on the moral level I propose that we view the whole of American life as a drama acted out upon the body of a Negro giant, who, lying trussed up like Gulliver, forms the stage and the scene upon which and within which the action unfolds. If we examine the beginning of the Colonies, the application of this view is not, in its economic connotations at least, too far-fetched or too difficult to see. For then the Negro's body was exploited as amorally as the soil and climate. It was later, when white men drew up a plan for a democratic way of life, that the Negro began slowly to exert an influence upon America's moral consciousness. Gradually he was recognized as the human factor placed outside the democratic master plan, a human "natural" resource who, so that white men could become more human, was elected to undergo a process of institutionalized dehumanization.

Until the Korean War this moral role had become obscured within the staggering growth of contemporary science and industry, but during the nineteenth century it flared nakedly in the American consciousness, only to be repressed after the Reconstruction. During periods of national crises, when the United States rounds a sudden curve on the pitch-black road of history, this moral awareness surges in the white American's conscience like a raging river revealed at his feet by a lightning flash. Only then is the veil of anti-Negro myths, symbols, stereotypes and taboos drawn somewhat aside. And when we look closely at our literature it is to be seen operating even when the Negro seems most patently the little man who isn't there.

I see no value either in presenting a catalogue of Negro characters appearing in twentieth-century fiction or in charting the racial attitudes of white writers. We are interested not in quantities but in qualities. And since it is impossible here to discuss the entire body of this writing, the next best thing is to select a framework in which the relationships with which we are concerned may be clearly seen. For brevity let us take three representative writers: Mark Twain, Hemingway and Faulkner. Twain for historical perspective and as an example of how a great nineteenth-century writer handled the Negro; Hemingway as the prime example of the artist who ignored the dramatic and symbolic possibilities presented by this theme; and Faulkner as an example of a writer who has confronted Negroes with such mixed motives that he has presented them in terms of both the "good nigger" and the "bad nigger" stereotypes, and who yet has explored perhaps more successfully than anyone else, either white or black, certain forms of Negro humanity.

For perspective let us begin with Mark Twain's great classic, *Huckleberry Finn*. Recall that Huckleberry has run away from his father, Miss Watson and the Widow Douglas (indeed the whole community, in relation to which he is a young outcast) and has with him as companion on the raft upon which they are sailing down the Mississippi the Widow Watson's runaway Negro slave, Jim. Recall, too, that Jim, during the critical moment of the novel, is stolen by two scoundrels and sold to another master, presenting Huck with the problem of freeing Jim once more. Two ways are open: he can rely upon his own ingenuity and "steal" Jim into freedom or he might write the Widow Watson and request reward money to have Jim returned to her. But there is a danger in this course, remember, since the angry widow might sell the slave down the river into a harsher slavery. It is this course which Huck starts to take, but as he composes the letter he wavers.

> "It was a close place." [he tells us] "I took it [the letter] up, and held it in my hand. I was trembling, because I'd got to decide, forever, 'twixt two things, and I knowed it. I studied a minute, sort of holding my breath, and then says to myself:
> " 'Alright, then, I'll *go* to hell'—and tore it up, . . . It was awful thoughts and awful words, but they was said . . . And I let them stay said, and never thought no more about reforming. I shoved the whole thing out of my head and said I would take up wickedness again, which was in my line, being brung up to it, and the other warn't. And for a starter I would . . . steal Jim out of slavery again. . . ."

And a little later, in defending his decision to Tom Sawyer, Huck comments, "I know you'll say it's dirty, low-down business but *I'm* low-down. And I'm going to steal him . . ."

We have arrived at a key point of the novel and, by an

ironic reversal, of American fiction, a pivotal moment announcing a change of direction in the plot, a reversal as well as a recognition scene (like that in which Oedipus discovers his true identity) wherein a new definition of necessity is being formulated. Huck Finn has struggled with the problem poised by the clash between property rights and human rights, between what the community considered to be the proper attitude toward an escaped slave and his knowledge of Jim's humanity, gained through their adventures as fugitives together. He has made his decision on the side of humanity. In this passage Twain has stated the basic moral issue centering around Negroes and the white American's democratic ethics. It dramatizes as well the highest point of tension generated by the clash between the direct, human relationships of the frontier and the abstract, inhuman, market-dominated relationships fostered by the rising middle class—which in Twain's day was already compromising dangerously with the most inhuman aspects of the defeated slave system. And just as politically these forces reached their sharpest tension in the outbreak of the Civil War, in *Huckleberry Finn* (both the boy and the novel) their human implications come to sharpest focus around the figure of the Negro.

Huckleberry Finn knew, as did Mark Twain, that Jim was not only a slave but a human being, a man who in some ways was to be envied, and who expressed his essential humanity in his desire for freedom, his will to possess his own labor, in his loyalty and capacity for friendship and in his love for his wife and child. Yet Twain, though guilty of the sentimentality common to humorists, does not idealize the slave. Jim is drawn in all his ignorance and superstition, with his good traits and his bad. He, like all men, is ambiguous, limited in circumstance but not in possibility. And it will be noted that when Huck makes his decision he identifies himself with Jim and accepts the judgment of his superego—that internalized representative of the community—that his action is evil. Like Prometheus, who for mankind stole fire from the gods, he embraces the evil implicit in his act in order to affirm his belief in humanity. Jim, therefore, is not simply a slave, he is a symbol of humanity, and in freeing Jim, Huck makes a bid to free himself of the conventionalized evil taken for civilization by the town.

This conception of the Negro as a symbol of Man—the reversal of what he represents in most contemporary thought—was organic to nineteenth-century literature. It occurs not only in Twain but in Emerson, Thoreau, Whitman and Melville (whose symbol of evil, incidentally, was white), all of whom were men publicly involved in various forms of deeply personal rebellion. And while the Negro and the color black were associated with the concept of evil and ugliness far back in the Christian era, the Negro's emergence as a symbol of value came, I believe, with Rationalism and the rise of the romantic individual of the eighteenth century. This, perhaps, because the romantic was in revolt against the old moral authority, and if he suffered a sense of guilt, his passion for personal freedom was such that he was willing to accept evil (a tragic attitude) even to identifying himself with the "noble slave"—who symbolized the darker, unknown potential side of his personality, that underground side, turgid with possibility, which might, if given a chance, toss a fistful of mud into the sky and create a "shining star."
Even that prototype of the bourgeois, Robinson Crusoe, stopped to speculate as to his slave's humanity. And the rising American industrialists of the late nineteenth century were to rediscover what their European counterparts had learned a century before: that the good man Friday was as sound an investment for Crusoe morally as he was economically, for not only did Friday allow Crusoe to achieve himself by working for him, but by functioning as a living scapegoat

to contain Crusoe's guilt over breaking with the institutions and authority of the past, he made it possible to exploit even his guilt economically. The man was one of the first missionaries.

Mark Twain was alive to this irony and refused such an easy (and dangerous) way out. Huck Finn's acceptance of the evil implicit in his "emancipation" of Jim represents Twain's acceptance of his personal responsibility in the condition of society. This was the tragic face behind his comic mask.

But by the twentieth century this attitude of tragic responsibility had disappeared from our literature along with that broad conception of democracy which vitalized the work of our greatest writers. After Twain's compelling image of black and white fraternity the Negro generally disappears from fiction as a rounded human being. And if already in Twain's time a novel which was optimistic concerning a democracy which would include all men could not escape being banned from public libraries, by our day his great drama of interracial fraternity had become, for most Americans at least, an amusing boy's story and nothing more. But, while a boy, Huck Finn has become by the somersault motion of what William Empson terms "pastoral," an embodiment of the heroic, and an exponent of humanism. Indeed, the historical and artistic justification for his adolescence lies in the fact that Twain was depicting a transitional period of American life; its artistic justification is that adolescence is the time of the "great confusion" during which both individuals and nations flounder between accepting and rejecting the responsibilities of adulthood. Accordingly, Huck's relationship to Jim, the river, and all they symbolize, is that of a humanist; in his relation to the community he is an individualist. He embodies the two major conflicting drives operating in nineteenth-century America. And if humanism is man's basic attitude toward a social order which he accepts, and individualism his basic attitude toward one he rejects, one might say that Twain, by allowing these two attitudes to argue dialectically in his work of art, was as highly moral an artist as he was a believer in democracy, and vice versa.

History, however, was to bring an ironic reversal to the direction which Huckleberry Finn chose, and by our day the divided ethic of the community had won out. In contrast with Twain's humanism, individualism was thought to be the only tenable attitude for the artist.

Thus we come to Ernest Hemingway, one of the two writers whose art is based most solidly upon Mark Twain's language, and one who perhaps has done most to extend Twain's technical influence upon our fiction. It was Hemingway who pointed out that all modern American writing springs from *Huckleberry Finn*. (One might add here that equally as much of it derives from Hemingway himself.) But by the twenties the element of rejection implicit in Twain had become so dominant an attitude of the American writer that Hemingway goes on to warn us to "stop where the Nigger Jim is stolen from the boys. That is the real end. The rest is just cheating."

So thoroughly had the Negro, both as man and as a symbol of man, been pushed into the underground of the American conscience that Hemingway missed completely the structural, symbolic and moral necessity for that part of the plot in which the boys rescue Jim. Yet it is precisely this part which gives the novel its significance. Without it, except as a boy's tale, the novel is meaningless. Yet Hemingway, a great artist in his own right, speaks as a victim of that culture of which he is himself so critical, for by his time that growing rift in the ethical fabric pointed out by Twain had become completely sundered—snagged upon the irrepressible moral reality of the Negro. Instead of the single democratic ethic for every man, there now existed two: one, the idealized ethic of the Constitution and the Declaration of Independence, reserved for white men; and the other, the pragmatic ethic designed for Negroes and other minorities, which took the form of discrimination. Twain had dramatized the conflict leading to this division in its earlier historical form, but what was new here was that such a moral division, always a threat to the sensitive man, was ignored by the artist in the most general terms, as when Hemingway rails against the rhetoric of the First World War.

Hemingway's blindess to the moral values of *Huckleberry Finn* despite his sensitivity to its technical aspects duplicated the one-sided vision of the twenties. Where Twain, seeking for what Melville called "the common continent of man," drew upon the rich folklore of the frontier (not omitting the Negro's) in order to "Americanize" his idiom, thus broadening his stylistic appeal, Hemingway was alert only to Twain's technical discoveries—the flexible colloquial language, the sharp naturalism, the thematic potentialities of adolescence. Thus what for Twain was a means to a moral end became for Hemingway an end in itself. And just as the trend toward technique for the sake of technique and production for the sake of the market lead to the neglect of the human need out of which they spring, so do they lead in literature to a marvelous technical virtuosity won at the expense of a gross insensitivity to fraternal values.

It is not accidental that the disappearance of the human Negro from our fiction coincides with the disappearance of deep-probing doubt and a sense of evil. Not that doubt in some form was not always present, as the works of the lost generation, the muckrakers and the proletarian writers make very clear. But it is a shallow doubt, which seldom turns inward upon the writer's own values; almost always it focuses outward, upon some scapegoat with which he is seldom able to identify himself as Huck Finn identified himself with the scoundrels who stole Jim and with Jim himself. This particular naturalism explored everything except the nature of man.

And when the artist would no longer conjure with the major moral problem in American life, he was defeated as a manipulator of profound social passions. In the United States, as in Europe, the triumph of industrialism had repelled the artist with the blatant hypocrisy between its ideals and its acts. But while in Europe the writer became the most profound critic of these matters, in our country he either turned away or was at best half-hearted in his opposition— perhaps because any profound probing of human values, both within himself and within society, would have brought him face to face with the rigidly tabooed subject of the Negro. And now the tradition of avoiding the moral struggle had led not only to the artistic segregation of the Negro but to the segregation of real fraternal, i.e., democratic, values.

The hard-boiled school represented by Hemingway, for instance, is usually spoken of as a product of World War I disillusionment, yet it was as much the product of a tradition which arose even before the Civil War—that tradition of intellectual evasion for which Thoreau criticized Emerson in regard to the Fugitive Slave Law, and which had been growing swiftly since the failure of the ideals in whose name the Civil War was fought. The failure to resolve the problem symbolized by the Negro has contributed indirectly to the dispossession of the artist in several ways. By excluding our largest minority from the democratic process, the United States weakened all national symbols and rendered sweeping public rituals which would dramatize the American dream impossible; it robbed the artist of a body of unassailable public beliefs upon which he could base his art; it deprived him of a personal faith in the ideals upon which society supposedly rested; and it provided him with no tragic mood indigenous to his society upon which he could erect a tragic art. The result was that he responded with an attitude of rejection, which he expressed as artistic individualism. But too often both his rejection and individualism were narrow; seldom was he able to transcend the limitations of pragmatic reality, and the quality of moral imagination—the fountainhead of great art—was atrophied within him.

Malraux has observed that contemporary American writing is the only important literature not created by intellectuals, and that the creators possess "neither the relative historical culture, nor the love of ideas (a prerogative of professors in the United States)" of comparable Europeans. And is there not a connection between the non-intellectual aspects of this writing (though many of the writers are far more intellectual than they admit or than Malraux would suspect) and its creators' rejection of broad social responsibility, between its non-concern with ideas and its failure to project characters who grasp the broad sweep of American life, or who even attempt to state its fundamental problems? And has not this affected the types of heroes of this fiction, is it not a partial explanation of why it has created no characters possessing broad insight into their situations or the emotional, psychological and intellectual complexity which would allow them to possess and articulate a truly democratic world view?

It is instructive that Hemingway, born into a civilization characterized by violence, should seize upon the ritualized violence of the culturally distant Spanish bullfight as a laboratory for developing his style. For it was, for Americans, an amoral violence (though not for the Spaniards) which he was seeking. Otherwise he might have studied that ritual of violence closer to home, that ritual in which the sacrifice is that of a human scapegoat, the lynching bee. Certainly this rite is not confined to the rope as agency, nor to the South as scene, nor even to the Negro as victim.

But let us not confuse the conscious goals of twentieth-century fiction with those of the nineteenth century, let us take it on its own terms. Artists such as Hemingway were seeking a technical perfection rather than moral insight. (Or should we say that theirs was a morality of technique?) They desired a style stripped of unessentials, one that would appeal without resorting to what was considered worn-out rhetoric, or best of all without any rhetoric whatsoever. It was felt that through the default of the powers that ruled society the artist had as his major task the "pictorial presentation of the evolution of a personal problem." Instead of re-creating and extending the national myth as he did this, the writer now restricted himself to elaborating his personal myth. And although naturalist in his general style, he was not interested, like Balzac, in depicting a society, or even, like Mark Twain, in portraying the moral situation of a nation. Rather he was engaged in working out a personal problem through the evocative, emotion-charged images and ritual-therapy available through the manipulation of art forms. And while art was still an instrument of freedom, it was now mainly the instrument of a questionable personal freedom for the artist, which too often served to enforce the "unfreedom" of the reader.

This because it is not within the province of the artist to determine whether his work is social or not. Art by its nature *is* social. And while the artist can determine within a certain narrow scope the type of social effect he wishes his art to create, here his will is definitely limited. Once introduced into society, the work of art begins to pulsate with those meanings, emotions, ideas brought to it by its audience and over which the artist has but limited control. The irony of the "lost generation" writers is that while disavowing a social role it was the fate of their works to perform a social function which re-enforced those very social values which they most violently opposed. How could this be? Because in its genesis the work of art, like the stereotype, is personal; psychologically it represents the socialization of some profoundly personal problem involving guilt (often symbolic murder—parricide, fratricide—incest, homosexuality, all problems at the base of personality) from which by expressing them along with other elements (images, memories, emotions, ideas) he seeks transcendence. To be effective as personal fulfillment, if it is to be more than dream, the work of art must simultaneously evoke images of reality and give them formal organization. And it must, since the individual's emotions are formed in society, shape them into socially meaningful patterns (even Surrealism and Dadaism depended upon their initiates). Nor, as we can see by comparing literature with reportage, is this all. The work of literature differs basically from reportage not merely in its presentation of a pattern of events, nor in its concern with emotion (for a report might well be an account of highly emotional events), but in the deep personal necessity which cries full-throated in the work of art and which seeks transcendence in the form of ritual.

Malcolm Cowley, on the basis of the rites which he believes to be the secret dynamic of Hemingway's work, has identified him with Poe, Hawthorne and Melville, "the haunted and nocturnal writers," he calls them, "the men who dealt with images that were symbols of an inner world." In Hemingway's work, he writes, "we can recognize rites of animal sacrifice . . . of sexual union . . . of conversion . . . and of symbolic death and rebirth." I do not believe, however, that the presence of these rites in writers like Hemingway is as important as the fact that here, beneath the dead-pan prose, the cadences of understatement, the anti-intellectualism, the concern with every "fundamental" of man except that which distinguishes him from the animal—that here is the twentieth-century form of that magical rite which during periods of great art has been to a large extent public and explicit. Here is the literary form by which the personal guilt of the pulverized individual of our rugged era is expatiated: not through his identification with the guilty acts of an Oedipus, a Macbeth or a Medea, by suffering their agony and loading his sins upon their "strong and passionate shoulders," but by being gored with a bull, hooked with a fish, impaled with a grasshopper on a fishhook; not by identifying himself with human heroes, but with those who are indeed defeated.

On the social level this writing performs a function similar to that of the stereotype: it conditions the reader to accept the less worthy values of society, and it serves to justify and absolve our sins of social irresponsibility. With unconscious irony it advises stoic acceptance of those conditions of life which it so accurately describes and which it pretends to reject. And when I read the early Hemingway I seem to be in the presence of Huckleberry Finn who, instead of identifying himself with humanity and attempting to steal Jim free, chose to write the letter which sent him back into slavery. So that now he is a Huck full of regret and nostalgia, suffering a sense of guilt that fills even his noondays with nightmares, and against which, like a terrified child avoiding the cracks in the sidewalk, he seeks protection through the compulsive minor rituals of his prose.

The major difference between nineteenth- and twentieth-century writers is not in the latter's lack of personal rituals—a property of all fiction worthy of being termed literature—but in the social effect aroused within their respective readers. Melville's ritual (and his rhetoric) was based upon materials that were more easily available, say, than Hemingway's. They represented a blending of his personal myth with universal myths as traditional as any used by Shakespeare or the Bible, while until *For Whom the Bell Tolls* Hemingway's was weighted on the personal side. The difference in terms of perspective of belief is that Melville's belief could still find a public object. Whatever else his works were "about" they also managed to be about democracy. But by our day the democratic dream had become too shaky a structure to support the furious pressures of the artist's doubt. And as always when the belief which nurtures a great social myth declines, large sections of society become prey to superstition. For man without myth is Othello with Desdemona gone: chaos descends, faith vanishes and superstitions prowl in the mind.

Hard-boiled writing is said to appeal through its presentation of sheer fact, rather than through rhetoric. The writer puts nothing down but what he pragmatically "knows." But actually one "fact" itself—which in literature must be presented simultaneously as image and as event—became a rhetorical unit. And the symbolic ritual which has set off the "fact"—that is, the fact unorganized by vital social myths (which might incorporate the findings of science and still contain elements of mystery)—is the rite of superstition. The superstitious individual responds to the capricious event, the fact that seems to explode in his face through blind fatality. For it is the creative function of myth to protect the individual from the irrational, and since it is here in the realm of the irrational that, impervious to science, the stereotype grows, we see that the Negro stereotype is really an image of the unorganized, irrational forces of American life, forces through which, by projecting them in forms of images of an easily dominated minority, the white individual seeks to be at home in the vast unknown world of America. Perhaps the object of the stereotype is not so much to crush the Negro as to console the white man.

Certainly there is justification for this view when we consider the work of William Faulkner. In Faulkner most of the relationships which we have pointed out between the Negro and contemporary writing come to focus: the social and the personal, the moral and the technical, the nineteenth-century emphasis upon morality and the modern accent upon the personal myth. And on the strictly literary level he is prolific and complex enough to speak for those Southern writers who are aggressively anti-Negro and for those younger writers who appear most sincerely interested in depicting the Negro as a rounded human being. What is more, he is the greatest artist the South has produced. While too complex to be given more than a glance in these notes, even a glance is more revealing of what lies back of the distortion of the Negro in modern writing than any attempt at a group survey might be.

Faulkner's attitude is mixed. Taking his cue from the Southern mentality in which the Negro is often dissociated into a malignant stereotype (the bad nigger) on the one hand and a benign stereotype (the good nigger) on the other, most often Faulkner presents characters embodying both. The dual function of this dissociation seems to be that of avoiding moral pain and thus to justify the South's racial code. But since such a social order harms whites no less than blacks, the sensitive Southerner, the artist, is apt to feel its effects acutely—and within the deepest levels of his personality. For not only is the social division forced upon the Negro by the ritualized ethic of discrimination, but upon the white man by the strictly enforced set of anti-Negro taboos. The conflict is always with him. Indeed, so rigidly has the recognition of Negro humanity been tabooed that the white Southerner is apt to associate any form of personal rebellion with the Negro. So that for the Southern artist the Negro becomes a symbol of his personal rebellion, his guilt and his repression of it. The Negro is thus a compelling object of fascination, and this we see very clearly in Faulkner.

Sometimes in Faulkner the Negro is simply a villain, but by an unconsciously ironic transvaluation his villainy consists, as with Loosh in *The Unvanquished,* of desiring his freedom. Or again the Negro appears benign, as with Ringo, of the same novel, who uses his talent not to seek personal freedom but to remain the loyal and resourceful retainer. Not that I criticize loyalty in itself, but that loyalty given where one's humanity is unrecognized seems a bit obscene. And yet in Faulkner's story, "The Bear," he brings us as close to the moral implication of the Negro as Twain or Melville. In the famous "difficult" fourth section, which Malcolm Cowley advises us to skip very much as Hemingway would have us skip the end of *Huckleberry Finn,* we find an argument in progress in which one voice (that of a Southern abolitionist) seeks to define Negro humanity against the other's enumeration of those stereotypes which many Southerners believe to be the Negro's basic traits. Significantly the mentor of the young hero of this story, a man of great moral stature, is socially a Negro.

Indeed, through his many novels and short stories. Faulkner fights out the moral problem which was repressed after the nineteenth century, and it was shocking for some to discover that for all his concern with the South, Faulkner was actually seeking out the nature of man. Thus we must turn to him for that continuity of moral purpose which made for the greatness of our classics. As for the Negro minority, he has been more willing perhaps than any other artist to start with the stereotype, accept it as true, and then seek out the human truth which it hides. Perhaps his is the example for our writers to follow, for in his work technique has been put once more to the task of creating value.

Which leaves these final things to be said. First, that this is meant as no plea for white writers to define Negro humanity, but to recognize the broader aspects of their own. Secondly, Negro writers and those of the other minorities have their own task of contributing to the total image of the American by depicting the experience of their own groups. Certainly theirs is the task of defining Negro humanity, as this can no more be accomplished by others than freedom, which must be won again and again each day, can be conferred upon another. A people must define itself, and minorities have the responsibility of having their ideals and images recognized as part of the composite image which is that of the still forming American people.

The other thing to be said is that while it is unlikely that American writing will ever retrace the way to the nineteenth century, it might be worth while to point out that for all its technical experimentation it is nevertheless an ethical instrument, and as such it might well exercise some choice in the kind of ethic it prefers to support. The artist is no freer than the society in which he lives, and in the United States the writers who stereotype or ignore the Negro and other minorities in the final analysis stereotype and distort their own humanity. Mark Twain knew that in *his* America humanity masked its face with blackness.

—Written in 1946. Published in *Confluence*, December 1953.

Change the Joke and Slip the Yoke

This essay originated in the form of a letter in which, from Rome, I expressed my reactions to a lecture which Stanley Edgar Hyman, an old friend and intellectual sparring partner, was preparing for what was to be the first of the Ludwig Lewisohn lectures at Brandeis University. Hyman wrote back suggesting that I work up my ideas as part of a publishable debate, and the two essays were presented in Partisan Review, Spring 1958. They were titled "The Negro Writer in America: An Exchange," and they are apt to yield their maximum return when read together. Hyman's part of the exchange, which is a most useful discussion of the Negro American's relation to the folk tradition, appears in his book of essays and reviews, "The Promised End," published by The World Publishing Company, 1963.

Stanley Edgar Hyman's essay on the relationship between Negro American literature and Negro American folklore concerns matters in which my own interest is such that the very news of his piece aroused my enthusiasm. Yet after reading it I find that our conceptions of the way in which folk tradition gets into literature—and especially into the novel; our conceptions of just what is *Negro* and what is *American* in Negro American folklore; and our conceptions of a Negro American writer's environment—are at such odds that I must disagree with him all along the way. And since much of his essay is given over so generously to aspects of my own meager writings, I am put in the ungrateful—and embarrassing—position of not only evaluating some of his statements from that highly dubious (but privileged) sanctuary provided by one's intimate knowledge of one's personal history, but of questioning some of his readings of my own novel by consulting the text.

Archetypes, like taxes, seem doomed to be with us always, and so with literature, one hopes; but between the two there must needs be the living human being in a specific texture of time, place and circumstance; who must respond, make choices, achieve eloquence and create specific works of art. Thus I feel that Hyman's fascination with folk tradition and the pleasure of archetype-hunting leads to a critical game that ignores the specificity of literary works. And it also causes him to blur the distinction between various archetypes and different currents of American folklore, and, generally, to oversimplify the American tradition.

Hyman's favorite archetypical figure is the trickster, but I see a danger here. From a proper distance *all* archetypes would appear to be tricksters and confidence men; part-God, part-man, no one seems to know he-she-its true name, because he-she-it is protean with changes of pace, location and identity. Further, the trickster is everywhere and anywhere at one and the same time, and, like the parts of some dismembered god, is likely to be found on stony as well as on fertile ground. Folklore is somewhat more stable, in its identity if not in its genealogy; but even here, if we are to discuss

Negro American folklore let us not be led astray by interlopers.

Certainly we should not approach Negro folklore through the figure Hyman calls the " 'darky' entertainer." For even though such performers as he mentions appear to be convenient guides, they lead us elsewhere, into a Cthonic labyrinth. The role with which they are identified is not, despite its "blackness," *Negro* American (indeed, Negroes are repelled by it); it does not find its popularity among Negroes but among whites; and although it resembles the role of the clown familiar to Negro variety-house audiences, it derives not from the Negro but from the Anglo-Saxon branch of American folklore. In other words, this " 'darky' entertainer" is white. Nevertheless, it might be worth while to follow the trail for a while, even though we seem more interested in interracial warfare than the question of literature.

These entertainers are, as Hyman explains, professionals, who in order to enact a symbolic role basic to the underlying drama of American society assume a ritual mask—the identical mask and role taken on by white minstrel men when *they* depicted comic Negroes. Social changes occurring since the 1930's have made for certain modifications (Rochester operates in a different climate of rhetoric, say, than did Stepin Fetchit) but the mask, stylized and iconic, was once required of anyone who would act the role—even those Negroes whose natural coloration should, for any less ritualistic purposes at least, have made it unnecessary.

Nor does the role, which makes use of Negro idiom, songs, dance motifs and word-play, grow out of the Negro American sense of the comic (although we too have our comedy of blackness), but out of the white American's Manichean fascination with the symbolism of blackness and whiteness expressed in such contradictions as the conflict between the white American's Judeo-Christian morality, his democratic political ideals and his daily conduct—indeed in his general anti-tragic approach to experience.

Being "highly pigmented," as the sociologists say, it was our Negro "misfortune" to be caught up associatively in the negative side of this basic dualism of the white folk mind, and to be shackled to almost everything it would repress from conscience and consciousness. The physical hardships and indignities of slavery were benign compared with this continuing debasement of our image. Because these things are bound up with their notion of chaos it is almost impossible for many whites to consider questions of sex, women, economic opportunity, the national identity, historic change, social justice—even the "criminality" implicit in the broadening of freedom itself—without summoning malignant images of black men into consciousness.

In the Anglo-Saxon branch of American folklore and in the entertainment industry (which thrives on the exploitation and debasement of all folk materials), the Negro is reduced to a negative sign that usually appears in a comedy of the grotesque and the unacceptable. As Constance Rourke has made us aware, the action of the early minstrel show—with its Negro-deprived choreography, its ringing of banjos and rattling of bones, its voices cackling jokes in pseudo-Negro dialect, with its nonsense songs, its bright costumes and sweating performers—constituted a ritual of exorcism. Other white cultures had their gollywogs and blackamoors but the fact of Negro slavery went to the moral heart of the American social drama and here the Negro was too real for easy fantasy, too serious to be dealt with in anything less than a national art. The mask was an inseparable part of the national iconography. Thus even when a Negro acted in an abstract role the national implications were unchanged. His costume made use of the "sacred" symbolism of the American flag—with red and white striped pants and coat and with stars set in a field of blue for a collar—but he could appear only with his hands gloved in white and his face blackened with burnt cork or greasepaint.

This mask, this willful stylization and modification of the natural face and hands, was imperative for the evocation of that atmosphere in which the fascination of blackness could be enjoyed, the comic catharsis achieved. The racial identity of the performer was unimportant, the mask was the thing (the "thing" in more ways than one) and its function was to veil the humanity of Negroes thus reduced to a sign, and to repress the white audience's awareness of its moral identification with its own acts and with the human ambiguities pushed behind the mask.

Hyman sees the comic point of the contemporary Negro's performance of the role as arising from the circumstance that a skilled man of intelligence is parodying a subhuman grotesque; this is all very kind, but when we move in from the wide-ranging spaces of the archetype for a closer inspection we see that the specific rhetorical situation involves the self-humiliation of the "sacrificial" figure, and that a psychological dissociation from this symbolic self-maiming is one of the powerful motives at work in the audience. Motives of race, status, economics and guilt are always clustered here. The comic point is inseparable from the racial identity of the performer—as is clear in Hyman's example from Wright's *Black Boy*—who by assuming the group-debasing role for gain not only substantiates the audience's belief in the "blackness" of things black, but relieves it, with dreamlike efficiency, of its guilt by accepting the very profit motive that was involved in the designation of the Negro as national scapegoat in the first place. There are all kinds of comedy: here one is reminded of the tribesman in *Green Hills of Africa* who hid his laughing face in shame at the sight of a gut-shot hyena jerking out its own intestines and eating them, in Hemingway's words, "with relish."

Down at the deep dark bottom of the melting pot, where

the private is public and the public private, where black is white and white black, where the immoral becomes moral and the moral is anything that makes one feel good (or that one has the power to sustain), the white man's relish is apt to be the black man's gall.

It is not at all odd that this black-faced figure of white fun is for Negroes a symbol of everything they rejected in the white man's thinking about race, in themselves and in their own group. When he appears, for example, in the guise of Nigger Jim, the Negro is made uncomfortable. Writing at a time when the blackfaced minstrel was still popular, and shortly after a war which left even the abolitionists weary of those problems associated with the Negro, Twain fitted Jim into the outlines of the minstrel tradition, and it is from behind this stereotype mask that we see Jim's dignity and human capacity—and Twain's complexity—emerge. Yet it is his source in this same tradition which creates that ambivalence between his identification as an adult and parent and his "boyish" naïveté, and which by contrast makes Huck, with his street-sparrow sophistication, seem more adult. Certainly it upsets a Negro reader, and it offers a less psychoanalytical explanation of the discomfort which lay behind Leslie Fiedler's thesis concerning the relation of Jim and Huck in his essay "Come Back to the Raft Ag'in, Huck Honey!"

A glance at a more recent fictional encounter between a Negro adult and a white boy, that of Lucas Beauchamp and Chick Mallison in Faulkner's *Intruder in The Dust,* will reinforce my point. For all the racial and caste differences between them, Lucas holds the ascendency in his mature dignity over the youthful Mallison and refuses to lower himself in the comic duel of status forced on him by the white boy whose life he has saved. Faulkner was free to reject the confusion between manhood and the Negro's caste status which is sanctioned by white Southern tradition, but Twain, standing closer to the Reconstruction and to the oral tradition, was not so free of the white dictum that Negro males must be treated either as boys or "uncles"—never as men. Jim's friendship for Huck comes across as that of a boy for another boy rather than as the friendship of an adult for a junior; thus there is implicit in it not only a violation of the manners sanctioned by society for relations between Negroes and whites, there is a violation of our conception of adult maleness.

In Jim the extremes of the private and the public come to focus, and before our eyes an "archetypal" figure gives way before the realism implicit in the form of the novel. Here we have, I believe, an explanation in the novel's own terms of that ambiguity which bothered Fiedler. Fiedler was accused of mere sensationalism when he named the friendship homosexual, yet I believe him so profoundly disturbed by the manner in which the deep dichotomies symbolized by blackness and whiteness are resolved that, forgetting to look at the specific form of the novel, he leaped squarely into the middle of that tangle of symbolism which he is dedicated to unsnarling, and yelled out his most terrifying name for chaos. Other things being equal, he might have called it "rape," "incest," "parricide" or— "miscegenation." It is ironic that what to a Negro appears to be a lost fall in Twain's otherwise successful wrestle with the ambiguous figure in black face is viewed by a critic as a symbolic loss of sexual identity. Surely for literature there is some rare richness here.

Although the figure in black face looks suspiciously homegrown, Western and Calvinist to me, Hyman identifies it as being related to an archetypical trickster figure, originating in Africa. Without arguing the point I shall say only that if it *is* a trickster, its adjustment to the contours of "white" symbolic needs is far more intriguing than its alleged origins, for it tells us something of the operation of American values as modulated by folklore and literature. We are back once more to questions of order and chaos, illusion and reality, nonentity and identity.

The trickster, according to Karl Kerenyi (in a commentary included in Paul Radin's study, *The Trickster*), represents a personification of the body

> which is . . . never wholly subdued, ruled by lust and hunger, forever running into pain and injury, cunning and stupid in action. Disorder belonging to the totality of life . . . the spirit of this disorder is the trickster. His function in an archaic society, or rather the function of his mythology, of tales told about him, is to add disorder to order and to make a whole, to render possible, within the fixed bounds of what is permitted, an experience of what is not permitted. . . .

But ours is no archaic society (although its archaic elements exert far more influence in our lives than we care to admit), and it is an ironic reversal that in what is regarded as the most "open" society in the world, the license of the black trickster figure is limited by the rigidities of racial attitudes, by political expediencies, and by the guilt bound with the white compulsion to identify with the ever-present man of flesh and blood whose irremediable features have been expropriated for "immoral" purposes. Hyman, incidentally, would have found in Louis Armstrong a much better example of the trickster, his medium being music rather than words and pantomime. Armstrong's clownish license and intoxicating powers are almost Elizabethan; he takes liberties with kings, queens and presidents; emphasizes the physicality of his music with sweat, spittle and facial contortions; he performs the magical feat of making romantic melody issue from a throat of gravel; and some few years ago was recommending to all and sundry his personal physic, "Pluto Water," as a purging way to health, happiness and international peace.

When the white man steps behind the mask of the trickster his freedom is circumscribed by the fear that he is not simply miming a personification of his disorder and chaos but that he will become in fact that which he intends only to symbolize; that he will be trapped somewhere in the mystery of hell (for there is a mystery in the whiteness of blackness, the innocence of evil and the evil of innocence, though, being initiates, Negroes express the joke of it in the blues) and thus lose that freedom which, in the fluid, "traditionless," "classless" and rapidly changing society, he would recognize as the white man's alone.

Here another ironic facet of the old American problem of identity crops up. For out of the counterfeiting of the black American's identity there arises a profound doubt in the white man's mind as to the authenticity of his own image of himself. He, after all, went into the business when he refused the king's shilling and revolted. He had put on a mask of his own, as it were; and when we regard our concern with identity in the light of what Robert Penn Warren has termed the "intentional" character of our national beginnings, a quotation from W. B. Yeats proves highly meaningful:

> There is a relation between discipline and the theatrical sense. If we cannot imagine ourselves as different from what we are and assume the second self, we cannot impose a discipline upon ourselves, though we may accept one from others. Active virtue, as distinct from the passive acceptance of a current code, is the wearing of a mask. It is the condition of an arduous full life.

For the ex-colonials, the declaration of an American identity meant the assumption of a mask, and it imposed not only the discipline of national self-consciousness, it gave Americans an ironic awareness of the joke that always lies between appearance and reality, between the discontinuity of social tradition and that sense of the past which clings to the mind. And perhaps even an awareness of the joke that society is man's creation, not God's. Americans began their revolt from the English fatherland when they dumped the tea into the Boston Harbor, masked as Indians, and the mobility of the society created in this limitless space has encouraged the use of the mask for good and evil ever since. As the advertising industry, which is dedicated to the creation of masks, makes clear, that which cannot gain authority from tradition may borrow it with a mask. Masking is a play upon possibility and ours is a society in which possibilities are many. When American life is most American it is apt to be most theatrical.

And it is this which makes me question Hyman's designation of the "smart man playing dumb" role as primarily Negro, if he means by "conflict situations" those in which racial pressure is uppermost. Actually it is a role which Negroes share with other Americans, and it might be more "Yankee" than anything else. It is a strategy common to the culture, and it is reinforced by our anti-intellectualism, by our tendency toward conformity and by the related desire of the individual to be left alone; often simply by the desire to put more money in the bank. But basically the strategy grows out of our awareness of the joke at the center of the American identity. Said a very dark Southern friend of mine in laughing reply to a white businessman who complained of his recalcitrance in a bargaining situation, "I know, you thought I was colored, didn't you." It is across this joke that Negro and white Americans regard one another. The white American has charged the Negro American with being without past or tradition (something which strikes the white man with a nameless horror), just as he himself has been so charged by European and American critics with a nostalgia for the stability once typical of European cultures; and the Negro knows that both were "mammy-made" right here at home. What's more, each secretly believes that he alone knows what is valid in the American experience, and that the other knows he knows but will not admit it, and each suspects the other of being at bottom a phony.

The white man's half-conscious awareness that his image of the Negro is false makes him suspect the Negro of always seeking to take him in, and assume his motives are anger and fear—which very often they are. On his side of the joke the Negro looks at the white man and finds it difficult to believe that the "grays"—a Negro term for white people—can be so absurdly self-deluded over the true interrelatedness of blackness and whiteness. To him the white man seems a hypocrite who boasts of a pure identity while standing with his humanity exposed to the world.

Very often, however, the Negro's masking is motivated not so much by fear as by a profound rejection of the image created to usurp his identity. Sometimes it is for the sheer joy of the joke; sometimes to challenge those who presume, across the psychological distance created by race manners, to know his identity. Nonetheless, it is in the American grain. Benjamin Franklin, the practical scientist, skilled statesman and sophisticated lover, allowed the French to mistake him for Rousseau's Natural Man. Hemingway poses as a non-literary sportsman, Faulkner as a farmer; Abe Lincoln allowed himself to be taken for a simple country lawyer—until the chips were down. Here the "darky" act makes brothers of us all. America is a land of masking jokers. We wear the mask for purposes of aggression as well as for defense; when we are projecting the future and preserving the past. In short, the motives hidden behind the mask are as numerous as the ambiguities the mask conceals.

My basic quarrel with Hyman is not over his belief in the importance of the folk tradition, nor over his interest in archetypes; but that when he turns to specific works of literature he tends to distort their content to fit his theory. Since he refers so generously to my own novel, let us take it as a case in point. So intense is Hyman's search for archetypical forms that he doesn't see that the narrator's grandfather in *Invisible Man* is no more involved in a "darky" act than was Ulysses in Polyphemus' cave. Nor is he so much a "smart-man-playing-dumb" as a weak man who knows the nature of his oppressor's weakness. There is a good deal of spite in the old man, as there comes to be in his grandson, and the strategy he advises is a kind of jiujitsu of the spirit, a denial and rejection through agreement. Samson, eyeless in Gaza, pulls the building down when his strength returns; politically weak, the grandfather has learned that conformity leads to a similar end, and so advises his children. Thus his mask of meekness conceals the wisdom of one who has learned the secret of saying the "yes" which accomplishes the expressive "no." Here, too, is a rejection of a current code and a denial become metaphysical. More important to the novel is the fact that he represents the ambiguity of the past for the hero, for whom his sphinxlike deathbed advice poses a riddle which points the plot in the dual direction which the hero will follow throughout the novel.

Certainly B. P. Rhinehart (the P. is for "Proteus," the B. for "Bliss") would seem the perfect example of Hyman's trickster figure. He is a cunning man who wins the admiration of those who admire skulduggery and know-how; an American virtuoso of identity who thrives on chaos and swift change; he is greedy, in that his masquerade is motivated by money as well as by the sheer bliss of impersonation; he is godlike, in that he brings new techniques—electric guitars, etc.—to the service of God, and in that there are many men in his image while he is himself unseen; he is phallic in his role of "lover"; as a numbers runner he is a bringer of manna and a worker of miracles, in that he transforms (for winners, of course) pennies into dollars, and thus he feeds (and feeds on) the poor. Indeed, one could extend this list in the manner of much myth-mongering criticism until the fiction dissolved into anthropology, but Rhinehart's role in the formal structure of the narrative is to suggest to the hero a mode of escape from Ras, and a means of applying, in yet another form, his grandfather's cryptic advice to his own situation. One could throw Rhinehart among his literary betters and link him with Mann's Felix Krull, the Baron Clappique of Malraux's *Man's Fate* and many others, but that would be to make a game of criticism and really say nothing.

The identity of fictional characters is determined by the implicit realism of the form, not by their relation to tradition; they are what they do or do not do. Archetypes are timeless, novels are time-haunted. Novels achieve timelessness through time. If the symbols appearing in a novel link up with those of universal myth they do so by virtue of their emergence from the specific texture of a specific form of social reality. The final act of *Invisible Man* is not that of a concealment in darkness in the Anglo-Saxon connotation of the word, but that of a voice issuing its little wisdom out of the substance of its own inwardness—after having undergone a transformation from ranter to w   If, by the way, the hero is pulling a "darky art" in ths, ne certainly is not a smart man playing dumb. For the novel, his memoir, is one long, loud rant, howl and laugh. Confession, not concealment, is his mode. His mobility is dual; geographical, as Hyman points out, but, more importantly, it is intellectual. And in keeping with the reverse English of the plot, and with the Negro American conception of blackness, his movement vertically downward (not into a "sewer," Freud notwithstanding, but into a coal cellar, a source of heat, light, power and, through association with the character's motivation, self-perception) is a process of *rising* to an understanding of his human condition. He gets his restless mobility not so much from the blues or from sociology but from the circumstance that he appears in a literary form which has time and social change as its special province.

Besides, restlessness of the spirit is an American condition that transcends geography, sociology and past condition of servitude.

Discussions of folk tradition and literature which slight the specific literary forms involved seem to me questionable. Most of the writers whom Hyman mentions are novelists, workers in a form which has absorbed folk tradition into its thematic structures, its plots, symbolism and rhetoric; and which has its special way with folklore as it has with manners, history, sociology and psychology. Besides, novelists in our time are more likely to be inspired by reading novels than by their acquaintance with any folk tradition.

I use folklore in my work not because I am Negro, but because writers like Eliot and Joyce made me conscious of the literary value of my folk inheritance. My cultural background, like that of most Americans, is dual (my middle name, sadly enough, is Waldo).

I knew the trickster Ulysses just as early as I knew the wily rabbit of Negro American lore, and I could easily imagine myself a pint-sized Ulysses but hardly a rabbit, no matter how human and resourceful or Negro. And a little later I could imagine myself as Huck Finn (I so nicknamed my brother) but not, though I racially identified with him, as Nigger Jim, who struck me as a white man's inadequate portrait of a slave.

My point is that the Negro American writer is also an heir of the human experience which is literature, and this might well be more important to him than his living folk tradition. For me, at least, in the discontinuous, swiftly changing and diverse American culture, the stability of the Negro American folk tradition became precious as a result of an act of literary discovery. Taken as a whole, its spirituals along with its blues, jazz and folk tales, it has, as Hyman suggests, much to tell us of the faith, humor and adaptability to reality necessary to live in a world which has taken on much of the insecurity and blues-like absurdity known to those who brought it into being. For those who are able to translate its meanings into wider, more precise vocabularies it has much to offer indeed. Hyman performs a service when he makes us aware that Negro American folk tradition constitutes a valuable source for literature, but for the novelist, of any cultural or racial identity, his form is his greatest freedom and his insights are where he finds them.

—From *Partisan Review*, Spring 1958.

Stephen Crane and the
Mainstream of
American Fiction

Of all our nineteenth-century masters of fiction—Hawthorne, Melville, Henry James, Mark Twain and Stephen Crane—it was Crane, the youngest, arrived most distantly from the Civil War in point of time, who was the most war-haunted. Born in Newark, New Jersey, six years after the firing ceased, Crane was the youngest of fourteen offspring of parents whose marriage marked the union of two lines of hard-preaching, fundamentalist Methodist ministers. The time and place of his birth and his parents' concern with conduct, morality and eloquence were, when joined with his self-dedication to precise feeling and writing, perhaps as portentous and as difficult a gift to bear as any seer's obligation to peer through walls and into the secret places of the heart, or around windy corners and into the enigmatic future. Indeed, such words as "clairvoyant," "occult" and "uncanny" have been used to describe his style, and while these tell us little, there was nonetheless an inescapable aura of the marvelous about Stephen Crane. For although there is no record of his eyes having been covered at birth with that caul which is said to grant one second sight, he revealed a unique vision of the human condition and an unusual talent for projecting it. His was a costly vision, won through personal suffering, hard living and harsh artistic discipline; and by the time of his death, at twenty-nine, he was recognized as one of the important innovators of American fictional prose and master of a powerful and original style.

Fortunately it was the style and not the myth which was important. Thus today, after sixty years during which there was little interest in the meaning and sources of Crane's art, the best of the work remains not only alive but capable of speaking to us with a new resonance of meaning. While recent criticism holds that the pioneer style, which leads directly to Ernest Hemingway, sprang from a dedication to the moral and aesthetic possibilities of literary form similar to that of Henry James, Crane's dedication to art was no less disciplined or deadly serious than that which characterized his preaching forefathers' concern with religion. Indeed, John Berryman and Robert Wooster Stallman, the most perceptive of Crane's recent critics, see much of the tension in the work as arising from his desperate struggle with the rejected angel of his parents' Methodism—an insight which we find highly suggestive.

Surely if fundamentalist Christianity could get so authoritatively into national politics (especially in the Bible Belt), so ambiguously into our system of education (as in the Scopes trial issue), into our style of crime (through prohibition's spawn of bootleggers, gangsters, jellybeans and flappers) and so powerfully into jazz—it is about time we recognized its deeper relationship to the art of our twentieth-century literature. And not simply as subject matter, but as a major source of its technique, its form and rhetoric. For while much has been made of the role of the high church in the development of modern poetry, and with Kierkegaard become a household god for many contemporary novelists, Crane's example suggests that for the writer a youthful contact with the emotional intensity and harsh authority of American fundamentalism can be as important an experience as contact with those churches which possess a ritual containing elements of high art and a theology spun subtle and fine through intellectualization. Undoubtedly the Methodist Church provided Crane an early schooling in the seriousness of spiritual questions—of the individual's ultimate relationship to his fellow men, to the universe and to God—and was one source of the youthful revolt which taught him to look upon life with his own eyes. Just as important, perhaps, is the discipline which the church provided him in keeping great emotion under the control of the intellect, as during the exciting services (which the boy learned to question quite early), along with an awareness of the disparity between the individual's public testimony (a rite common to evangelical churches) and his private deeds—a matter intensified by the fact that the celebrant of this rite of public confession was his own father. In brief, Crane was concerned very early with private emotions publicly displayed as an act of purification and self-definition; an excellent beginning for a writer interested in the ordeals of the private individual struggling to define himself as against the claims of society. Crane, who might well have become a minister, turned from religion but transferred its forms to his art.

For his contemporaries much of the meaning of Crane's art was obscured by a personal myth compounded of ele-

ments ever fascinating to the American mind: his youth and
his early mastery of a difficult and highly technical skill (like
a precocious juvenile delinquent possessed of an uncanny
knowledge not of pocket pool, craps or tap dancing, but of
advanced literary technique) coupled with that highly individual way of feeling and thinking which is the basis of all
significant innovation in art; his wild bohemian way of life;
his maverick attitude toward respectability; his gallantry toward prostitutes no less than toward their respectable sisters;
his friendship with Bowery outcasts—"What Must I Do to Be
Saved?" was the title of a tract by his mother's uncle, the
Methodist Bishop of Syracuse and a founder of the university
there; his gambler's prodigality with fame and money; his
search for wars to observe and report; and, finally, the fatality of "genius" which followed the fair, slight, gifted youth
from obscurity to association with the wealthy and gifted in
England (Joseph Conrad, H. G. Wells, Ford Madox Ford
and Henry James were among his friends), to his death from
tuberculosis, one of the period's most feared and roman-
ticized scourges, in the far Black Forest of Germany.

Blind to the cost of his knowledge, many of his contemporaries regarded Crane's adventures as undertaken merely
to provide them with entertainment: Crane chasing bandits
in Mexico; Crane shipwrecked while running guns to Cuba;
Crane reporting the Greco-Turkish War; Crane taking on the
New York police force and being obliged to abandon the city;
Crane marrying a woman said to have been an ex-madam;
Crane on a spree. And there was, in fact, some truth to their
assumption. Crane was as gifted at acting out good newspaper copy as Hemingway or F. Scott Fitzgerald were to be
and no less a delight to the reporters.

Yet despite the headlines and malicious gossip concerning
his wife's past (which motivated their taking up residence
in England), the fiction presented here testifies that whatever else Crane might have been seeking, the playboy author

was engaged in a most desperate moral struggle. At a time when the capacity for moral seriousness appeared to have disappeared from American society, Crane was attempting to live his own life as cleanly, as imaginatively and with as much immediacy and realistic poetry as he aspired to convey in his writing. If there was something of the entertainer in his public role (and this was still the time of that great popular entertainer, Mark Twain) there was also an element of the self-sacrificial, and the sensational features of the public adventures hint at the cost of the art. There was in Crane something of Emerson and Thoreau as well as the fundamentalist moralist-designate, and the quiet, desperate, unthinking life was to be avoided at the cost of life itself.

At the center of Crane's myth there lay, of course, the mystery of the creative talent with which a youth of twenty-one was able to write what is considered one of the world's foremost war novels when he had neither observed nor participated in combat. And, indeed, with this second book, *The Red Badge of Courage,* Crane burst upon the American public with the effect of a Civil War projectile lain dormant beneath a city square for thirty years. Two years before he had appeared with *Maggie: A Girl of the Streets,* a stripped little novel of social protest written in a strange new idiom. But although Hamlin Garland and William Dean Howells had recognized the work's importance, the reading public was prepared neither for such a close look at the devastating effect of the Bowery upon the individual's sense of life, nor for the narrow choice between the sweatshop and prostitution which Crane saw as the fate of such girls as Maggie. Besides, with its ear attuned to the languid accents of genteel fiction it was unprepared for the harsh, although offbeat, poetic realism of Crane's idiom.

In a famous inscription in which he exhorted a reader to have the "courage" to read his book to the end, Crane explained that he had tried to show that environment is a tremendous thing in the world, and frequently shapes lives regardless. If one proves that theory, one makes room in heaven for all sorts of souls, notably an occasional street girl, who are not confidently expected to be there by many excellent people. . . .

a statement which reveals that the young author knew the mood of his prospective audience much better than it was prepared to know him. For although Crane published *Maggie* at his own expense (significantly, under a pseudony and paid four men to read it conspicuously while travel up and down Manhattan on the El, it failed.

This was for American literature a most significant failure indeed; afterward, following *Maggie,* Crane developed the strategy of understatement and the technique of impressionism which was to point the way for Hemingway and our fiction of the twenties. Crane was not to return to an explicit projection of his social criticism until "The Monster," a work written much later in his career; he turned, instead, to exploring the psychology of the individual under extreme pressure. *Maggie,* which is omitted here in favor of the neglected and more mature "The Monster," stands with *The Adventures of Huckleberry Finn* as one of the parents of the modern American novel; but it is *The Red Badge of Courage* which claims our attention with all the authority of a masterpiece.

One cannot help but feel, however, that the romantic mystery made of the fact that Crane had no direct experience of war before writing *The Red Badge* has served to obscure much of its true importance. For even while rejecting the assumption that the creative act is completely accountable, it is evident that Crane was the type of writer upon whom, to use Henry James's phrase, "nothing was lost," and the possessor of an imagination for which minor experiences ever revealed their more universal implications. It is not necessary for even the most unimaginative of us to be consumed by flame in order to envision hellfire—the hot head of a match against the fingernail suffices—and the embers of the Civil War, let us recall, had far from ceased their burning in the American mind.

Factually we know that one of Crane's brothers was an expert on the Civil War; that while attending the Hudson River Institute at Claverack, N.Y., Crane had listened to the exciting war experiences of Lieutenant John Van Petten, a hero of the old 34th New York, then teaching elocution and drill at the little military academy; that he possessed an excellent memory for detail and a marvelous ear for speech accents, rhythms and idioms; and that as a college athlete he had gained some notion of the psychology of men engaged in mass action while on the football field. As for his concern with the ambiguities of fear and of courage, cowardice and heroism, and the problem of the relation of the individual to the group and to God, these were a part of his religious and family background; while the deeper insights were available to him (as they are to each of us) through a ruthless plunging into the dark depths of his own heart and mind. More than this, we know truly that although the fighting had ceased six years before Crane's birth, the moral climate which it created formed the only climate Crane was ever to know. Having been born in the world which the war had brought into being, much of his activity was a search for ways of living within it with meaningful intensity. Historically wars and revolutions form the background for the high periods of the novel, and civil wars, Hemingway has written, are the best wars for the writer. To which we would add, yes, because they have a way of continuing long after wars between nations are resolved; because, with the combatants being the same people, civil wars are never really won; and because their most devastating engagements are fought within the individual human heart.

For all our efforts to forget it, the Civil War was the great shaping event not only of our political and economic life, but following Crane, of our twentieth-century fiction. It was the agency through which many of the conflicting elements within the old republic were brought to maximum tension, leaving us a nation fully aware of the continental character of our destiny, preparing the emergence of our predominantly industrial economy and our increasingly urban way of life, and transforming us from a nation consisting of two major regions which could pretend to a unity of values, despite their basic split over fundamental issues, to one which was now consciously divided. To put it drastically, if war, as Clausewitz insisted, is the continuation of politics by other means, it requires little imagination to see American life since the abandonment of the Reconstruction as an abrupt reversal of that formula: the continuation of the Civil War by means other than arms. In this sense the conflict has not only gone unresolved but the line between civil war and civil peace has become so blurred as to require of the sensitive man a questioning attitude toward every aspect of the nation's self-image. Stephen Crane, in his time, was such a man.

The America into which Crane was born was one of mirrorlike reversals in which the victors were the defeated and the defeated the victors; with the South, its memory frozen at the fixed moment of its surrender, carrying its aggression to the North in the form of guerrilla politics, and with the North, compromising as it went, retreating swiftly into the vast expanse of its new industrial development, eager to lose any memory traces of those values for which it had gone to war. Mark Twain had attacked this postwar society, infamous for its carpetbaggers, its Hayes-Tilden Compromise, its looting of the nation's resources during the Grant administrations, in *The Man That Corrupted Hadleyburg,* and Henry James depicted the inversion of its moral values in *The Bos-*

tonians and was stimulated by it to those subtleties of moral perception which inform his major fiction. For all of this, however, Twain's bitter satire was taken for comedy and the best of James was left unread. Despite the prosperity and apparent openness and freedom of the society, it was as though a rigid national censorship had been imposed—not by an apparatus set up in Washington, but within the center of the American mind. Now there was much of which Americans were morally aware but little which they wished to confront in literature, and the compelling of such confrontation was the challenge flung down to Crane by history.

Let us not forget, then, that while the setting of *The Red Badge* is the Civil War, its issues are drawn from the lax society of the eighteen-eighties and nineties; a society which Crane viewed as hostile to those who would achieve manhood and moral identity, whose tendency toward moral evasion he set out to overcome with his technique of understatement, and whose capacity for reality and moral responsibility he sought to ensnare through the realistic poetry of his diction.

Thus in *The Red Badge* social reality is filtered through the sensibility of a young Northern soldier who is only vaguely aware of the larger issues of the war, and we note that for all the complex use of the symbolic connotations of blackness, only one Negro, a dancing teamster, appears throughout the novel. The reader is left to fill in the understated background, to re-create those matters of which the hero, Henry Fleming, is too young, too self-centered and too concerned with the more immediate problems of courage, honor and self-preservation to be aware. This leaves the real test of moral courage as much a challenge to the reader as to the hero; he must decide for himself whether or not to confront the public issues evoked by Henry's private ordeal. *The Red Badge* is a novel about a lonely individual's struggle for self-definition, written for lonely individualists, and its style, which no longer speaks in terms of the traditional

American rhetoric, implies a deep skepticism as to the possibility of the old American ideals being revived by a people which had failed to live up to them after having paid so much to defend them in hardship and blood. Here in place of the conventional plot—which implies the public validity of private experiences—we find a series of vividly impressionistic episodes that convey the discontinuity of feeling and perception of one caught up in a vast impersonal action, and a concentration upon the psychology of one who seeks first to secede from society and then to live in it with honor and courage.

Indeed, for a novel supposedly about the war, *The Red Badge* is intensely concerned with invasion of the private life, a theme announced when the men encounter the body of their first dead soldier, whose shoe soles, "worn to the thinness of writing paper," strike Henry as evidence of a betrayal by fate which in death had exposed to the dead Confederate's enemies "that poverty which in life he had perhaps concealed from his friends." But war is nothing if not an invasion of privacy, and so is death (the "invulnerable" dead man forces his way between the men as they open ranks to avoid him); and society, more so. For society, even when reduced to a few companions, invades personality and demands of the individual an almost impossible consistency while guaranteeing the individual hardly anything. Or so it seems to the naïve Henry, much of whose anguish springs from the fear that his friends will discover that the wound which he received from the rifle butt of another frightened soldier is not the red badge of courage they assume but a badge of shame. Thus the Tattered Soldier's questions as to the circumstance of his injury (really questions as to his moral identity) fill Henry with fear and hostility, and he regards them as

> the assertion of a society that probed pitilessly at secrets until all is apparent. . . . His late companion's chance per-

sistency made him feel that he could not keep his crime [of malingering] concealed in his bosom. It was sure to be brought plain by one of those arrows which cloud the air and are constantly pricking, discovering, proclaiming those things which are willed to be forever hidden. He admitted that he could not defend himself against this agency. It was not within the power of vigilance. . . .

In time Henry learns to act with honor and courage and to perceive something of what it means to be a man, but this perception depends upon the individual fates of those who make up his immediate group; upon the death of Jim Conklin, the most mature and responsible of the men, and upon the Loud Soldier's attainment of maturity and inner self-confidence. But the cost of perception is primarily personal, and for Henry it depends upon the experience of the moral discomfort which follows the crimes of malingering and assuming a phony identity, and the further crime of allowing the voice of conscience, here symbolized by the Tattered Soldier, to wander off and die. Later he acquits himself bravely and comes to feel that he has attained

> a quiet manhood, non-assertive but of sturdy and strong blood. He knew that he would no more quail before his guides wherever they should point. He had been to touch the great death, and found that, after all, it was but the great death. He was a man.

Obviously although Henry has been initiated into the battle of life, he has by no means finished with illusion—but that, too, is part of the human condition.

That *The Red Badge* was widely read during Crane's own time was a triumph of his art, but the real mystery lay not in his re-creation of the simpler aspects of battle: the corpses, the wounds, the sound of rifle fire, the panic and high elation of combat; the real mystery lay in the courage out of which one so young could face up to the truth which so many Americans were resisting with a noisy clamor of opti-

mism and with frantic gestures of materialistic denial. War,
the jungle and hostile Nature became Crane's underlying
metaphors for the human drama and the basic situations in
which the individual's capacity for moral and physical courage were put to their most meaningful testing.

And so with "The Open Boat." In January, 1897, Crane
was one of four men who spent thirty hours in a ten-foot
dinghy after their ship, bound on a gun-running expedition
to Cuba, developed a leak and sank. It was from this experience that Crane shaped what is considered his most perfect
short story. When "The Open Boat" is compared with the report which Crane wrote for the New York *Press*, we can see
that it keeps to the order of events as they actually occurred;
but such is the power of Crane's shaping vision that the
reader is made to *experience* the events as a complete, dynamic, symbolic action. We become one with the men in the
boat, who pit their skill and courage against the raging sea,
living in their hope and despair and sharing the companion-
ship won within the capricious hand of fate. Under the shaping grace of Crane's imagination the actual event is reduced
to significant form, with each wave and gust of wind, each
intonation of voice and gesture of limb combining toward a
single effect of meaning.

And as with most of Crane's fiction, the point at issue is
the cost of moral perception, of achieving an informed sense
of life, in a universe which is essentially hostile to man and
in which skill and courage and loyalty are virtues which
help in the struggle but by no means exempt us from the
necessary plunge into the storm-sea-war of experience. For
it is thus and thus only that humanity is won, and often the
best are destroyed in the trial—as with Higgins, the oiler,
whose skill and generosity have helped save the men from
the sea but who in the end lies dead upon the shore. Through
their immersion into the raging sea of life, and through Higgins's sacrificial death, the survivors are initiated into a per-

sonal knowledge of the human condition—and "when the wind brought the sound of the great sea's voice to the men on the shore . . . they felt that they could be interpreters."

In his essay on storytelling, Mark Twain informs us that the humorous story is especially American and that

> it depends for its effect upon the manner of its telling . . . [it] is told gravely; the teller doing his best to conceal the fact that he even dimly suspects that there is anything funny about it. . . .

It is this same noncommittal manner which Stephen Crane brings to the depiction of events which are far from humorous, and while he is seldom comic in the manner of Twain, the method gives his fiction an endless complexity of meaning, and among those matters of which his style pretends unawareness are the social and historical references of his stories. Here, too, the effect depends upon a collaboration between the teller, who conceals the range of his intention, and the listener, who must pit his sense of reality against the enigmatic order of the narrated events . . . as in "The Bride Comes to Yellow Sky," a story which dances over its apparent terrain with such a tight choreography of ironic reversals that the reader must be extremely light-footed lest he fall out of the pattern of the dance.

Scratchy Wilson, the drunken badman of deadly marksmanship, terrorizes the town and appears to have Jack Potter at his mercy—until the unarmed marshal's announcement of his marriage unnerves him. For Scratchy, who is the last of a local gang, the news is like a "glimpse of another world," and he sees the bride as foreshadowing the end of his way of life. The point, it would seem, is that history has played a joke on Scratchy; the man with the gun is defeated by the unarmed man who has embraced those civilized values symbolized by marriage. But is this all? Doesn't the story pivot at this point and return to the westward-moving train of its beginning?

When the marshal faces the badman's pistol it is clear that despite being unarmed he reacts out of an old habit of courage; he has fought Scratchy many times and even shot him once—in the leg (the red-topped boots with gilded imprints "of the kind beloved in winter by little sledding boys on the hillsides of New England" robs Scratchy of much of his menace for the contemporary reader). But he is also sustained by a vision of the Pullman car from which he and his bride have just departed. He sees in its sea-green velvet, its glass and its gleaming surfaces of silver, brass and darkly brilliant wood "all the glory of marriage, the environment of [his] new estate," and it is this vision, when conveyed to Scratchy, which defeats the badman.

But here we have a double reversal. Because for all of Scratchy's simple-mindedness, his moment of defeat is also one of perception; he has learned where he is. While in his moment of unarmed triumph the marshal is even more unarmed than he knows; for he is unaware that his new estate has its own complications—even though he has already been subjected to them. In the actual Pullman car the Negro porter has played with him and his bride much as the gunman has played with the town (and as Crane plays with the reader's susceptibilities), and they have been bullied

> with skill in ways that did not make it exactly plain to them that they were bullied. He [the porter] subtly used all the manners of the most unconquerable kinds of snobbery. He oppressed them; but of his oppression they had small knowledge, and they speedily forgot that infrequently a number of travelers covered them with stares of derisive enjoyment.

And again, in the dining car the waiter's patronage had been so entwined with deference that when they returned to their coach their faces revealed "a sense of escape."

"Historically," we are told, "there was supposed to be some-thing infinitely humorous in their situation . . ." And there is indeed something humorous in their situation which is limited neither to the circumstances of their middle-aged wedlock nor to their provincial discomfort in the Pullman car; there is the humor arising from their *historical* situation. For in face of the complexities of American civilization represented by the bullying yet patronizing Negro servants, the marshal is no less a "child of the earlier plains" than Scratchy Wilson. The Stephen Crane who wrote "The Bride" was essentially the same moral man who wrote the social protest of *Maggie*, only he has learned to hide his perceptions behind a sardonic smile. Still, the form of the story is one with its meaning: the necessity for vigilance in confronting historical change is unending, and living with American change is much like Crane's description of keeping a small boat afloat in an angry sea, where "after successfully sur-mounting one wave you discover that there is another behind it just as important and just as nervously anxious to do something effective in the way of swamping boats." A sim-ilar vigilance is required when reading his fiction.

Perhaps at the root of our American fascination with the humorous story lies the awareness that if we don't know *where* we are, we have little chance of knowing *who* we are, that if we confuse the *time* we confuse the *place;* and that when we confuse these we endanger our humanity, both physically and morally. "Any room," writes Crane in "The Blue Hotel," "can present a tragic front; any room be comic." Thus men determine their own social weather, and human fate is a creation of human confusion.

The background of "The Blue Hotel" is that same confu-sion of time and place underlying "The Bride," and the Swede's failure to understand the rapidity of American his-torical change and its effect upon social relationships and personality is his undoing. Frightened and believing himself to be in a West that has long since passed, he evokes the violence which he associates with it out of the very intensity of his illusion. Arriving at a place where he believes he is to be killed, he forces a fight from men who are usually peaceful, wins it and then goes full of his victory to a peaceful barroom and there, confused perhaps by his ten years of hiding the reality of the human form (he is a tailor) as well as by drinking, he picks on the man who appears least likely to defend himself and is killed. No other Crane fiction—except, perhaps, "The Monster"—expresses such a violence of disgust with man and his condition, and one feels behind the noncommittal mask of the prose a conviction that man exists in the universe ever at the mercy of a capricious fate, a hostile nature, an indifferent and unjust god—*and* his own misconceptions.

And yet, for all the self-destructive actions of the Swede, the Easterner sees his death as the corporate sin of society. Society is responsible to itself *for* itself; the death is thus a failure of social charity. It is the same failure of social charity which characterizes "The Monster." Here Crane presents the cost of two acts of human loyalty and courage when they occur in a small, smug Northern town. Henry Johnson's self-sacrificial act, which destroys his face and his mind, is repaid first with applause and then with demands for his death or banishment. Dr. Trescott's loyalty to his oath as physician and to the man who has saved his son's life costs him his practice, his friends and ultimately his social identity. In short, "The Monster" places us in an atmosphere like that of post-Civil War America, and there is no question as to the Negro's part in it, nor to the fact that the issues go much deeper than the question of race. Indeed, the work is so fresh that the daily papers tell us all we need to know of its background and the timeliness of its implications.

As for Crane the conscious artist, "The Monster" reminds us that he not only anticipated many of the techniques and themes of Hemingway, but that he also stands as the link between the Twain of *Pudd'nhead Wilson* and *Huckleberry Finn* and the Faulkner of *The Sound and the Fury*. The point is not simply that in *The Sound and the Fury*, as in Crane's work, a young boy is warned against "projecking" with flowers, or that Benjy is as much a "monster" as Henry Johnson, or Henry as much an idiot as Benjy, or that their communities are more monstrous than either, or that to touch either is considered a test of courage by the small fry, or even that both suffer when young white girls are frightened by them. The important point is that between Twain and the emergence of the driving honesty and social responsibility of Faulkner, no artist of Crane's caliber looked so steadily at the wholeness of American life and discovered such far-reaching symbolic equivalents for its unceasing state of civil war. Crane's work remains fresh today because he was a great artist, but perhaps he became a great artist because under conditions of pressure and panic he stuck to his guns.

—Introduction to *The Red Badge of Courage*, 1960.

Richard Wright's Blues

> *If anybody ask you*
> *who sing this song,*
> *Say it was ole [Black Boy]*
> *done been here and gone.*[1]

As a writer, Richard Wright has outlined for himself a dual
role: to discover and depict the meaning of Negro experience; and to reveal to both Negroes and whites those problems of a psychological and emotional nature which arise
between them when they strive for mutual understanding.

Now, in *Black Boy*, he has used his own life to probe what
qualities of will, imagination and intellect are required of a
Southern Negro in order to possess the meaning of his life in
the United States. Wright is an important writer, perhaps
the most articulate Negro American, and what he has to say
is highly perceptive. Imagine Bigger Thomas projecting his
own life in lucid prose, guided, say, by the insights of Marx
and Freud, and you have an idea of this autobiography.

---

[1] Signature formula used by blues singers at conclusion of song.

Published at a time when any sharply critical approach to Negro life has been dropped as a wartime expendable, it should do much to redefine the problem of the Negro and American Democracy. Its power can be observed in the shrill manner with which some professional "friends of the Negro people" have attempted to strangle the work in a noose of newsprint.

What in the tradition of literary autobiography is it like, this work described as a "great American autobiography"? As a non-white intellectual's statement of his relationship to Western culture, *Black Boy* recalls the conflicting pattern of identification and rejection found in Nehru's *Toward Freedom*. In its use of fictional techniques, its concern with criminality (sin) and the artistic sensibility, and in its author's judgment and rejection of the narrow world of his origin, it recalls Joyce's rejection of Dublin in *A Portrait of the Artist*. And as a psychological document of life under oppressive conditions, it recalls *The House of the Dead*, Dostoievsky's profound study of the humanity of Russian criminals.

Such works were perhaps Wright's literary guides, aiding him to endow his life's incidents with communicable significance; providing him with ways of seeing, feeling and describing his environment. These influences, however, were encountered only after these first years of Wright's life were past and were not part of the immediate folk culture into which he was born. In that culture the specific folk-art form which helped shape the writer's attitude toward his life and which embodied the impulse that contributes much to the quality and tone of his autobiography was the Negro blues. This would bear a word of explanation:

The blues is an impulse to keep the painful details and episodes of a brutal experience alive in one's aching consciousness, to finger its jagged grain, and to transcend it, not by the consolation of philosophy but by squeezing from it a near-tragic, near-comic lyricism. As a form, the blues is an autobiographical chronicle of personal catastrophe expressed lyrically. And certainly Wright's early childhood was crammed with catastrophic incidents. In a few short years his father deserted his mother, he knew intense hunger, he became a drunkard begging drinks from black stevedores in Memphis saloons; he had to flee Arkansas, where an uncle was lynched; he was forced to live with a fanatically religious grandmother in an atmosphere of constant bickering; he was lodged in an orphan asylum; he observed the suffering of his mother, who became a permanent invalid, while fighting off the blows of the poverty-stricken relatives with whom he had to live; he was cheated, beaten and kicked off jobs by white employees who disliked his eagerness to learn a trade; and to these objective circumstances must be added the subjective fact that Wright, with his sensitivity, extreme shyness and intelligence, was a problem child who rejected his family and was by them rejected.

Thus along with the themes, equivalent descriptions of milieu and the perspectives to be found in Joyce, Nehru, Dostoievsky, George Moore and Rousseau, *Black Boy* is filled with blues-tempered echoes of railroad trains, the names of Southern towns and cities, estrangements, fights and flights, deaths and disappointments, charged with physical and spiritual hungers and pain. And like a blues sung by such an artist as Bessie Smith, its lyrical prose evokes the paradoxical, almost surreal image of a black boy singing lustily as he probes his own grievous wound.

In *Black Boy,* two worlds have fused, two cultures merged, two impulses of Western man become coalesced. By discussing some of its cultural sources I hope to answer those critics who would make of the book a miracle and of its author a mystery. And while making no attempt to probe the mystery of the artist (who Hemingway says is "forged in injustice as a sword is forged"), I do hold that basically the prerequisites to the writing of *Black Boy* were, on the one hand, the microscopic degree of cultural freedom which Wright found in the South's stony injustice, and, on the other, the existence of a personality agitated to a state of almost manic restlessness. There were, of course, other factors, chiefly ideological; but these came later.

Wright speaks of his journey north as

> . . . taking a part of the South to transplant in alien soil, to see if it could grow differently, if it could drink of new an: cool rains, bend in strange winds, respond to the warmth of other suns, and perhaps, to bloom. . . .

And t as Wright, the man, represents the blooming of the deli ent child of the autobiography, just so does *Black Boy* esent the flowering—cross-fertilized by pollen blo oy the winds of strange cultures—of the humble blues lyric. There is, as in all acts of creation, a world of mystery in this, but there is also enough that is comprehensible for Americans to create the social atmosphere in which other black boys might freely bloom.

For certainly, in the historical sense, Wright is no exception. Born on a Mississippi plantation, he was subjected to all those blasting pressures which in a scant eighty years have sent the Negro people hurtling, without clearly defined trajectory, from slavery to emancipation, from log cabin to city tenement, from the white folks' fields and kitchens to factory assembly lines; and which, between two wars, have shattered the wholeness of its folk consciousness into a thousand writhing pieces.

Black Boy describes this process in the personal terms of *one* Negro childhood. Nevertheless, several critics have complained that it does not "explain" Richard Wright. Which, aside from the notion of art involved, serves to remind us that the prevailing mood of American criticism has so thoroughly excluded the Negro that it fails to recognize some of the most basic tenets of Western democratic thought when encountering them in a black skin. They forget that human life possesses an innate dignity and mankind an innate sense of nobility; that all men possess the tendency to dream and the compulsion to make their dreams reality; that the need to be ever dissatisfied and the urge ever to seek satisfaction is implicit in the human organism; and that all men are the victims and the beneficiaries of the goading, tormenting, commanding and informing activity of that imperious process known as the Mind—the Mind, as Valéry describes it, "armed with its inexhaustible questions."

Perhaps all this (in which lies the very essence of the human, and which Wright takes for granted) has been forgotten because the critics recognize neither Negro humanity nor the full extent to which the Southern community renders the fulfillment of human destiny impossible. And while it is true that *Black Boy* presents an almost unrelieved picture of a personality corrupted by brutal environment, it also presents those fresh, human responses brought to its world by the sensitive child:

There was the *wonder* I felt when I first saw a brace of mountainlike, spotted, black-and-white horses clopping down a dusty road . . . the *delight* I caught in seeing long straight rows of red and green vegetables stretching away in the sun . . . the faint, cool kiss of *sensuality* when dew came on to my cheeks . . . the vague *sense of the infinite* as I looked down upon the yellow, dreaming waters of the Mississippi . . . the echoes of *nostalgia* I heard in the crying strings of wild geese . . . the *love* I had for the mute regality of tall, moss-clad oaks . . . the hint of *cosmic cruelty* that I *felt* when I saw the curved timbers of a wooden shack that had been warped in the summer sun . . . and there was the *quiet terror* that suffused my senses when vast hazes of gold washed earthward from star-heavy skies on silent nights. . . .[2]

---

[2] Italics mine.

And a bit later, his reactions to religion:

> Many of the religious symbols appealed to my sensibilities
> and I responded to the dramatic vision of life held by the
> church, feeling that to live day by day with death as one's
> sole thought was to be so compassionately sensitive toward
> all life as to view all men as slowly dying, and the trembling
> sense of fate that welled up, sweet and melancholy, from
> the hymns blended with the sense of fate that I had already
> caught from life.

There was also the influence of his mother—so closely
linked to his hysteria and sense of suffering—who (though
he only implies it here) taught him, in the words of the dedication prefacing *Native Son*, "to revere the fanciful and the
imaginative." There were also those white men—the one
who allowed Wright to use his library privileges and the
other who advised him to leave the South, and still others
whose offers of friendship he was too frightened to accept.

Wright assumed that the nucleus of plastic sensibility is a
human heritage: the right and the opportunity to dilate,
deepen and enrich sensibility—democracy. Thus the drama
of *Black Boy* lies in its depiction of what occurs when Negro
sensibility attempts to fulfill itself in the undemocratic
South. Here it is not the n᷍ ᷍ al that is the immediate focus, as in Joyce's *Stephen Hero*, but that upon which his
sensibility was nourished.

Those critics who complain that Wright has omitted the
development of his own sensibility hold that the work thus
fails as art. Others, because it presents too little of what they
consider attractive in Negro life, charge that it distorts reality. Both groups miss a very obvious point: That whatever
else the environment contained, it had as little chance of
prevailing against the overwhelming weight of the child's
unpleasant experiences as Beethoven's Quartets would have
of destroying the stench of a Nazi prison.

We come, then, to the question of art. The function, the

psychology, of artistic selectivity is to eliminate from art form all those elements of experience which contain no compelling significance. Life is as the sea, art a ship in which man conquers life's crushing formlessness, reducing it to a course, a series of swells, tides and wind currents inscribed on a chart. Though drawn from the world, "the organized significance of art," writes Malraux, "is stronger than all the multiplicity of the world; . . . that significance alone enables man to conquer chaos and to master destiny."

Wright saw his destiny—that combination of forces before which man feels powerless—in terms of a quick and casual violence inflicted upon him by both family and community. His response was likewise violent, and it has been his need to give that violence significance which has shaped his writings.

What were the ways by which other Negroes confronted their destiny?

In the South of Wright's childhood there were three general ways: They could accept the role created for them by the whites and perpetually resolve the resulting conflicts through the hope and emotional catharsis of Negro religion; they could repress their dislike of Jim Crow social relations while striving for a middle way of respectability, becoming —consciously or unconsciously—the accomplices of the whites in oppressing their brothers; or they could reject the situation, adopt a criminal attitude, and carry on an unceasing psychological scrimmage with the whites, which often flared forth into physical violence.

Wright's attitude was nearest the last. Yet in it there was an all-important qualitative difference: it represented a groping for *individual* values, in a black community whose values were what the young Negro critic, Edward Bland, has defined as "pre-individual." And herein lay the setting for the extreme conflict set off, both within his family and in the community, by Wright's assertion of individuality. The clash was sharpest on the psychological level, for, to quote Bland:

> In the pre-individualistic thinking of the Negro the stress is on the group. Instead of seeing in terms of the individual, the Negro sees in terms of "races," masses of peoples separated from other masses according to color. Hence, an act rarely bears intent against him as a Negro individual. He is singled out not as a person but as a specimen of an ostracized group. He knows that he never exists in his own right but only to the extent that others hope to make the race suffer vicariously through him.

This pre-individual state is induced artificially—like the regression to primitive states noted among cultured inmates of Nazi prisons. The primary technique in its enforcement is to impress the Negro child with the omniscience and omnipotence of the whites to the point that whites appear as ahuman as Jehovah, and as relentless as a Mississippi flood. Socially it is effected through an elaborate scheme of taboos supported by a ruthless physical violence, which strikes not only the offender but the entire black community. To wander from the paths of behavior laid down for the group is to become the agent of communal disaster.

In such a society the development of individuality depends upon a series of accidents, which often arise, as in Wright's case, from conditions within the Negro family. In Wright's life there was the accident that as a small child he could not distinguish between his fair-skinned grandmother and the white women of the town, thus developing skepticism as to their special status. To this was linked the accident of his having no close contacts with whites until after the child's normal formative period.

But these objective accidents not only link forward to these qualities of rebellion, criminality and intellectual questioning expressed in Wright's work today. They also link backward into the shadow of infancy where environment and consciousness are so darkly intertwined as to require the skill of a psychoanalyst to define their point of juncture. Nevertheless, at the age of four, Wright set the house afire and was beaten near to death by his frightened mother. This beating, followed soon by his father's desertion of the family, seems to be the initial psychological motivation of his quest for a new identification. While delirious from this beating Wright was haunted "by huge wobbly white bags like the full udders of a cow, suspended from the ceiling above me [and] I was gripped by the fear that they were going to fall and drench me with some horrible liquid . . ."

It was as though the mother's milk had turned acid, and with it the whole pattern of life that had produced the ignorance, cruelty and fear that had fused ⸱ ͺth mother-love and exploded in the beating. It is s͗ ᷒ᴧ᷉t that the bags were of the hostile color white, and the female symbol that of the cow, the most stupid (and, to the small child, the most frightening) of domestic animals. Here in dream symbolism is expressed an attitude worthy of an Orestes. And the significance of the crisis is increased by virtue of the historical fact that the lower-class Negro family is matriarchal; the child turns not to the father to compensate if he feels mother-rejection, but to the grandmother, or to an aunt—and Wright rejected both of these. Such rejection leaves the child open to psychological insecurity, distrust and all of those hostile environmental forces from which the family functions to protect it.

One of the Southern Negro family's methods of protecting the child is the severe beating—a homeopathic dose of the violence generated by black and white relationships. Such beatings as Wright's were administered for the child's own good; a good which the child resisted, thus giving family relationships an undercurrent of fear and hostility, which differs qualitatively from that found in patriarchal middle-class families, because here the severe beating is administered by the mother, leaving the child no parental sanctuary. He must ever embrace violence along with maternal tenderness, or else reject, in his helpless way, the mother.

The division between the Negro parents of Wright's mother's generation, whose sensibilities were often bound by their proximity to the slave experience, and their children, who historically and through the rapidity of American change stand emotionally and psychologically much farther away, is quite deep. Indeed, sometimes as deep as the cultural distance between Yeats' *Autobiographies* and a Bessie Smith blues. This is the historical background to those incidents of family strife in *Black Boy* which have caused reviewers to question Wright's judgment of Negro emotional relationships.

We have here a problem in the sociology of sensibility that is obscured by certain psychological attitudes brought to Negro life by whites.

The first is the attitude which compels whites to impute to Negroes sentiments, attitudes and insights which, as a group living under certain definite social conditions, Negroes could not humanly possess. It is the identical mechanism which William Empson identifies in literature as "pastoral." It implies that since Negroes possess the richly human virtues credited to them, then their social position is advantageous and should not be bettered; and, continuing syllogistically, the white individual need feel no guilt over his participation in Negro oppression.

The second attitude is that which leads whites to misjudge Negro passion, looking upon it as they do, out of the turgidity of their own frustrated yearning for emotional warmth, their capacity for sensation having been constricted by the impersonal mechanized relationships typical of bourgeois society. The Negro is idealized into a symbol of sensation, of unhampered social and sexual relationships. And when *Black Boy* questions their illusion they are thwarted much in the manner of the occidental who, after observing the erotic character of a primitive dance, "shacks up" with a native woman—only to discover that far from possessing the hair-trigger sexual responses of a Stork Club "babe," she is relatively phlegmatic.

The point is not that American Negroes are primitives, but that as a group their social situation does not provide for the type of emotional relationships attributed them. For how could the South, recognized as a major part of the backward third of the nation, nurture in the black, most brutalized section of its population, those forms of human relationships achievable only in the most highly developed areas of civilization?

Champions of this "Aren't-Negroes-Wonderful?" school of thinking often bring Paul Robeson and Marian Anderson forward as examples of highly developed sensibility, but actually they are only its *promise*. Both received their development from an extensive personal contact with European culture, free from the influences which shape Southern Negro personality. In the United States, Wright, who is the only Negro literary artist of equal caliber, had to wait years and escape to another environment before discovering the moral and ideological equivalents of his childhood attitudes.

Man cannot express that which does not exist—either in the form of dreams, ideas or realities—in his environment. Neither his thoughts nor his feelings, his sensibility nor his intellect are fixed, innate qualities. They are processes which arise out of the interpenetration of human instinct with environment, through the process called experience; each changing and being changed by the other. Negroes cannot possess many of the sentiments attributed to them because the same changes in environment which, through experience, enlarge man's intellect (and thus his capacity for still greater change) also modify his feelings; which in turn increase his sensibility, i.e., his sensitivity, to refinements of impression and subtleties of emotion. The extent of these changes depends upon the quality of political and cultural freedom in the environment.

Intelligence tests have measured the quick rise in intellect which takes place in Southern Negroes after moving north, but little attention has been paid to the mutations effected in their sensibilities. However, the two go hand in hand. Intellectual complexity is accompanied by emotional complexity; refinement of thought, by refinement of feeling. The movement north affects more than the Negro's wage scale, it affects his entire psychosomatic structure.

The rapidity of Negro intellectual growth in the North is due partially to objective factors present in the environment, to influences of the industrial city and to a greater political freedom. But there are also changes within the "inner world." In the North energies are released and given *intellectual* channelization—energies which in most Negroes in the South have been forced to take either a *physical* form or, as with potentially intellectual types like Wright, to be expressed as nervous tension, anxiety and hysteria. Which is nothing mysterious. The human organism responds to environmental stimuli by converting them into either physical and/or intellectual energy. And what is called hysteria is suppressed intellectual energy expressed physically.

The "physical" character of their expression makes for much of the difficulty in understanding American Negroes. Negro music and dances are frenziedly erotic; Negro religious ceremonies violently ecstatic; Negro speech strongly rhythmical and weighted with image and gesture. But there is more in this sensuousness than the unrestraint and insensitivity found in primitive cultures; nor is it simply the relatively spontaneous and undifferentiated responses of a people living in close contact with the soil. For despite Jim Crow, Negro life does not exist in a vacuum, but in the seething vortex of those tensions generated by the most highly industrialized of Western nations. The welfare of the most humble black Mississippi sharecropper is affected less by the flow of the seasons and the rhythm of natural events than by the fluctuations of the stock market; even though, as Wright states of his father, the sharecropper's memories, actions and emotions are shaped by his immediate contact with nature and the crude social relations of the South.

All of this makes the American Negro far different from the "simple" specimen for which he is taken. And the "physical" quality offered as evidence of his primitive simplicity is actually the form of his complexity. The American Negro is a Western type whose social condition creates a state which is almost the reverse of the cataleptic trance: Instead of his consciousness being lucid to the reality around it while the body is rigid, here it is the body which is alert, reacting to pressures which the constricting forces of Jim Crow block off from the transforming, concept-creating activity of the brain. The "eroticism" of Negro expression springs from much the same conflict as that displayed in the violent gesturing of a man who attempts to express a complicated concept with a limited vocabulary; thwarted ideational energy is converted into unsatisfactory pantomime, and his words are burdened with meanings they cannot convey. Here lies the source of the basic ambiguity of *Native Son*, wherein in order to translate Bigger's complicated feelings into universal ideas, Wright had to force into Bigger's consciousness concepts and ideas which his intellect could not formulate. Between Wright's skill and knowledge and the potentials of Bigger's mute feelings lay a thousand years of conscious culture.

In the South the sensibilities of both blacks and whites are inhibited by the rigidly defined environment. For the Negro there is relative safety as long as the impulse toward individuality is suppressed. (Lynchings have occurred because Negroes painted their homes.) And it is the task of the Negro family to adjust the child to the Southern milieu; through it the currents, tensions and impulses generated within the human organism by the flux and flow of events are given their distribution. This also gives the group its distinctive character. Which, because of Negroes' suppressed minority position, is very much in the nature of an elaborate but limited defense mechanism. Its function is dual: to protect the Negro from whirling away from the undifferentiated mass of his people into the unknown, symbolized in its most abstract form by insanity, and most concretely by lynching; and to protect him from those unknown forces *within him-f* which might urge him to reach out for that social and human equality which the white South says he cannot have. Rather than throw himself against the charged wires of his prison he annihilates the impulses within him.

The pre-individualistic black community discourages individuality out of self-defense. Having learned through experience that the whole group is punished for the actions of the single member, it has worked out efficient techniques of behavior control. For in many Southern communities everyone knows everyone else and is vulnerable to his opinions. In some communities everyone is "related" regardless of blood-ties. The regard shown by the group for its members, its general communal character and its cohesion are often mentioned. For by comparison with the coldly impersonal relationships of the urban industrial community, its relationships are personal and warm.

Black Boy, however, illustrates that this personal quality, shaped by outer violence and inner fear, is ambivalent. Personal warmth is accompanied by an equally personal coldness, kindliness by cruelty, regard by malice. And these opposites are as quickly set off against the member who gestures toward individuality as a lynch mob forms at the cry of rape. Negro leaders have often been exasperated by this phenomenon, and Booker T. Washington (who demanded far less of Negro humanity than Richard Wright) described the Negro community as a basket of crabs, wherein should one attempt to climb out, the others immediately pull him back.

The member who breaks away is apt to be more impressed by its negative than by its positive character. He becomes a stranger even to his relatives and he interprets gestures of protection as blows of oppression—from which there is no hiding place, because every area of Negro life is affected. Even parental love is given a qualitative balance akin to "sadism." And the extent of beatings and psychological maimings meted out by Southern Negro parents rivals those described by the nineteenth-century Russian writers as characteristic of peasant life under the Czars. The horrible thing is that the cruelty is also an expression of concern, of love.

In discussing the inadequacies for democratic living typical of the education provided Negroes by the South, a Negro educator has coined the term *mis-education*. Within the ambit of the black family this takes the form of training the child away from curiosity and adventure, against reaching out for those activities lying beyond the borders of the black community. And when the child resists, the parent discourages him; first with the formula, "That there's for white folks. Colored can't have it," and finally with a beating.

It is not, then, the family and communal violence described by *Black Boy* that is unusual, but that Wright *recognized* and made no peace with its essential cruelty—even when, like a babe freshly emerged from the womb, he could not discern where his own personality ended and it began. Ordinarily both parent and child are protected against this cruelty—seeing it as love and finding subjective sanction for it in the spiritual authority of the Fifth Commandment, and on the secular level in the legal and extralegal structure of the Jim Crow system. The child who did not rebel, or who was unsuccessful in his rebellion, learned a masochistic submissiveness and a denial of the impulse toward Western culture when it stirred within him.

Why then have Southern whites, who claim to "know" the Negro, missed all this? Simply because they, too, are armored against the horror and the cruelty. Either they deny the Negro's humanity and feel no cause to measure his actions against civilized norms; or they protect themselves from their guilt in the Negro's condition and from their fear that their cooks might poison them, or that their nursemaids might strangle their infant charges, or that their field hands might do them violence, by attributing to them a superhuman capacity for love, kindliness and forgiveness. Nor does this in any way contradict their stereotyped conviction that all Negroes (meaning those with whom they have no contact) are given to the most animal behavior.

It is only when the individual, whether white or black, *rejects* the pattern that he awakens to the nightmare of his life. Perhaps much of the South's regressive character springs from the fact that many, jarred by some casual crisis into wakefulness, flee hysterically into the sleep of violence or the coma of apathy again. For the penalty of wakefulness is to encounter ever more violence and horror than the sensibilities can sustain unless translated into some form of social action. Perhaps the impassioned character so noticeable among those white Southern liberals so active in the Negro's cause is due to their sense of accumulated horror; their passion—like the violence in Faulkner's novels—is evidence of a profound spiritual vomiting.

This compulsion is even more active in Wright and the increasing number of Negroes who have said an irrevocable "no" to the Southern pattern. Wright learned that it is not enough merely to reject the white South, but that he had also to reject that part of the South which lay within. As a rebel he formulated that rejection negatively, because it was the negative face of the Negro community upon which he looked most often as a child. It is this he is contemplating when he writes:

> Whenever I thought of the essential bleakness of black life in America, I knew that Negroes had never been allowed to catch the full spirit of Western civilization, that they lived somehow in it but not of it. And when I brooded upon the cultural barrenness of black life, I wondered if clean, positive tenderness, love, honor, loyalty and the capacity to remember were native to man. I asked myself if these human qualities were not fostered, won, struggled and suffered for, preserved in ritual from one generation to another.

But far from implying that Negroes have no capacity for culture, as one critic interprets it, this is the strongest affirmation that they have. Wright is pointing out what should be obvious (especially to his Marxist critics) that Negro sensibility is socially and historically conditioned; that Western culture must be won, confronted like the animal in a Spanish bullfight, dominated by the red shawl of codified experience and brought heaving to its knees.

Wright knows perfectly well that Negro life is a by-product of Western civilization, and that in it, if only one possesses the humanity and humility to see, are to be discovered all those impulses, tendencies, life and cultural forms to be found elsewhere in Western society.

The problem arises because the special condition of Negroes in the United States, including the defensive character of Negro life itself (the "will toward organization" noted in the Western capitalist appears in the Negro as a will to camouflage, to dissimulate), so distorts these forms as to render their recognition as difficult as finding a wounded quail against the brown and yellow leaves of a Mississippi thicket—even the spilled blood blends with the background. Having himself been in the position of the quail—to expand the metaphor—Wright's wounds have told him both the question and the answer which every successful hunter must discover for himself: "Where would I hide if *I* were a wounded quail?" But perhaps that requires more sympathy with one's quarry than most hunters possess. Certainly it requires such a sensitivity to the shifting guises of humanity under pressure as to allow them to identify themselves with the human content, whatever its outer form; and even with those Southern Negroes to whom Paul Robeson's name is only a rolling sound in the fear-charged air.

Let us close with one final word about the blues: Their attraction lies in this, that they at once express both the agony of life and the possibility of conquering it through sheer toughness of spirit. They fall short of tragedy only in that they provide no solution, offer no scapegoat but the self. Nowhere in America today is there social or political action based upon the solid realities of Negro life depicted in *Black Boy;* perhaps that is why, with its refusal to offer solutions, it is like the blues. Yet in it thousands of Negroes will for the first time see their destiny in public print. Freed here of fear and the threat of violence, their lives have at last been organized, scaled down to possessable proportions. And in this lies Wright's most important achievement: He has converted the American Negro impulse toward self-annihilation and "going-under-ground" into a will to confront the world, to evaluate his experience honestly and throw his findings unashamedly into the guilty conscience of America.

—From *The Antioch Review,* Summer 1945.

Beating That Boy

During these post-military-phase-of-the-war days when a Negro is asked what occurs when he visits with white friends, he is likely to chuckle and drily reply, "Oh, we beat that boy," meaning to belabor in polite conversation what is commonly called the "Negro problem." Though Negroes laugh when the phrase is used, beneath its folksy surface there lies—like a booby trap in a music box of folk tunes—a disillusionment that only its attitude of detached participation saves from exploding into violent cynicism: its counterpart among those Negroes who know no whites as friends.

For the racial situation has become like an irrational sea in which Americans flounder like convoyed ships in a gale. The phrase rotates like a gyroscope of irony of which the Negro maintains a hazardous stability as the sea-tossed ship of his emotions whirls him willy-nilly along: lunging him toward the shoals of bitter rejection (of the ideology that makes

him the sole sacrifice of America's tragedy); now away toward the mine-strewn shores of hopelessness (that despite
the war democracy is still discussed on an infantile level
and himself in pre-adult terms); now smashing him flush
against waves of anger that threaten to burst his seams in revolt (that his condition is so outrageously flagrant); now
teetering him clear on a brief, calm, sunlit swell of self-
amusement (that he must cling to the convoy though he
doubts its direction); now knocking him erect, like a whale
on its tail, before plunging again into the still dark night of
the one lone "rational" thing—the pounding irrational sea.

This is a nightmarishly "absurd" situation, and perhaps no
major problem affecting the destiny of a nation has ever received such superficial discussion. As Bucklin Moon knew
when he conceived *Primer for White Folks*, a great deal of
the superficiality comes from the general ignorance prevailing in our society of the historical and social condition of the
black tenth of the population. He might have subtitled his
anthology, *A Short Course on the American Negro for Those
Who "Beat That Boy."*

Primer for White Folks comes as a result of the long fight
which Negroes have made to make their story known, and
the aroused efforts of liberal whites, many of them Southerners, to chart more accurately that heart-lashing sea of irra-
tionality called the "Negro problem." The fair-minded but
uninformed should read the book to learn how much they
have been humiliated, insulted and injured by the Rankins
and Bilbos who speak in their name to the world.

Primer for White Folks is something new in its genre. Unlike similar anthologies, it does not consist solely of Negro
contributions, but of writings on the racial situation as seen
by both white and Negro authors. The book, which presents
such writers as Will W. Alexander, Kay Boyle, Sterling
Brown, Henrietta Buckmaster, Fanny Kemble, Langston
Hughes, Wendell Wilkie, Lillian Smith, Dorothy Parker,

James T. Farrell and Richard Wright, divides into three major sections. The first, "Heritage," covers slavery, the Civil War and the end of Reconstruction in Negro disfranchisement, and presents unfamiliar information on Negro slave revolts and heroism; the second consists of short stories about the mores of our society and the relationships, "sometimes ludicrous, sometimes tragic, between Negroes and whites"; and the third, "Today and Tomorrow," presents the thoughts of contemporary white and Negro writers on the "Negro question" and their recommendations for its solution. This section is especially valuable and will bear repeated reference as the tense period we have just entered unfolds. Here are the most democratically informed discussions of the racial situation to appear in print since Pearl Harbor.

But if you believe you have read many of these pieces before, then you're mistaken; even if you *have*, you haven't. For here, under Bucklin Moon's creative editing, they have been placed in a fresh context of meaning, where, like the subtle relationships of forms in a great painting, they ever reveal something new. Encountering some of them here, one wonders whether Moon's conception was not superior to even the best images which he found to give it articulation. What an astounding book this could have been had every piece been on a par with its conception! Since hardly any aspect of our culture escapes the blight of hypocrisy implicit in our social institutions, it is not surprising that many of the pieces mix appeal for fair play with double-talk; or that most are much too fearful of that absolute concept "democracy," circling above it like planes being forced to earth in a fog. They seemed concerned most often with patching up the merry-go-round-that-broke-down than with the projection of that oh, so urgently needed new American humanism. Here, too, the boy comes in for a bit of a beating.

These negative criticisms of its parts do not, however, apply to the anthology as a whole. For the negative when piled up quantitatively often assumes a positive value; and certainly it is valuable to detect the cracks in the tones of our most Liberty Bell voices. Then, too, such studies inevitably reveal as much about the white American as about the American Negro—which lends them a value that is generally ignored. When viewed from a perspective which takes this circumstance into account, *Primer for White Folks* will be prized for the oblique light it throws upon an aspect of American writing which was not its immediate concern.

One notices, for instance, that most of the fiction presented here, with the exception of stories by Dorothy Parker, Kay Boyle, Erskine Caldwell and William March, is by writers who have appeared since the Depression; and that most of the widely read authors of the between-wars period are, with the exceptions of James T. Farrell and Richard Wright, conspicuously missing. We are reminded that from 1776 to 1876 there was a conception of democracy current in this country that allowed the writer to identify himself with the Negro; and that had such an anthology been conceivable during the nineteenth century, it could have included such writers as Whitman, Emerson, Thoreau, Hawthorne, Melville and Mark Twain. For slavery (it was not termed a "Negro problem" then) was a vital issue in the American consciousness, symbolic of the condition of Man, and a valid aspect of the writer's reality. Only after the Emancipation and the return of the Southern ruling class to power in the counter-revolution of 1876, was the Negro issue pushed into the underground of the American conscience and ignored.

To ignore, however, is not to nullify, and the fact that so many of our important writers are missing from *Primer for White Folks* raises the question whether the existence of the race problem in our culture has not had an insidiously powerful effect upon twentieth-century writing that has not been generally suspected. Perhaps here, too, lies a partial explanation of why we have come to regard certain faults of this writing as excellences.

But first let me hasten to say that I do not mean to imply that whites had any obligation to write of Negroes, nor that in the depiction of the racial situation lies any blueprint for a supreme fiction (if so, all Negro writers would rate with Tolstoy and Balzac, Shakespeare and Dostoievsky). Unfortunately, the connection between literature and society is seldom so naïvely direct. There is, nevertheless, an inescapable connection between the writer and the beliefs and attitudes current in his culture, and it is here exactly that the "Negro problem" begins to exert a powerful, uncalculated influence.

For since 1876 the race issue has been like a stave driven into the American system of values, a stave so deeply imbedded in the American *ethos* as to render America a nation of ethical schizophrenics. Believing truly in democracy on one side of their minds, they act on the other in violation of its most sacred principles; holding that all men are created equal, they treat thirteen million Americans as though they were not.

There are, as always, political and economic motives for this rending of values, but in terms of the ethical and psychological, what was opportunistically labeled the "Negro problem" is actually a guilt problem charged with pain. Just how painful, might be judged from the ceaseless effort expended to dull its throbbings with the anesthesia of legend, myth, hypnotic ritual and narcotic modes of thinking. And not only have our popular culture, our newspapers, radio and cinema been devoted to justifying the Negro's condition and the conflict created thereby, but even our social sciences and serious literature have been conscripted—all in the effort to drown out the persistent voice of outraged conscience.

This unwillingness to resolve the conflict in keeping with

his democratic ideals has compelled the white American, figuratively, to force the Negro down into the deeper level of his consciousness, into the inner world, where reason and madness mingle with hope and memory and endlessly give birth to nightmare and to dream; down into the province of the psychiatrist and the artist, from whence spring the lunatic's fancy and the work of art. It is a dangerous region even for the artist, and his tragedy lies in the fact that in order to tap the fluid fire of inspiration, he must perpetually descend and re-encounter not only the ghosts of his former selves, but all of the unconquered anguish of his living.

Obviously this position need not be absolutely disadvantageous for the Negro. It might, in a different culture, be highly strategic, enlisting in his cause the freedom-creating powers of art. For imprisoned in the deepest drives in human society, it is practically impossible for the white American to think of sex, of economics, his children or womenfolk, or of sweeping socio-political changes, without summoning into consciousness fear-flecked images of black men. Indeed, it seems that the Negro has become identified with those unpleasant aspects of conscience and consciousness which it is part of the American's character to avoid. Thus when the literary artist attempts to tap the charged springs issuing from his inner world, up float his misshapen and bloated images of the Negro, like the fetid bodies of the drowned, and he turns away, discarding an ambiguous substance which the artists of other cultures would confront boldly and humanize into the stuff of a tragic art. It is as though we were to discard the beneficial properties of the x-ray simply because when used without the protection of a leaden screen they might burn us or produce sterility.

Indeed, the racial situation has exerted an influence upon the writer similar to that of an x-ray concealed in a radio. Moving about, perhaps ignoring, perhaps enjoying Jack—Rochester or a hot jazz band, he is unaware of his exposure

to a force that shrivels his vital sperm. Not that it has rendered him completely sterile, but that it has caused him to
produce deformed progeny: literary offspring without
hearts, without brains, viscera or vision, and some even
without genitalia.

Thus it has not been its failure to depict racial matters
that has determined the quality of American writing, but
that the writer has formed the habit of living and thinking in
a culture that is opposed to the deep thought and feeling necessary to profound art; hence its avoidance of emotion, its
fear of ideas, its obsession with mere physical violence and
pain, its overemphasis of understatement, its precise and
complex verbal constructions for converting goatsong into
carefully modulated squeaks.

Nor are the stories and articles included in *Primer for
White Folks* free of these faults. But if they bear the mark of
the culture out of which they spring, they are also appeals
for a superior society and a more vital literature. As ar-
ranged here, they offer a vivid statement of the strengths
and weaknesses of the new mood born in the hearts of Americans during the war, a mood more precise in its fears (of
racial bloodshed) than definite in its hopes (symbolized
most concretely in the frantic efforts of interracial organizations and mayors' committees to discover a foolproof technique of riot control); but more significant than their obvious fears and vacillations, they are valuable for something
practically missing from American writing since *Huckleberry Finn:* a search for images of black and white fraternity.

—From *The New Republic*, October 22, 1945.

Brave Words for a Startling Occasion

First, as I express my gratitude for this honor which you have bestowed on me, let me say that I take it that you are rewarding my efforts rather than my not quite fully achieved attempt at a major novel. Indeed, if I were asked in all seriousness just what I considered to be the chief significance of *Invisible Man* as a fiction, I would reply: Its experimental attitude, and its attempt to return to the mood of personal moral responsibility for democracy which typified the best of our nineteenth-century fiction. That my first novel should win this most coveted prize must certainly indicate that there is a crisis in the American novel. You as critics have told us so, and current fiction sales would indicate that the reading public agrees. Certainly the younger novelists concur. The explosive nature of events mocks our brightest efforts. And the very "facts" which the naturalists assumed would make us free have lost the power to protect us from despair. Controversy now rages over just what aspects of American experience are suitable for novelistic treatment. The prestige of the theorists of the so-called novel of manners has been challenged. Thus after a long period of stability we find our assumptions concerning the novel being called into question. And though I was only vaguely aware, it was this growing crisis which shaped the writing of *Invisible Man*.

After the usual apprenticeship of imitation and seeking with delight to examine my experience through the discipline of the novel, I became gradually aware that the forms of so many of the works which impressed me were too restricted to contain the experience which I knew. The diversity of American life with its extreme fluidity and openness seemed too vital and alive to be caught for more than the briefest instant in the tight well-made Jamesian novel, which was, for all its artistic perfection, too concerned with "good taste" and stable areas. Nor could I safely use the forms of the "hard-boiled" novel, with its dedication to physical violence, social cynicism and understatement. Understatement depends, after all, upon commonly held assumptions and my minority status rendered all such assumptions questionable. There was also a problem of language, and even dialogue, which, with its hard-boiled stance and its monosyllabic utterance, is one of the shining achievements of twentieth-century American writing. For despite the notion that its rhythms were those of everyday speech, I found that when compared with the rich babel of idiomatic expression around me, a language full of imagery and gesture and rhetorical canniness, it was embarrassingly austere. Our speech I found resounding with an alive language swirling with over three hundred years of American living, a mixture of the folk, the Biblical, the scientific and the political. Slangy in one stance, academic in another, loaded poetically with imagery at one moment, mathematically bare of imagery in the next. As for the rather rigid concepts of reality which informed a number of the works which impressed me and to which I owe a great deal, I was forced to conclude that reality was far more mysterious and uncertain, and more exciting, and still, despite its raw violence and capriciousness, more promising. To attempt to express that American experience which has carried one back and forth and up and down the land and across, and across again the great river, from freight train to Pullman car, from contact with slavery to contact with a world of advanced scholarship, art and science, is simply to burst such neatly understated forms of the novel asunder.

A novel whose range was both broader and deeper was needed. And in my search I found myself turning to our classical nineteenth-century novelists. I felt that except for the work of William Faulkner something vital had gone out of American prose after Mark Twain. I came to believe that the writers of that period took a much greater responsibility for the condition of democracy and, indeed, their works were imaginative projections of the conflicts within the human heart which arose when the sacred principles of the Constitution and the Bill of Rights clashed with the practical exigencies of human greed and fear, hate and love. Naturally I was attracted to these writers as a Negro. Whatever they thought of my people per se, in their imaginative economy the Negro symbolized both the man lowest down and the mysterious, underground aspect of human personality. In a sense the Negro was the gauge of the human condition as it waxed and waned in our democracy. These writers were willing to confront the broad complexities of American life and we are the richer for their having done so.

Thus to see America with an awareness of its rich diversity and its almost magical fluidity and freedom, I was forced

to conceive of a novel unburdened by the narrow naturalism which has led, after so many triumphs, to the final and
unrelieved despair which marks so much of our current fiction. I was to dream of a prose which was flexible, and swift
as American change is swift, confronting the inequalities
and brutalities of our society forthrightly, but yet thrusting
forth its images of hope, human fraternity and individual
self-realization. It would use the richness of our speech, the
idiomatic expression and the rhetorical flourishes from past
periods which are still alive among us. And despite my personal failures, there must be possible a fiction which, leaving sociology to the scientists, can arrive at the truth about
the human condition, here and now, with all the bright
magic of a fairy tale.

What has been missing from so much experimental writing has been the passionate will to dominate reality as well
as the laws of art. This will is the true source of the experimental attitude. We who struggle with form and with America should remember Eidothea's advice to Menelaus when in
the *Odyssey* he and his friends are seeking their way home.
She tells him to seize her father, Proteus, and to hold him
fast "however he may struggle and fight. He will turn into
all sorts of shapes to try you," she says, "into all the creatures
that live and move upon the earth, into water, into blazing
fire; but you must hold him fast and press him all the
harder. When he is himself, and questions you in the same
shape that he was when you saw him in his bed, let the old
man go; and then, sir, ask which god it is who is angry, and
how you shall make your way homewards over the fish-giv-
ing sea."

For the novelist, Proteus stands for both America and the
inheritance of illusion through which all men must fight to
achieve reality; the offended god stands for our sins against
those principles we all hold sacred. The way home we seek is
that condition of man's being at home in the world, which is

called love, and which we term democracy. Our task then is always to challenge the apparent forms of reality—that is, the fixed manners and values of the few, and to struggle with it until it reveals its mad, vari-implicated chaos, its false faces, and on until it surrenders its insight, its truth. We are fortunate as American writers in that with our variety of racial and national traditions, idioms and manners, we are yet one. On its profoundest level American experience is of a whole. Its truth lies in its diversity and swiftness of change. Through forging forms of the novel worthy of it, we achieve not only the promise of our lives, but we anticipate the resolution of those world problems of humanity which f.... mo- ment seem to those who are in awe of statist .....etely insoluble.

Whenever we as Americans hav. ...d ser ....ses we have returned to fundamentals; this, in brief, .. .hat I have tried to do.

> —Address for Presentation Ceremony,
> National Book Award, January 27, 1953.

The World and the Jug

"The World and the Jug" is actually a combination of two separate pieces. The first, bearing the original title, was written at the suggestion of Myron Kolatch of The New Leader, *who was interested in my reactions, via telephone, to an essay by Irving Howe titled "Black Boys and Native Sons," which appeared in the Autumn 1963 issue of Howe's magazine,* Dissent.

Usually such a reply would have appeared in the same magazine in which the original essay was published, but in this instance, and since it hadn't occurred to me to commit my reactions to paper, they went to the editor who asked for them. The second section of the essay, originally entitled, "A Rejoinder," was written after Irving Howe had consented to reply, in The New Leader, *of February 3, 1964, to my attack. There is, unfortunately, too little space here to do justice to Howe's arguments, and it is recommended that the interested reader consult Mr. Howe's book of essays,* A World More Attractive—*a book worthy of his attention far beyond the limits of our exchange —published by Horizon Press in 1963.*

> What runs counter to the revolutionary convention is, in revolutionary histories, suppressed more imperiously than embarrassing episodes in private memoirs, and by the same obscure forces. . . .
>
> —André Malraux

I

First, three questions: Why is it so often true that when critics confront the American as *Negro* they suddenly drop their advanced critical armament and revert with an air of confident superiority to quite primitive modes of analysis?

Why is it that sociology-oriented critics seem to rate literature so far below politics and ideology that they would rather
kill a novel than modify their presumptions concerning a
given reality which it seeks in its own terms to project?
Finally, why is it that so many of those who would tell us the
meaning of Negro life never bother to learn how varied it
really is?

These questions are aroused by "Black Boys and Native
Sons," an essay by Irving Howe, the well-known critic and editor of *Dissent,* in the Autumn 1963 issue of that magazine.
It is a lively piece, written with something of the Olympian
authority that characterized Hannah Arendt's "Reflections
on Little Rock" in the Winter 1959 *Dissent* (a dark foreshadowing of the Eichmann blowup). And in addition to a
hero, Richard Wright, it has two villians, James Baldwin and
Ralph Ellison, who are seen as "black boys" masquerading as
false, self-deceived "native sons." Wright himself is given a
diversity of roles (all conceived by Howe): He is not only the
archetypal and true-blue black boy—the "honesty" of his famous autobiography established this for Howe—but the spiritual father of Ellison, Baldwin and all other Negroes of literary bent to come. Further, in the platonic sense he is his own
father and the culture hero who freed Ellison and Baldwin
to write more "modulated" prose.

Howe admires Wright's accomplishments, and is frankly
annoyed by the more favorable evaluation currently placed
upon the works of the younger men. His claims for *Native
Son* are quite broad:

> The day [it] appeared, American culture was changed
> forever . . . it made impossible a repetition of the old lies
> . . . it brought into the open . . . the fear and violence
> that have crippled and may yet destroy our culture. . . . A
> blow at the white man, the novel forced him to recognize
> himself as an oppressor. A blow at the black man, the novel
> forced him to recognize the cost of his submission. *Native*

Son assaulted the most cherished of American vanities: the hope that the accumulated injustices of the past would bring with it no lasting penalties, the fantasy that in his humiliation the Negro somehow retained a sexual potency . . . that made it necessary to envy and still more to suppress him. Speaking from the black wrath of retribution, Wright insisted that history can be a punishment. He told us the one thing even the most liberal whites preferred not to hear: that Negroes were far from patient or forgiving, that they were scarred by fear, that they hated every moment of their suppression even when seeming most acquiescent, and that often enough they hated *us*, the decent and cultivated white men who from complicity or neglect shared in the responsibility of their plight. . . .

There are also negative criticisms: that the book is "crude," "melodramatic" and marred by "claustrophobia" of vision, that its characters are "cartoons," etc. But these defects Howe forgives because of the book's "clenched militancy." One wishes he had stopped there. For in his zeal to champion Wright, it is as though he felt it necessary to stage a modern version of the Biblical myth of Noah, Ham, Shem and Japheth (based originally, I'm told, on a castration ritual), with first Baldwin and then Ellison acting out the impious role of Ham: Baldwin by calling attention to Noah–Wright's artistic nakedness in his famous essays, "Everybody's Protest Novel" (1949) and "Many Thousands Gone" (1951); Ellison by rejecting "narrow naturalism" as a fictional method, and by alluding to the "diversity, fluidity and magical freedom of American life" on that (for him at least) rather magical occasion when he was awarded the National Book Award. Ellison also offends by having the narrator of *Invisible Man* speak of his life (Howe either missing the irony or assuming that *I* did) as one of "infinite possibilities" while living in a hole in the ground.

Howe begins by attacking Baldwin's rejection in "Everybody's Protest Novel" of the type of literature he labeled "protest fiction" (*Uncle Tom's Cabin* and *Native Son* being prime examples), and which he considered incapable of dealing adequately with the complexity of Negro experience. Howe, noting that this was the beginning of Baldwin's career, sees the essay's underlying motive as a declaration of Baldwin's intention to transcend "the sterile categories of 'Negroness,' whether those enforced by the white world or those defensively erected by the Negroes themselves. No longer mere victim or rebel, the Negro would stand free in a self-achieved humanity. As Baldwin put it some years later, he hoped to 'prevent himself from becoming merely a Negro; or even, merely, a Negro writer.' " Baldwin's elected agency for self-achievement would be the novel—as it turns out, it was the essay *and* the novel—but the novel, states Howe, "is an inherently ambiguous genre: it strains toward formal autonomy and can seldom avoid being public gesture."

I would have said that it is *always* a public gesture, though not necessarily a political one. I would also have pointed out that the American Negro novelist is himself "inherently ambiguous." As he strains toward self-achievement as artist (and here he can only "integrate" and free himself), he moves toward fulfilling his dual potentialities as Negro and American. While Howe agrees with Baldwin that "literature and sociology are not one and the same," he notes nevertheless that, "it is equally true that such statements hardly begin to cope with the problem of how a writer's own experience affects his desire to represent human affairs in a work of fiction." Thus Baldwin's formula evades "through rhetorical sweep, the genuinely difficult issue of the relationship between social experience and literature." And to Baldwin's statement that one writes "out of one thing only—one's own experience" (I would have added, for the novelist, this qualification: one's own experience as understood and ordered

through one's knowledge of self, culture and literature),
Howe, appearing suddenly in blackface, replies with a rhetorical sweep of his own:

> What, then, was the experience of a man with a black skin,
> what *could* it be here in this country? How could a Negro
> put pen to paper, how could he so much as think or breathe,
> without some impulsion to protest, be it harsh or mild,
> political or private, released or buried?" . . . The "soci-
> ology" of his existence forms a constant pressure on his
> literary work, and not merely in the way this might be true
> of any writer, but with a pain and ferocity that nothing
> could remove.

I must say that this brought a shock of recognition. Some
twelve years ago, a friend argued with me for hours that I
could not possibly write a novel because my experience as a
Negro had been too excruciating to allow me to achieve that
psychological and emotional distance necessary to artistic
creation. Since he "knew" Negro experience better than I, I
could not convince him that he might be wrong. Evidently
Howe feels that unrelieved suffering is the only "real" Negro
experience, and that the true Negro writer must be fero-
cious.

But there is also an American Negro tradition which
teaches one to deflect racial provocation and to master and
contain pain. It is a tradition which abhors as obscene any
trading on one's own anguish for gain or sympathy; which
springs not from a desire to deny the harshness of existence
but from a will to deal with it as men at their best have always done. It takes fortitude to be a man and no less to be an
artist. Perhaps it takes even more if the black man would be
an artist. If so, there are no exemptions. It would seem to
me, therefore, that the question of how the "sociology of his
existence" presses upon a Negro writer's work depends upon
how much of his life the individual writer is able to trans-

form into art. What moves a writer to eloquence is less meaningful than what he makes of it. How much, by the way, do
we know of Sophocles' wounds?

One unfamiliar with what Howe stands for would get the
impression that when he looks at a Negro he sees not a human being but an abstract embodiment of living hell. He
seems never to have considered that American Negro life
(and here he is encouraged by certain Negro "spokesmen")
is, for the Negro who must live it, not only a burden (and
not always that) but also a *discipline*—just as any human
life which has endured so long is a discipline teaching its
own insights into the human condition, its own strategies of
survival. There is a fullness, even a richness here; and here
despite the realities of politics, perhaps, but nevertheless
here and real. Because it is *human* life. And Wright, for all
of his indictments, was no less its product than that other
talented Mississippian, Leontyne Price. To deny in the interest of revolutionary posture that such possibilities of human
richness exist for others, even in Mississippi, is not only to
deny us our humanity but to betray the critic's commitment
to social reality. Critics who do so should abandon literature
for politics.

For even as his life toughens the Negro, even as it brutal-
izes him, sensitizes him, dulls him, goads him to anger,
moves him to irony, sometimes fracturing and sometimes
affirming his hopes; even as it shapes his attitudes toward
family, sex, love, religion; even as it modulates his humor,
tempers his joy—it *conditions* him to deal with his life and
with himself. Because it is *his* life and no mere abstraction
in someone's head. He must live it and try consciously to
grasp its complexity until he can change it; must live it *as* he
changes it. He is no mere product of his socio-political predicament. He is a product of the interaction between his
racial predicament, his individual will and the broader American cultural freedom in which he finds his ambiguous ex-

istence. Thus he, too, in a limited way, is his own creation.

In his loyalty to Richard Wright, Howe considers Ellison and Baldwin guilty of filial betrayal because, in their own work, they have rejected the path laid down by *Native Son*, phonies because, while actually "black boys," they pretend to be mere American writers trying to react to something of the pluralism of their predicament.

In his myth Howe takes the roles of both Shem and Japheth, trying mightily (his face turned backward so as not to see what it is he's veiling) to cover the old bare belly, and then becoming Wright's voice from beyond the grave by uttering the curses which Wright was too ironic or too proud to have uttered himself, at least in print:

> In response to Baldwin and Ellison, Wright would have said (I virtually quote the words he used in talking to me during the summer of 1958) that only through struggle could men with black skins, and for that matter, all the oppressed of the world, achieve their humility. It was a lesson, said Wright, with a touch of bitterness yet not without kindness, that the younger writers would have to learn in their own way and their own time. All that has happened since bears him out.

What, coming eighteen years after *Native Son* and thirteen years after World War II, does this rather limp cliché mean? Nor is it clear what is meant by the last sentence—or is it that today Baldwin has come to out-Wrighting Richard? The real questions seem to be: How does the Negro writer participate *as a writer* in the struggle for human freedom? To whom does he address his work? What values emerging from Negro experience does he try to affirm?

I started with the primary assumption that men with black skins, having retained their humanity before all of the conscious efforts made to dehumanize them, especially following the Reconstruction, are unquestionably human. Thus they have the obligation of freeing themselves—whoever their allies might be—by depending upon the validity of their own experience for an accurate picture of the reality which they seek to change, and for a gauge of the values they would see made manifest. Crucial to this view is the belief that their resistance to provocation, their coolness under pressure, their sense of timing and their tenacious hold on the ideal of their ultimate freedom are indispensable values in the struggle, and are at least as characteristic of American Negroes as the hatred, fear and vindictiveness which Wright chose to emphasize.

Wright believed in the much abused idea that novels are "weapons"—the counterpart of the dreary notion, common among most minority groups, that novels are instruments of good public relations. But I believe that true novels, even when most pessimistic and bitter, arise out of an impulse to celebrate human life and therefore are ritualistic and ceremonial at their core. Thus they would preserve as they destroy, affirm as they reject.

In *Native Son*, Wright began with the ideological proposition that what whites think of the Negro's reality is more important than what Negroes themselves know it to be. Hence Bigger Thomas was presented as a near-subhuman indictment of white oppression. He was designed to shock whites out of their apathy and end the circumstances out of which Wright insisted Bigger emerged. Here environment is all— and interestingly enough, environment conceived solely in terms of the physical, the non-conscious. Well, cut off my legs and call me Shorty! Kill my parents and throw me on the mercy of the court as an orphan! Wright could imagine Bigger, but Bigger could not possibly imagine Richard Wright. Wright saw to that.

But without arguing Wright's right to his personal vision, I would say that he was himself a better argument for my approach than Bigger was for his. And so, to be fair and as inclusive as Howe, is James Baldwin. Both are true Negro Americans, and both affirm the broad possibility of personal realization which I see as a saving aspect of American life. Surely, this much can be admitted without denying the injustice which all three of us have protested.

Howe is impressed by Wright's pioneering role and by the ". . . enormous courage, the discipline of self-conquest required to conceive Bigger Thomas. . . ." And earlier: "If such younger novelists as Baldwin and Ralph Ellison were able to move beyond Wright's harsh naturalism toward more supple modes of fiction, that was only possible because Wright had been there first, courageous enough to release the full weight of his anger."

It is not for me to judge Wright's courage, but I must ask just why it was possible for me to write as I write "only" because Wright released his anger? Can't I be allowed to release my own? What does Howe know of my acquaintance with violence, or the shape of my courage or the intensity of my anger? I suggest that my credentials are at least as valid as Wright's, even though he began writing long before I did, and it is possible that I have lived through and committed even more violence than he. Howe must wait for an autobiography before he can be responsibly certain. Everybody wants to tell us what a Negro is, yet few wish, even in a joke, to be one. But if you would tell me who I am, at least take the trouble to discover what I have been.

Which brings me to the most distressing aspect of Howe's thinking: his Northern white liberal version of the white Southern myth of absolute separation of the races. He implies that Negroes can only aspire to contest other Negroes (this at a time when Baldwin has been taking on just about everyone, including Hemingway, Faulkner and the United States Attorney General!), and must wait for the appearance of a Black Hope before they have the courage to move.

Howe is so committed to a sociological vision of society that he apparently cannot see (perhaps because he is dealing with Negroes—although not because he would suppress us socially or politically, for in fact he is anxious to end such suppression) that whatever the efficiency of segregation as a socio-political arrangement, it has been far from absolute on the level of *culture*. Southern whites cannot walk, talk, sing, conceive of laws or justice, think of sex, love, the family or freedom without responding to the presence of Negroes.

Similarly, no matter how strictly Negroes are segregated socially and politically, on the level of the imagination their ability to achieve freedom is limited only by their individual aspiration, insight, energy and will. Wright was able to free himself in Mississippi because he had the imagination and the will to do so. He was as much a product of his reading as of his painful experiences, and he made himself a writer by subjecting himself to the writer's discipline—as he understood it. The same is true of James Baldwin, who is not the product of a Negro store-front church but of the library, and the same is true of me.

Howe seems to see segregation as an opaque steel jug with the Negroes inside waiting for some black messiah to come along and blow the cork. Wright is his hero and he sticks with him loyally. But if we are in a jug it is transparent, not opaque, and one is allowed not only to see outside but to read what is going on out there; to make identifications as to values and human quality. So in Macon County, Alabama, I read Marx, Freud, T. S. Eliot, Pound, Gertrude Stein and Hemingway. Books which seldom, if ever, mentioned Negroes were to release me from whatever "segregated" idea I might have had of my human possibilities. I was freed not by propagandists or by the example of Wright—I did not know him at the time and was earnestly trying to learn enough to write a symphony and have it performed by the time I was twenty-six, because Wagner had done so and I admired his music—but by composers, novelists, and poets who spoke to me of more interesting and freer ways of life.

These were works which, by fulfilling themselves as works of art, by being satisfied to deal with life in terms of their own sources of power, were able to give me a broader sense of life and possibility. Indeed, I understand a bit more about myself as Negro because literature has taught me something of my identity as Western man, as political being. It has also taught me something of the cost of being an individual who aspires to conscious eloquence. It requires real poverty of the imagination to think that this can come to a Negro *only* through the example of *other Negroes*, especially after the performance of the slaves in re-creating themselves, in good part, out of the images and myths of the Old Testament Jews.

No, Wright was no spiritual father of mine, certainly in no sense I recognize—nor did he pretend to be, since he felt that I had started writing too late. It was Baldwin's career, not mine, that Wright proudly advanced by helping him attain the Eugene Saxton Fellowship, and it was Baldwin who found Wright a lion in his path. Being older and familiar with quite different lions in quite different paths, I simply stepped around him.

But Wright was a friend for whose magazine I wrote my first book review and short story, and a personal hero in the same way Hot Lips Paige and Jimmy Rushing were friends and heroes. I felt no need to attack what I considered the limitations of his vision because I was quite impressed by what he had achieved. And in this, although I saw with the black vision of Ham, I was, I suppose, as pious as Shem and Japheth. Still I would write my own books and they would be in themselves, implicitly, criticisms of Wright's; just as all novels of a given historical moment form an argument over the nature of reality and are, to an extent, criticisms each of the other.

While I rejected Bigger Thomas as any *final* image of Negro personality, I recognized *Native Son* as an achievement; as one man's essay in defining the human condition as seen from a specific Negro perspective at a given time in a given place. And I was proud to have known Wright and happy for the impact he had made upon our apathy. But Howe's ideas notwithstanding, history is history, cultural contacts ever mysterious, and taste exasperatingly personal. Two days after arriving in New York I was to read Malraux's *Man's Fate* and *The Days of Wrath*, and after these how could I be impressed by Wright as an ideological novelist. Need my skin blind me to all other values? Yet Howe writes:

> When Negro liberals write that despite the prevalence of bias there has been an improvement in the life of their people, such statements are reasonable and necessary. But what have these to do with the way Negroes feel, with the power of the memories they must surely retain? About this we know very little and would be well advised not to nourish preconceptions, for their feelings may well be closer to Wright's rasping outbursts than to the more modulated tones of the younger Negro novelists. *Wright remembered,* and what he remembered other Negroes must also have remembered. And in that way he kept faith with the experience of the boy who had fought his way out of the depths, to speak for those who remained there.

Wright, for Howe, is the genuine article, the authentic Negro writer, and his tone the only authentic tone. But why strip Wright of his individuality in order to criticize other writers. He had his memories and I have mine, just as I suppose Irving Howe has his—or has Marx spoken the final word for him? Indeed, very early in *Black Boy*, Wright's memory and his contact with literature come together in a way revealing, at least to the eye concerned with Wright the literary man, that his manner of keeping faith with the Negroes who remained in the depths is quite interesting:

(After I had outlived the shocks of childhood, after the habit of reflection had been born in me, I used to mull over the strange absence of real kindness in Negroes, how unstable was our tenderness, how lacking in genuine passion we were, how void of great hope, how timid our joy, how bare our traditions, how hollow our memories, how lacking we were in those intangible sentiments that bind man to man and how shallow was even our despair. After I had learned other ways of life I used to brood upon the unconscious irony of those who felt that Negroes led so passional an existence! I saw that what had been taken for our emotional strength was our negative confusions, our flights, our fears, our frenzy under pressure.

(Whenever I thought of the essential bleakness of black life in America, I knew that Negroes had never been allowed to catch the full spirit of Western civilization, that they lived somehow in it but not of it. And when I brooded upon the cultural barrenness of black life, I wondered if clean, positive tenderness, love, honor, loyalty and the capacity to remember were native with man. I asked myself if these human qualities were not fostered, won, struggled and suffered for, preserved in ritual from one generation to another.)

Must I be condemned because my sense of Negro life was quite different? Or because for me keeping faith would never allow me to even raise such a question about any segment of humanity? *Black Boy* is not a sociological case history but an autobiography, and therefore a work of art shaped by a writer bent upon making an ideological point. Doubtlessly, this was the beginning of Wright's exile, the making of a decision which was to shape his life and writing thereafter. And it is precisely at this point that Wright is being what I would call, in Howe's words, "literary to a fault."

For just as *How Bigger Was Born* is Wright's Jamesian preface to *Native Son*, the passage quoted above is his paraphrase of Henry James' catalogue of those items of a high civilization which were absent from American life during Hawthorne's day, and which seemed so necessary in order for the novelist to function. This, then, was Wright's list of those items of high humanity which he found missing among Negroes. Thank God, I have never been quite that literary.

How awful that Wright found the facile anwers of Marxism before he learned to use literature as a means for discovering the forms of American Negro humanity. I could not and cannot question their existence, I can only seek again and again to project that humanity as I see it and feel it. To me Wright as *writer* was less interesting than the enigma he personified: that he could so dissociate himself from the complexity of his background while trying so hard to improve the condition of black men everywhere; that he could be so wonderful an example of human possibility but could not for ideological reasons depict a Negro as intelligent, as creative or as dedicated as himself.

In his effort to resuscitate Wright, Irving Howe would designate the role which Negro writers are to play more rigidly than any Southern politician—and for the best of reasons. We must express "black" anger and "clenched militancy"; most of all we should not become too interested in the problems of the art of literature, even though it is through these that we seek our individual identities. And between writing well and being ideologically militant, we must choose militancy.

Well, it all sounds quite familiar and I fear the social order which it forecasts more than I do that of Mississippi. Ironically, during the 1940s it was one of the main sources of Wright's rage and frustration.

II

I am sorry Irving Howe got the impression that I was throwing bean-balls when I only meant to pitch him a hyperbole. It would seem, however, that he approves of angry Negro writers only until one questions his ideas; then he reaches for his honor, cries "misrepresentation" and "distortion," and charges the writer with being both out of control of himself and with fashioning a "strategy calculated to appeal, ready-made, to the preconceptions of the liberal audience." Howe implies that there are differences between us which I disguised in my essay, yet whatever the validity of this attempt at long-distance psychoanalysis, it was not his honor which I questioned but his thinking; not his good faith but his critical method.

And the major differences which these raised between us I tried to describe. They are to be seen by anyone who reads Howe's "Black Boys and Native Sons" not as a collection of thematically related fragments but as the literary exposition of a considered point of view. I tried to interpret this essay in the light of the impact it made upon my sense of life and literature, and I judged it through its total form—just as I would have Howe base his judgments of writers and their circumstances on as much of what we know about the actual complexity of men living in a highly pluralistic society as is possible. I realize that the *un*common sense of a critic, his special genius, is a gift to be thankful for whenever we find it. The very least I expected of Howe, though, was that he would remember his *common* sense, that he would not be carried away by that intellectual abandon, that lack of restraint, which seizes those who regard blackness as an absolute and who see in it a release from the complications of the real world.

Howe is interested in militant confrontation and suffering, yet evidently he recognizes neither when they involve some act of his own. He *really* did not know the subject was loaded. Very well, but I was brought into the booby-trapped field of his assumptions and finding myself in pain, I did not choose to "hold back from the suffering" inflicted upon me there. Out of an old habit I yelled—without seeking Howe's permission, it is true—where it hurt the most. For oddly enough, I found it far less painful to have to move to the back of a Southern bus, or climb to the peanut gallery of a movie house—matters about which I could do nothing except walk, read, hunt, dance, sculpt, cultivate ideas, or seek other uses for my time—than to tolerate concepts which distorted the actual reality of my situation or my reactions to it.

I could escape the reduction imposed by unjust laws and customs, but not that imposed by ideas which defined me as no more than the *sum* of those laws and customs. I learned to outmaneuver those who interpreted my silence as submission, my efforts at self-control as fear, my contempt as awe before superior status, my dreams of faraway places and room at the top of the heap as defeat before the barriers of their stifling, provincial world. And my struggle became a desperate battle which was usually fought, though not always, in silence; a guerrilla action in a larger war in which I found some of the most treacherous assaults against me committed by those who regarded themselves either as neutrals, as sympathizers, or as disinterested military advisers.

I recall this not in complaint, for thus was I disciplined to endure the absurdities of both conscious and unconscious prejudice, to resist racial provocation and, before the ready violence of brutal policemen, railroad "bulls," and casual white citizens, to hold my peace and bide my time. Thus was I forced to evaluate my own self-worth, and the narrow freedom in which it existed, against the power of those who would destroy me. In time I was to leave the South, although it has never left me, and the interests which I discovered there became my life.

But having left the South I did not leave the battle—for how could I leave Howe? He is a man of words and ideas, and since I, too, find my identity in the world of ideas and words, where would I flee? I still endure the nonsense of fools with a certain patience, but when a respected critic distorts my situation in order to feel comfortable in the abstractions he would impose upon American reality, then it is indeed "in accordance with my nature" to protest. Ideas are important in themselves, perhaps, but when they are interposed between me and my sense of reality I feel threatened; they are too elusive, they move with missile speed and are too often fired from altitudes rising high above the cluttered terrain upon which I struggle. And too often those with a facility for ideas find themselves in the councils of power representing me at the double distance of racial alienation and inexperience.

Taking leave of Howe for a moment—for his lapse is merely symptomatic—let me speak generally. Many of those who write of Negro life today seem to assume that as long as their hearts are in the right place they can be as arbitrary as they wish in their formulations. Others seem to feel that they can air with impunity their most private Freudian fantasies as long as they are given the slightest camouflage of intellectuality and projected as "Negro." They have made of the no-man's land created by segregation a territory for infantile self-expression and intellectual anarchy. They write as though Negro life exists only in light of their belated regard, and they publish interpretations of Negro experience which would not hold true for their own or for any other form of human life.

Here the basic unity of human experience that assures us of some possibility of empathic and symbolic identification with those of other backgrounds is blasted in the interest of specious political and philosophical conceits. Prefabricated Negroes are sketched on sheets of paper and superimposed upon the Negro community; then when someone thrusts his head through the page and yells, "Watch out there, Jack, there're people living under here," they are shocked and indignant. I am afraid, however, that we shall hear much more of such protest as these interpositions continue. And I predict this, not out of any easy gesture of militancy (and what an easy con-game for ambitious, publicity-hungry Negroes this stance of "militancy" has become!) but because as Negroes express increasingly their irritation in this critical area, many of those who make so lightly with our image shall find their own subjected to a most devastating scrutiny.

One of the most insidious crimes occurring in this democracy is that of designating another, politically weaker, less socially acceptable, people as the receptacle for one's own self-disgust, for one's own infantile rebellions, for one's own fears of, and retreats from, reality. It is the crime of reducing the humanity of others to that of a mere convenience, a counter in a banal game which involves no apparent risk to ourselves. With us Negroes it started with the appropriation of our freedom and our labor; then it was our music, our speech, our dance and the comic distortion of our image by burnt-corked, cotton-gloved corn-balls yelling, "Mammy!" And while it would be futile, non-tragic, and un-Negro American to complain over the processes through which we have become who and what we are, it is perhaps permissible to say that the time for such misappropriations ran out long ago.

For one thing, Negro American consciousness is not a product (as so often seems true of so many American groups) of a will to historical forgetfulness. It is a product of our memory, sustained and constantly reinforced by events, by our watchful waiting, and by our hopeful suspension of final judgment as to the meaning of our grievances. For another, most Negroes recognize themselves as themselves despite what others might believe them to be. Thus, although the sociologists tell us that thousands of light-skinned Negroes become white each year undetected, most Negroes can spot a paper-thin "white Negro" every time simply because those who masquerade missed what others were forced to pick up along the way: discipline—a discipline which these heavy thinkers would not undergo even if guaranteed that combined with their own heritage it would make of them the freest of spirits, the wisest of men and the most sublime of heroes.

The rhetorical strategy of my original reply was not meant, as Howe interprets it, to strike the stance of a "free artist" against the "ideological critic," although I *do* recognize that I can be free only to the extent that I detect error and grasp the complex reality of my circumstances and work to dominate it through the techniques which are my means of confronting the world. Perhaps I am only free enough to recognize those tendencies of thought which, actualized, would render me even less free.

Even so, I did not intend to take the stance of the "knowing Negro writer" against the "presuming white intellectual." While I am without doubt a Negro, and a writer, I am also an *American* writer, and while I am more knowing than Howe where my own life and its influences are concerned, I took the time to question his presumptions as one responsible for contributing as much as he is capable to the clear perception of American social reality. For to think unclearly about that segment of reality in which I find my existence is to do myself violence. To allow others to go unchallenged when they distort that reality is to participate not only in that distortion but to accept, as in this instance, a violence inflicted upon the art of criticism. And if I am to recognize those aspects of my role as writer which do not depend primarily upon my racial identity, if I am to fulfill the writer's basic responsibilities to his craft, then surely I must insist upon the maintenance of a certain level of precision in language, a maximum correspondence between the form of a piece of writing and its content, and between words and ideas and the things and processes of his world.

Whatever my role as "race man" (and it knocks me out whenever anyone, black or white, tries to tell me—and the white Southerners have no monopoly here—how to become their conception of a "good Negro"), I am as writer no less a custodian of the American language than is Irving Howe. Indeed, to the extent that I am a writer—I lay no claims to being a thinker—the American language, including the Negro idiom, is all that I have. So let me emphasize that my reply to Howe was neither motivated by racial defensiveness nor addressed to his own racial identity.

It is fortunate that it was not, for considering how Howe identifies himself in this instance, I would have missed the target, which would have been embarrassing. Yet it would have been an innocent mistake, because in situations such as this many Negroes, like myself, make a positive distinction between "whites" and "Jews." Not to do so could be either offensive, embarrassing, unjust or even dangerous. If I would know who I am and preserve who I am, then I must see others distinctly whether they see me so or no. Thus I feel uncomfortable whenever I discover Jewish intellectuals writing as though *they* were guilty of enslaving my grandparents, or as though the *Jews* were responsible for the system of segregation. Not only do they have enough troubles of their own, as the saying goes, but Negroes know this only too well.

The real guilt of such Jewish intellectuals lies in their facile, perhaps unconscious, but certainly unrealistic, identification with what is called the "power structure." Negroes call that "passing for white." Speaking personally, both as writer and as Negro American, I would like to see the more positive distinctions between whites and Jewish Americans maintained. Not only does it make for a necessary bit of historical and social clarity, at least where Negroes are concerned, but I consider the United States freer politically and richer culturally because there are Jewish Americans to bring it the benefit of their special forms of dissent, their humor and their gift for ideas which are based upon the uniqueness of their experience. The diversity of American life is often painful, frequently burdensome and always a source of conflict, but in it lies our fate and our hope.

To Howe's charge that I found his exaggerated claims for Richard Wright's influence upon my own work presumptuous, I plead guilty. Was it necessary to impose a line of succession upon Negro writers simply because Howe identified with Wright's cause? And why, since he grasps so readily the intentional absurdity of my question regarding his relationship to Marx, couldn't he see that the notion of an intellectual or artistic succession based upon color or racial background is no less absurd than one based upon a common religious background? (*Of course, Irving, I know that you haven't believed in final words for twenty years—not even your own—and I know, too, that the line from Marx to Howe is as complex and as dialectical as that from Wright to Ellison. My point was to try to see to it that certain laspes in your thinking did not become final.*) In fact, this whole exchange would never have started had I not been dragged into the discussion. Still, if Howe could take on the role of man with a "black skin," why shouldn't I assume the role of critic-of-critic?

But how surprising are Howe's ideas concerning the ways of controversy. Why, unless of course he holds no respect for his opponent, should a polemicist be expected to make things *hard* for himself? As for the "preconceptions of the liberal audience," I had not considered them, actually, except as they appear in Howe's own thinking. Beyond this I wrote for anyone who might hesitate to question his formulations, especially very young Negro writers who might be bewildered by the incongruity of such ideas coming from such an authority. Howe himself rendered complicated rhetorical strategies unnecessary by lunging into questionable territory with his flanks left so unprotected that any schoolboy sniper could have routed him with a bird gun. Indeed, his reaction to my reply reminds me of an incident which occurred during the 1937 Recession when a companion and I were hunting the country outside Dayton, Ohio.

There had been a heavy snowfall and we had just put up a covey of quail from a thicket which edged a field when, through the rising whirr of the rocketing, snow-shattering birds, we saw, emerging from a clump of trees across the field, a large, red-faced, mackinawed farmer, who came running toward us shouting and brandishing a rifle. I could see strands of moisture tearing from his working mouth as he came on, running like a bear across the whiteness, the brown birds veering and scattering before him; and standing there against the snow, a white hill behind me and with no tree nor foxhole for cover I felt as exposed as a Black Muslim caught at a meeting of the K.K.K.

He had appeared as suddenly as the quail, and although the rifle was not yet to his shoulder, I was transfixed, watching him zooming up to become the largest, loudest, most aggressive-sounding white man I'd seen in my life, and I was, quite frankly, afraid. Then I was measuring his approach to the crunching tempo of his running and praying silently that he'd come within range of my shotgun before he fired; that I would be able to do what seemed necessary for me to do; that, shooting from the hip with an old twelve-gauge shotgun, I could stop him before he could shoot either me or my companion; and that, though stopped effectively, he would be neither killed, nor blinded, nor maimed.

It was a mixed-up prayer in an icy interval which ended in a smoking fury of cursing, when, at a warning from my companion, the farmer suddenly halted. Then we learned that the reckless man had meant only to warn us off of land which was not even his but that of a neighbor—my companion's foster father. He stood there between the two shotguns pointing short-ranged at his middle, his face quite drained of color now by the realization of how close to death he'd come, sputtering indignantly that we'd interpreted his rifle, which wasn't loaded, in a manner other than he'd intended. He truly did not realize that situations can be more loaded than guns and gestures more eloquent than words.

Fortunately, words are not rifles, but perhaps Howe is just as innocent of the rhetorical eloquence of situations as the farmer. He does not see that the meaning which emerges from his essay is not determined by isolated statements, but by the juxtaposition of those statements in a context which creates a larger statement. Or that contributing to the judgment rendered by that larger statement is the one in which it is uttered. When Howe pits Baldwin and Ellison against Wright and then gives Wright the better of the argument by using such emotionally weighted terms as "remembered" and "kept faith," the implication to me is that Baldwin and Ellison did *not* remember or keep faith with those who remained behind. If this be true, then I think that in this instance "villain" is not too strong a term.

Howe is not the first writer given to sociological categories who has had unconscious value judgments slip into his "analytical" or "scientific" descriptions. Thus I can believe that his approach was meant to be "analytic, not exhortatory; descriptive, not prescriptive." The results, however, are something else again. And are we to believe that he simply does not recognize rhetoric when he practices it? That when he asks, "what *could* [his italics] the experience of a man with a black skin be . . ." etc., he thinks he is describing a situation as viewed by each and every Negro writer rather than expressing, yes, and in the mode of "exhortation," the views of Irving Howe? Doesn't he recognize that just as the anti-Negro stereotype is a command to Negroes to mold themselves in its image, there sounds through his descriptive "thus it is" the command "thus you become"? And doesn't he realize that in this emotion-charged area definitive description is, in effect, prescription? If he does not, how then can we depend upon his "analysis" of politics or his reading of fiction?

Perhaps Howe could relax his views concerning the situation of the writers with a "black skin" if he examined some of the meanings which he gives to the word "Negro." He contends that I "cannot help being caught up with *the idea* of the Negro," but I have never said that I could or wished to do so—only Howe makes a problem for me here. When he uses the term "Negro" he speaks of it as a "stigma," and again, he speaks of "Negroness" as a "sterile category." He sees the Negro writer as experiencing a "constant pressure upon his literary work" from the "sociology of his existence . . . not merely in the way this might be true of any writer, but with a *pain* and *ferocity* that nothing could remove." [1]

Note that this is a condition arising from a *collective* experience which leaves no room for the individual writer's unique existence. It leaves no room for that intensity of personal anguish which compels the artist to seek relief by projecting it into the world in conjunction with other things; that anguish which might take the form of an acute sense of inferiority for one, homosexuality for another, an overwhelming sense of the absurdity of human life for still another. Nor does it leave room for the experience that might be caused by humiliation, by a harelip, by a stutter, by epilepsy—indeed, by any and everything in this life which plunges the talented individual into solitude while leaving him the will to transcend his condition through art. The individual Negro writer must create out of his own special needs and through his own sensibilities, and these alone. Otherwise, all those who suffer in anonymity would be creators.

Howe makes of "Negroness" a metaphysical condition, one that is a state of irremediable agony which all but engulfs the

---

[1] Italics mine.

mind. Happily, the view from inside the skin is not so dark as it appears to be from Howe's remote position, and therefore my view of "Negroness" is neither his nor that of the exponents of *negritude*. It is not skin color which makes a Negro American but cultural heritage as shaped by the American experience, the social and political predicament; a sharing of that "concord of sensibilities" which the group expresses through historical circumstance and through which it has come to constitute a subdivision of the larger American culture. Being a Negro American has to do with the memory of slavery and the hope of emancipation and the betrayal by allies and the revenge and contempt inflicted by our former masters after the Reconstruction, and the myths, both Northern and Southern, which are propagated in justification of that betrayal. It involves, too, a special attitude toward the waves of immigrants who have come later and passed us by.

It has to do with a special perspective on the national ideals and the national conduct, and with a tragicomic attitude toward the universe. It has to do with special emotions evoked by the details of cities and countrysides, with forms of labor and with forms of pleasure; with sex and with love, with food and with drink, with machines and with animals; with climates and with dwellings, with places of worship and places of entertainment; with garments and dreams and idioms of speech; with manners and customs, with religion and art, with life styles and hoping, and with that special sense of predicament and fate which gives direction and resonance to the Freedom Movement. It involves a rugged initiation into the mysteries and rites of color which makes it possible for Negro Americans to suffer the injustice which race and color are used to excuse without losing sight of either the humanity of those who inflict that injustice or the motives, rational or irrational, out of which they act. It imposes the uneasy burden and occasional joy of a complex double vision, a fluid, ambivalent response to men and events which represents, at its finest, a profoundly civilized adjustment to the cost of being human in this modern world.

More important, perhaps, being a Negro American involves a *willed* (who wills to be a Negro? *I* do!) affirmation of self as against all outside pressures—an identification with the group as extended through the individual self which rejects all possibilities of escape that do not involve a basic resuscitation of the original American ideals of social and political justice. And those white Negroes (and I do not mean Norman Mailer's dream creatures) are Negroes too—if they wish to be.

Howe's defense against my charge that he sees unrelieved suffering as the basic reality of Negro life is to quote favorable comments from his review of *Invisible Man*. But this does not cancel out the restricted meaning which he gives to "Negroness," or his statement that "the sociology of [the Negro writer's] existence forms a constant pressure with a *pain* and *ferocity* that nothing could remove." He charges me with unfairness for writing that he believes ideological militancy is more important than writing well, yet he tells us that "there may of course be times when one's obligation as a human being supersedes one's obligation as a writer. . . ." I think that the writer's obligation in a struggle as broad and abiding as the one we are engaged in, which involves not merely Negroes but all Americans, is best carried out through his role as writer. And if he chooses to stop writing and take to the platform, then it should be out of personal choice and not under pressure from would-be managers of society.

Howe plays a game of pitty-pat with Baldwin and Ellison. First he throws them into the pit for lacking Wright's "pain," "ferocity," "memory," "faithfulness" and "clenched militance," then he pats them on the head for the quality of their writing. If he would see evidence of this statement, let him observe how these terms come up in his original essay when he traces Baldwin's move toward Wright's position. Howe's rhetoric is weighted against "more modulated tones" in favor of "rasping outbursts," the Baldwin of *Another Country* becomes "a voice of anger, rasping and thrusting," and he is no longer "held back" by the "proprieties of literature." The character of Rufus in that novel displays a "ferocity" quite new in Baldwin's fiction, and Baldwin's essays gain resonance from "the tone of unrelenting protest . . . from [their] very anger, even the violence," etc. I am afraid that these are "good" terms in Howe's essay and they led to part of my judgment.

In defense of Wright's novel *The Long Dream*, Howe can write:

> . . . This book has been attacked for presenting Negro life in the South through "old-fashioned" images of violence, but [and now we have "prescription"] one ought to hesitate before denying the relevance of such images or joining in the criticism of their use. *For Wright was perhaps justified* in not paying attention to the changes that have occurred in the South these past few decades.[2]

If this isn't a defense, if not of bad writing at least of an irresponsible attitude toward good writing, I simply do not understand the language. I find it astonishing advice, since novels exist, since the fictional spell comes into existence precisely through the care which the novelist gives to selecting the details, the images, the tonalities, the specific social and psychological processes of specific characters in specific milieus at specific points in time. Indeed, it is one of the main tenets of the novelist's morality that he should write of that which he knows, and this is especially crucial for novelists who deal with a society as mobile and rapidly changing as ours. To justify ignoring this basic obligation is to encour-

---

[2] Italics mine.

age the downgrading of literature in favor of other values, in this instance "anger," "protest" and "clenched militancy." Novelists create not simply out of "memory" but out of memory modified, extended, transformed by social change. For a novelist to heed such advice as Howe's is to commit an act of artistic immorality. Amplify this back through society and the writer's failure could produce not order but chaos.

Yet Howe proceeds on the very next page of his essay to state, with no sense of contradiction, that Wright failed in some of the stories which comprise *Eight Men* ("The Man Who Lived Underground" was first published, by the way, in 1944) because he needed the "accumulated material of circumstance." If a novelist ignores social change, how can he come by the "accumulated material of circumstance"? Perhaps if Howe could grasp the full meaning of that phrase he would understand that Wright did not report in *Black Boy* much of his life in Mississippi, and he would see that Ross Barnett is not the whole state, that there is also a Negro Mississippi which is much more varied than that which Wright depicted.

For the critic there simply exists no substitute for the knowledge of history and literary tradition. Howe stresses Wright's comment that when he went into rooms where there were naked white women he felt like a "non-man . . . doubly cast out." But had Howe thought about it he might have questioned this reaction, since most young men would have been delighted with the opportunity to study, at first hand, women usually cloaked in an armor of taboos. I wonder how Wright felt when he saw Negro women acting just as shamelessly? Clearly this was an ideological point, not a factual report. And anyone aware of the folk sources of Wright's efforts to create literature would recognize that the situation is identical with that of the countless stories which Negro men tell of the male slave called in to wash the mistress' back in the bath, of the Pullman porter invited in to share the beautiful white passenger's favors in the berth, of the bellhop seduced by the wealthy blond guest.

It is interesting that Howe should interpret my statement about Mississippi as evidence of a loss of self-control. So allow me to repeat it coldly: I fear the implications of Howe's ideas concerning the Negro writer's role as actionist more than I do the State of Mississippi. Which is not to deny the viciousness which exists there but to recognize the degree of freedom which also exists there precisely because the repression is relatively crude, or at least it was during Wright's time, and it left the world of literature alone. William Faulkner lived neither in Jefferson nor Frenchman's Bend but in Oxford. He, too, was a Mississippian, just as the boys who helped Wright leave Jackson were the sons of a Negro college president. Both Faulkner and these boys must be recognized as part of the social reality of Mississippi. I said nothing about Ross Barnett, and I certainly did not say that Howe was a "cultural authoritarian," so he should not spread his honor so thin. Rather, let him look to the implications of his thinking.

Yes, and let him learn more about the South and about Negro Americans if he would speak with authority. When he points out that "the young Ralph Ellison, even while reading these great writers, could not in Macon County attend the white man's school or movie house," he certainly appears to have me cornered. But here again he does not know the facts and he underplays choice and will. I rode freight trains to Macon County, Alabama, during the Scottsboro trial because I desired to study with the Negro conductor-composer William L. Dawson, who was, and probably still is, the greatest classical musician in that part of the country. I had no need to attend a white university when the master I wished to study with was available at Tuskegee. Besides, why should I have wished to attend the white state-controlled university where the works of the great writers might not have been so easily available.

As for the movie-going, it is ironic but nonetheless true that one of the few instances where "separate but equal" was truly separate and equal was in a double movie house in the town of Tuskegee, where Negroes and whites were accommodated in parallel theaters, entering from the same street level through separate entrances and with the Negro side viewing the same pictures shortly after the showing for whites had begun. It was a product of social absurdity and, of course, no real relief from our resentment over the restriction of our freedom, but the movies were just as enjoyable or boring. And yet, is not knowing the facts more interesting, even as an isolated instance, and more stimulating to real thought than making abstract assumptions? I went to the movies to see pictures, not to be with whites. I attended a certain college because what I wanted was there. What is more, I *never* attended a white school from kindergarten through my three years of college, and yet, like Howe, I have taught and lectured for some years now at Northern, predominantly white, colleges and universities.

Perhaps this counts for little, changes little of the general condition of society, but it *is* factual and it does form a part of my sense of reality because, though it was not a part of Wright's life, it is my own. And if Howe thinks mine is an isolated instance, let him do a bit of research.

I do not really think that Howe can make a case for himself by bringing up the complimentary remarks which he made about *Invisible Man*. I did not quarrel with them in 1952, when they were first published, and I did not quarrel with them in my reply. His is the right of any critic to make judgment of a novel, and I do not see the point of arguing that I achieved an aesthetic goal if it did not work for him. I can only ask that my fiction be judged as art; if it fails, it fails aesthetically, not because I did or did not fight some ideological battle. I repeat, however, that Howe's strategy of bringing me into the public quarrel between Baldwin and Wright was inept. I simply did not belong in the conflict, since I knew, even then, that protest is *not* the source of the inadequacy characteristic of most novels by Negroes, but the simple failure of craft, bad writing; the desire to have protest perform the difficult tasks of art; the belief that racial suffering, social injustice or ideologies of whatever mammy-made variety, is enough. I know, also, that when the work of Negro writers has been rejected they have all too often protected their egos by blaming racial discrimination, while turning away from the fairly obvious fact that good art—and Negro musicians are ever present to demonstrate this—commands attention of itself, whatever the writer's politics or point of view. And they forget that publishers will publish almost anything which is written with even a minimum of competency, and that skill is developed by hard work, study and a conscious assault upon one's own fear and provincialism.

I agree with Howe that protest is an element of all art, though it does not necessarily take the form of speaking for a political or social program. It might appear in a novel as a technical assault against the styles which have gone before, or as protest against the human condition. If *Invisible Man* is even "apparently" free from "the ideological and emotional penalties suffered by Negroes in this country," it is because I tried to the best of my ability to transform these elements into art. My goal was not to escape, or hold back, but to work through; to transcend, as the blues transcend the painful conditions with which they deal. The protest is there, not because I was helpless before my racial condition, but because I *put* it there. If there is anything "miraculous" about the book it is the result of hard work undertaken in the belief that the work of art is important in itself, that it is a social action in itself.

I cannot hope to persuade Irving Howe to this view, for it seems quite obvious that he believes there are matters more important than artistic scrupulousness. I will point out, though, that the laws of literary form exert their validity upon all those who write, and that it is his slighting of the formal necessities of his essay which makes for some of our misunderstanding. After reading his reply, I gave in to my ear's suggestion that I had read certain of his phrases somewhere before, and I went to the library, where I discovered that much of his essay was taken verbatim from a review in the *Nation* of May 10, 1952, and that another section was published verbatim in the *New Republic* of February 13, 1962; the latter, by the way, being in its original context a balanced appraisal and warm farewell to Richard Wright.

But when Howe spliced these materials together with phrases from an old speech of mine, swipes at the critics of the *Sewanee* and *Kenyon* reviews (journals in which I have never published), and the Baldwin-Wright quarrel, the effect was something other than he must have intended. A dialectical transformation into a new quality took place and despite the intention of Howe's content, the form made its own statement. If he would find the absurdities he wants me to reduce to a quotation, he will really have to read his essay whole. One gets the impression that he did a paste-and-scissors job and, knowing what he intended, knowing how the separated pieces had operated by themselves, did not bother to read very carefully their combined effect. It could happen to anyone; nevertheless, I'm glad he is not a scientist or a social engineer.

I do not understand why Howe thinks I said anything on the subject of writing about "Negro experience" in a manner which excludes what he calls "plight and protest"; he must have gotten his Negroes mixed. But as to answering his question concerning the "ways a Negro writer can achieve personal realization apart from the common effort of his people to win their full freedom," I suggest that he ask himself in what way shall a Negro writer achieve personal realization (as writer) *after* his people shall have won their full freedom? The answer appears to be the same in both instances: He will have to go it alone! He must suffer alone even as he shares the suffering of his group, and he must write alone and pit his talents against the standards set by the best practitioners of the craft, both past and present, in any case. For the writer's real way of sharing the experience of his group is to convert its mutual suffering into lasting value. Is Howe suggesting, incidentally, that Heinrich Heine did not exist?

His question is silly, really, for there is no such thing as "full freedom" (Oh, how Howe thirsts and hungers for the absolute for *Negroes!*), just as the notion of an equality of talent is silly. I am a Negro who once played trumpet with a certain skill, but alas, I am no Louis Armstrong or Clark Terry. Willie Mays has realized himself quite handsomely as an individual despite coming from an impoverished Negro background in oppressive Alabama; and Negro Americans, like most Americans who know the value of baseball, exult in his success. I am, after all, only a minor member, not the whole damned tribe; in fact, most Negroes have never heard of me. I could shake the nation for a while with a crime or with indecent disclosures, but my pride lies in earning the right to call myself quite simply "writer." Perhaps if I write well enough the children of today's Negroes will be proud that I did, and so, perhaps, will Irving Howe's.

Let me end with a personal note: Dear Irving, I have no objections to being placed beside Richard Wright in any estimation which is based not upon the irremediable ground of our common racial identity, but upon the quality of our achievements as writers. I respected Wright's work and I knew him, but this is not to say that he "influenced" me as significantly as you assume. Consult the text! I *sought out* Wright because I had read Eliot, Pound, Gertrude Stein and Hemingway, and as early as 1940 Wright viewed me as a potential rival, partially, it is true, because he feared I would allow myself to be used against him by political manipulators who were not Negro and who envied and hated him. But perhaps you will understand when I say he did not influence me if I point out that while one can do nothing about choosing one's relatives, one can, as artist, choose one's "ancestors." Wright was, in this sense, a "relative"; Hemingway an "ancestor." Langston Hughes, whose work I knew in grade school and whom I knew before I knew Wright, was a "relative"; Eliot, whom I was to meet only many years later, and Malraux and Dostoievsky and Faulkner, were "ancestors"—if you please or don't please!

Do you still ask why Hemingway was more important to me than Wright? Not because he was white, or more "accepted." But because he appreciated the things of this earth which I love and which Wright was too driven or deprived or inexperienced to know: weather, guns, dogs, horses, love *and* hate and impossible circumstances which to the courageous and dedicated could be turned into benefits and victories. Because he wrote with such precision about the processes and techniques of daily living that I could keep myself and my brother alive during the 1937 Recession by following his descriptions of wing-shooting; because he knew the difference between politics and art and something of their true relationship for the writer. Because all that he wrote—and this is very important—was imbued with a spirit beyond the tragic with which I could feel at home, for it was very close to the feeling of the blues, which are, perhaps, as close as Americans can come to expressing the spirit of tragedy. (And if you think Wright knew anything about the blues, listen to a "blues" he composed with Paul Robeson singing, a *most* unfortunate collaboration!; and read his introduction to Paul Oliver's *Blues Fell This Morning*.) But most important, because Hemingway was a greater artist than Wright, who although a Negro like myself, and perhaps a great man, understood little if anything of these, at least to me, important things. Because Hemingway loved the American language and the joy of writing, making the flight of birds, the loping of lions across an African plain, the mysteries of drink and moonlight, the unique styles of diverse peoples and individuals come alive on the page. Because he was in many ways the true father-as-artist of so many of us who came to writing during the late thirties.

I will not dwell upon Hemingway's activities in Spain or during the liberation in Paris, for you know all of that. I will remind you, however, that any writer takes what he needs to get his own work done from wherever he finds it. I did not need Wright to tell me how to be a Negro, or how to be angry or to express anger—Joe Louis was doing that very well— or even to teach me about socialism; my mother had canvassed for the socialists, not the communists, the year I was born. No, I had been a Negro for twenty-two or twenty-three years when I met Wright, and in more places and under a greater variety of circumstances than he had then known. He was generously helpful in sharing his ideas and information, but I needed instruction in other values and I found them in the works of other writers—Hemingway was one of them, T. S. Eliot initiated the search.

I like your part about Chekhov arising from his sickbed to visit the penal colony at Sakhalin Island. It was, as you say, a noble act. But shouldn't we remember that it was significant only because Chekhov was *Chekhov*, the great writer? You compliment me truly, but I have not written so much or so well, even though I *have* served a certain apprenticeship in the streets and even touch events in the Freedom Movement in a modest way. But I can also recall the story of a certain writer who succeeded with a great fanfare of publicity in having a talented murderer released from prison. It made for another very short story which ended quite tragically—though not for the writer: A few months after his release the man killed the mother of two young children. I also know of another really quite brilliant writer who, under the advice of certain wise men who were then managing the consciences of artists, abandoned the prison of his writing to go to Spain, where he was allowed to throw away his life defending a worthless hill. I have not heard his name in years but I remember it vividly; it was Christopher Cauldwell, *né* Christopher St. John Sprigg. There are many such stories, Irving. It's heads you win, tails you lose, and you are quite right about my not following Baldwin, who is urged on by a nobility—or is it a demon—quite different from my own. It has cost me quite a pretty penny, indeed, but then I was always poor and not (and I know this is a sin in our America) too uncomfortable.

Dear Irving, I am still yakking on and there's many a thousand gone, but I assure you that no Negroes are beating down my door, putting pressure on me to join the Negro Freedom Movement, for the simple reason that they realize that I am enlisted for the duration. Such pressure is coming only from a few disinterested "military advisers," since Negroes want no more fairly articulate would-be Negro leaders cluttering up the airways. For, you see, my Negro friends recognize a certain division of labor among the members of the tribe. Their demands, like that of many whites, are that I publish more novels—and here I am remiss and vulnerable perhaps. You will recall what the Talmud has to say about the trees of the forest and the making of books, etc. But then, Irving, they recognize what you have not allowed yourself to see; namely, that my reply to your essay is in itself a small though necessary action in the Negro struggle for freedom. You should not feel unhappy about this or think that I regard you either as dishonorable or an enemy. I hope, rather, that you will come to view this exchange as an act of, shall we say, "antagonistic co-operation"?

—From *The New Leader*, December 9, 1963, and
February 3, 1964.

Hidden Name and
Complex Fate

A Writer's Experience in the United States

In *Green Hills of Africa,* Ernest Hemingway reminds us that both Tolstoy and Stendhal had seen war, that Flaubert had seen a revolution and the Commune, that Dostoievsky had been sent to Siberia and that such experiences were important in shaping the art of these great masters. And he goes on to observe that "writers are forged in injustice as a sword is forged." He declined to describe the many personal forms which injustice may take in this chaotic world—who would be so mad as to try?—nor does he go into the personal wounds which each of these writers sustained. Now, however, thanks to his brother and sister, we do know something of the injustice in which he himself was forged, and this knowledge has been added to what we have long known of Hemingway's artistic temper.

In the end, however, it is the quality of his art which is primary. It is the art which allows the wars and revolutions which he knew, and the personal and social injustice which he suffered, to lay claims upon our attention; for it was through his art that they achieved their most enduring meaning. It is a matter of outrageous irony, perhaps, but in literature the great social clashes of history no less than the painful experience of the individual are secondary to the meaning which they take on through the skill, the talent, the imagination and personal vision of the writer who transforms them into art. Here they are reduced to more manageable proportions; here they are imbued with humane values; here, injustice and catastrophe become less important in themselves than what the writer makes of them. This is *not* true, however, of the writer's struggle with that recalcitrant angel called Art; and it was through *this* specific struggle that Ernest Hemingway became *Hemingway* (now refined to a total body of transcendent work, after forty years of being endlessly dismembered and resurrected, as it continues to be, in the styles, the themes, the sense of life and literature of countless other writers). And it was through this struggle with form that he became the master, the culture hero, whom we have come to know and admire.

It was suggested that it might be of interest if I discussed here this evening some of my notions of the writer's experience in the United States, hence I have evoked the name of Hemingway, not by way of inviting far-fetched comparisons but in order to establish a perspective, a set of assumptions from which I may speak, and in an attempt to avoid boring you by emphasizing those details of racial hardship which for some forty years now have been evoked whenever writers of my own cultural background have essayed their experience in public.

I do this *not* by way of denying totally the validity of these by now stylized recitals, for I have shared and still share many of their detailed injustices—what Negro can escape them?—but by way of suggesting that they are, at least in a discussion of a writer's experience, as *writer,* as artist, somewhat beside the point.

For we select neither our parents, our race nor our nation; these occur to us out of the love, the hate, the circumstances, the fate, of others. But we *do* become writers out of an act of will, out of an act of choice; a dim, confused and ofttimes regrettable choice, perhaps, but choice nevertheless. And what happens thereafter causes all those experiences which occurred before we began to function as writers to take on a special quality of uniqueness. If this does not happen then as far as writing goes, the experiences have been misused. If we do not make of them a value, if we do not transform them into forms and images of meaning which they did not possess before, then we have failed as artists.

Thus for a writer to insist that his personal suffering is of special interest in itself, or simply because he belongs to a particular racial or religious group, is to advance a claim for special privileges which members of his group who are not writers would be ashamed to demand. The kindest judgment one can make of this point of view is that it reveals a sad misunderstanding of the relationship between suffering and art. Thomas Mann and André Gide have told us much of this and there are critics, like Edmund Wilson, who have told of the connection between the wound and the bow.

As I see it, it is through the process of making artistic forms—plays, poems, novels—out of one's experience that one becomes a writer, and it is through this process, this struggle, that the writer helps give meaning to the experience of the group. And it is the process of mastering the discipline, the techniques, the fortitude, the culture, through which this is made possible that constitutes the writer's real experience as *writer*, as artist. If this sounds like an argument for the artist's withdrawal from social struggles, I would recall to you W. H. Auden's comment to the effect that:

> In our age, the mere making of a work of art is itself a political act. So long as artists exist, making what they please, and think they ought to make, even if it is not terribly good, even if it appeals to only a handful of people, they remind the Management of something managers need to be reminded of, namely, that the managed are people with faces, not anonymous members, that *Homo Laborans* is also *Homo Ludens*. . . .

Without doubt, even the most *engagé* writer—and I refer to true artists, not to artists *manqués*—begin their careers in play and puzzlement, in dreaming over the details of the world in which they become conscious of themselves.

Let Tar Baby, that enigmatic figure from Negro folklore, stand for the world. He leans, black and gleaming, against the wall of life utterly noncommittal under our scrutiny, our questioning, starkly unmoving before our naïve attempts at intimidation. Then we touch him playfully and before we can say *Sonny Liston!* we find ourselves stuck. Our playful investigations become a labor, a fearful struggle, an *agon*. Slowly we perceive that our task is to learn the proper way of freeing ourselves to develop, in other words, technique.

Sensing this, we give him our sharpest attention, we question him carefully, we struggle with more subtlety; while he, in his silent way, holds on, demanding that we perceive the necessity of calling him by his true name as the price of our freedom. It is unfortunate that he has so many, many "true names"—all spelling chaos; and in order to discover even one of these we must first come into the possession of our own names. For it is through our names that we first place ourselves in the world. Our names, being the gift of others, must be made our own.

Once while listening to the play of a two-year-old girl who did not know she was under observation, I heard her saying over and over again, at first with questioning and then with sounds of growing satisfaction, "I am Mimi Livisay? . . . I am Mimi Livisay. I *am* Mimi Livisay . . . I am *Mimi* Li-vi-say! I am Mimi . . ."

And in deed and in fact she was—or became so soon thereafter, by working playfully to establish the unity between herself and her name.

For many of us this is far from easy. We must learn to wear our names within all the noise and confusion of the environment in which we find ourselves; make them the center of all of our associations with the world, with man and with nature. We must charge them with all our emotions, our hopes, hates, loves, aspirations. They must become our masks and our shields and the containers of all those values and traditions which we learn and/or imagine as being the meaning of our familial past.

And when we are reminded so constantly that we bear, as Negroes, names originally possessed by those who owned our enslaved grandparents, we are apt, especially if we are potential writers, to be more than ordinarily concerned with the veiled and mysterious events, the fusions of blood, the furtive couplings, the business transactions, the violations of faith and loyalty, the assaults; yes, and the unrecognized and unrecognizable loves through which our names were handed down unto us.

So charged with emotion does this concern become for some of us, that we have, earlier, the example of the followers of Father Divine and, now, the Black Muslims, discarding their original names in rejection of the bloodstained, the brutal, the sinful images of the past. Thus they would declare new identities, would clarify a new program of intention and destroy the verbal evidence of a willed and ritualized discontinuity of blood and human intercourse.

Not all of us, actually only a few, seek to deal with our names in this manner. We take what we have and make of them what we can. And there are even those who know where the old broken connections lie, who recognize their relatives across the chasm of historical denial and the artificial barriers of society, and who see themselves as bearers of many of the qualities which were admirable in the original sources of their common line (Faulkner has made much of this); and I speak here not of mere forgiveness, nor of obsequious insensitivity to the outrages symbolized by the denial and the division, but of the conscious acceptance of the harsh realities of the human condition, of the ambiguities and hypocrisies of human history as they have played themselves out in the United States.

Perhaps, taken in aggregate, these European names which (sometimes with irony, sometimes with pride, but always with personal investment) represent a certain triumph of the spirit, speaking to us of those who rallied, reassembled and transformed themselves and who under dismembering pressures refused to die. "Brothers and sisters," I once heard a Negro preacher exhort, "let us make up our faces before the world, and our names shall sound throughout the land with honor! For we ourselves are our *true* names, not their epithets! So let us, I say, Make Up Our Faces and Our Minds!"

Perhaps my preacher had read T. S. Eliot, although I doubt it. And in actuality, it was unnecessary that he do so, for a concern with names and naming was very much a part of that special area of American culture from which I come, and it is precisely for this reason that this example should come to mind in a discussion of my own experience as a writer.

Undoubtedly, writers begin their *conditioning* as manipulators of words long before they become aware of literature—certain Freudians would say at the breast. Perhaps.

But if so, that is far too early to be of use at this moment. Of this, though, I am certain: that despite the misconceptions of those educators who trace the reading difficulties experienced by large numbers of Negro children in Northern schools to their Southern background, these children are, in *their* familiar South, facile manipulators of words. I know, too, that the Negro community is deadly in its ability to create nicknames and to spot all that is ludicrous in an unlikely name or that which is incongruous in conduct. Names are not qualities; nor are words, in this particular sense, actions. To assume that they are could cost one his life many times a day. Language skills depend to a large extent upon a knowledge of the details, the manners, the objects, the folkways, the psychological patterns, of a given environment. Humor and wit depend upon much the same awareness, and so does the suggestive power of names.

"A small brown bowlegged Negro with the name 'Franklin D. Roosevelt Jones' might sound like a clown to someone who looks at him from the outside," said my friend Albert Murray, "but on the other hand he just might turn out to be a hell of a fireside operator. He might just lie back in all of that comic juxtaposition of names and manipulate you deaf, dumb and blind—and you not even suspecting it, because you're thrown out of stance by his name! There you are, so dazzled by the F.D.R. image—which you *know* you can't see—and so delighted with your own superior position that you don't realize that its *Jones* who must be confronted."

Well, as you must suspect, all of this speculation on the matter of names has a purpose, and now, because it is tied up so ironically with my own experience as a writer, I must turn to my own name.

For in the dim beginnings, before I ever thought consciously of writing, there was my own name, and there was, doubtless, a certain magic in it. From the start I was uncomfortable with it, and in my earliest years it caused me much puzzlement. Neither could I understand what a poet was, nor why, exactly, my father had chosen to name me after one. Perhaps I could have understood it perfectly well had he named me after his own father, but that name had been given to an older brother who died and thus was out of the question. But why hadn't he named me after a hero, such as Jack Johnson, or a soldier like Colonel Charles Young, or a great seaman like Admiral Dewey, or an educator like Booker T. Washington, or a great orator and abolitionist like Frederick Douglass? Or again, why hadn't he named me (as so many Negro parents had done) after President Teddy Roosevelt?

Instead, he named me after someone called Ralph Waldo Emerson, and then, when I was three, he died. It was too early for me to have understood his choice, although I'm sure he must have explained it many times, and it was also too soon for me to have made the connection between my name and my father's love for reading. Much later, after I began to write and work with words, I came to suspect that he was aware of the suggestive powers of names and of the magic involved in naming.

I recall an odd conversation with my mother during my early teens in which she mentioned their interest in, of all things, prenatal culture! But for a long time I actually knew only that my father read a lot, and that he admired this remote Mr. Emerson, who was something called a "poet and philosopher"—so much so that he named his second son after him.

I knew, also, that whatever his motives, the combination of names he'd given me caused me no end of trouble from the moment when I could talk well enough to respond to the ritualized question which grownups put to very young children. Emerson's name was quite familiar to Negroes in Oklahoma during those days when World War I was brewing, and adults, eager to show off their knowledge of literary figures, and obviously amused by the joke implicit in such a small brown nubbin of a boy carrying around such a heavy moniker, would invariably repeat my first two names and then to my great annoyance, they'd add "Emerson."

And I, in my confusion, would reply, "No, *no, I'm* not Emerson; he's the little boy who lives next door." Which only made them laugh all the louder. "Oh no," they'd say, *"you're* Ralph Waldo Emerson," while I had fantasies of blue murder.

For a while the presence next door of my little friend, Emerson, made it unnecessary for me to puzzle too often over this peculiar adult confusion. And since there were other Negro boys named Ralph in the city, I came to suspect that there was something about the combination of names which produced their laughter. Even today I know of only one other Ralph who had as much comedy made out of his name, a campus politician and deep-voiced orator whom I knew at Tuskegee, who was called in friendly ribbing, *Ralph Waldo Emerson Edgar Allan Poe,* spelled Powe. This must have been quite a trial for him, but I had been initiated much earlier.

During my early school years the name continued to puzzle me, for it constantly evoked in the faces of others some secret. It was as though I possessed some treasure or some defect, which was invisible to my own eyes and ears; something which I had but did not *possess*, like a piece of property in South Carolina, which was mine but which I could not have until some future time. I recall finding, about this time, while seeking adventure in back alleys—which possess for boys a superiority over playgrounds like that which kitchen utensils possess over toys designed for infants—a large photographic lens. I remember nothing of its optical qualities, of its speed or color correction, but it gleamed with crystal mystery and it was beautiful.

Mounted handsomely in a tube of shiny brass, it spoke to

me of distant worlds of possibility. I played with it, looking through it with squinted eyes, holding it in shafts of sunlight, and tried to use it for a magic lantern. But most of this was as unrewarding as my attempts to make the music come from a phonograph record by holding the needle in my fingers.

I could burn holes through newspapers with it, or I could pretend that it was a telescope, the barrel of a cannon, or the third eye of a monster—*I* being the monster—but I could do nothing at all about its proper function of making images; nothing to make it yield its secret. But I could not discard it.

Older boys sought to get it away from me by offering knives or tops, agate marbles or whole zoos of grass snakes and horned toads in trade, but I held on to it. No one, not even the white boys I knew, had such a lens, and it was my own good luck to have found it. Thus I would hold on to it until such time as I could acquire the parts needed to make it function. Finally I put it aside and it remained buried in my box of treasures, dusty and dull, to be lost and forgotten as I grew older and became interested in music.

I had reached by now the grades where it was necessary to learn something about Mr. Emerson and what he had written, such as the "Concord Hymn" and the essay "Self-Reliance," and in following his advice, I reduced the "Waldo" to a simple and, I hoped, mysterious "W," and in my own reading I avoided his works like the plague. I could no more deal with my name—I shall never really master it—than I could find a creative use for my lens. Fortunately there were other problems to occupy my mind. Not that I forgot my fascination with names, but more about that later.

Negro Oklahoma City was starkly lacking in writers. In fact, there was only Roscoe Dungee, the editor of the local Negro newspaper and a very fine editorialist in that valuable tradition of personal journalism which is now rapidly disappearing; a writer who in his emphasis upon the possibilities for justice offered by the Constitution anticipated the anti-segregation struggle by decades. There were also a few reporters who drifted in and out, but these were about all. On the level of *conscious* culture the Negro community was biased in the direction of music.

These were the middle and late twenties, remember, and the state was still a new frontier state. The capital city was one of the great centers for southwestern jazz, along with Dallas and Kansas City. Orchestras which were to become famous within a few years were constantly coming and going. As were the blues singers—Ma Rainey and Ida Cox, and the old bands like that of King Oliver. But best of all, thanks to Mrs. Zelia N. Breaux, there was an active and enthusiastic school music program through which any child who had the interest and the talent could learn to play an instrument and take part in the band, the orchestra, the brass quartet. And there was a yearly operetta and a chorus and a glee club. Harmony was taught for four years and the music appreciation program was imperative. European folk dances were taught throughout the Negro school system, and we were also taught complicated patterns of military drill.

I tell you this to point out that although there were no incentives to write, there was ample opportunity to receive an artistic discipline. Indeed, once one picked up an instrument it was difficult to escape. If you chafed at the many rehearsals of the school band or orchestra and were drawn to the many small jazz groups, you were likely to discover that the jazzmen were apt to rehearse far more than the school band; it was only that they seemed to enjoy themselves better and to possess a freedom of imagination which we were denied at school. And one soon learned that the wild, transcendent moments which occurred at dances or "battles of music," moments in which memorable improvisations were ignited, depended upon a dedication to a discipline which was observed even when rehearsals had to take place in the crowded quarters of Halley Richardson's shoeshine parlor. It was not the place which counted, although a large hall with good acoustics was preferred, but what one did to perfect one's performance.

If this talk of musical discipline gives the impression that there were no forces working to nourish one who would one day blunder, after many a twist and turn, into writing, I am misleading you. And here I might give you a longish lecture on the Ironies and Uses of Segregation. When I was a small child there was no library for Negroes in our city; and not until a Negro minister invaded the main library did we get one. For it was discovered that there was no law, only custom, which held that we could not use these public facilities. The results were the quick renting of two large rooms in a Negro office building (the recent site of a pool hall), the hiring of a young Negro librarian, the installation of shelves and a hurried stocking of the walls with any and every book possible. It was, in those first days, something of a literary chaos.

But how fortunate for a boy who loved to read! I started with the fairy tales and quickly went through the junior fiction; then through the Westerns and the detective novels, and very soon I was reading the classics—only I didn't know it. There were also the Haldeman Julius Blue Books, which seem to have floated on the air down from Girard, Kansas; the syndicated columns of O. O. McIntyre, and the copies of *Vanity Fair* and the *Literary Digest* which my mother brought home from work—how could I ever join uncritically in the heavy-handed attacks on the so-called Big Media which have become so common today?

There were also the pulp magazines and, more important, that other library which I visited when I went to help my adopted grandfather, J. D. Randolph (my parents had been living in his rooming house when I was born), at his work as custodian of the law library of the Oklahoma State Capitol. Mr. Randolph had been one of the first teachers in what became Oklahoma City; and he'd also been one of the leaders of a group who walked from Gallatin, Tennessee, to the Oklahoma Territory. He was a tall man, as brown as smoked leather, who looked like the Indians with whom he'd herded horses in the early days.

And while his status was merely the custodian of the law library, I was to see the white legislators come down on many occasions to question him on points of law, and often I was to hear him answer without recourse to the uniform rows of books on the shelves. This was a thing to marvel at in itself, and the white lawmakers did so, but even more marvelous, ironic, intriguing, haunting—call it what you will—is the fact that the Negro who knew the answers was named after Jefferson Davis. What Tennessee lost, Oklahoma was to gain, and after gaining it (a gift of courage, intelligence, fortitude and grace), used it only in concealment and, one hopes, with embarrassment.

So, let us, I say, make up our faces and our minds!

In the loosely structured community of that time, knowledge, news of other ways of living, ancient wisdom, the latest literary fads, hate literature—for years I kept a card warning Negroes away from the polls, which had been dropped by the thousands from a plane which circled over the Negro community—information of all kinds, found its level, catch-as-catch can, in the minds of those who were receptive to it. Not that there was no conscious structuring—I read my first Shaw and Maupassant, my first Harvard Classics in the home of a friend whose parents were products of that stream of New England education which had been brought to Negroes by the young and enthusiastic white teachers who staffed the schools set up for the freedmen after the Civil

War. These parents were both teachers and there were others like them in our town.

But the places where a rich oral literature was truly functional were the churches, the schoolyards, the barbershops, the cotton-picking camps; places where folklore and gossip thrived. The drug store where I worked was such a place, where on days of bad weather the older men would sit with their pipes and tell tall tales, hunting yarns and homely versions of the classics. It was here that I heard stories of searching for buried treasure and of headless horsemen, which I was told were my own father's versions told long before. There were even recitals of popular verse, "The Shooting of Dan McGrew," and, along with these, stories of Jesse James, of Negro outlaws and black United States marshals, of slaves who became the chiefs of Indian tribes and of the exploits of Negro cowboys. There was both truth and fantasy in this, intermingled in the mysterious fashion of literature.

Writers, in their formative period, absorb into their consciousness much that has no special value until much later, and often much which is of no special value even then—perhaps, beyond the fact that it throbs with affect and mystery and in it "time and pain and royalty in the blood" are suspended in imagery. So, long before I thought of writing, I was claimed by weather, by speech rhythms, by Negro voices and their different idioms, by husky male voices and by the high shrill singing voices of certain Negro women, by music; by tight spaces and by wide spaces in which the eyes could wander; by death, by newly born babies, by manners of various kinds, company manners and street manners; the manners of white society and those of our own high society; and by interracial manners; by street fights, circuses and minstrel shows; by vaudeville and moving pictures, by prize fights and foot races, baseball games and football matches. By spring floods and blizzards, catalpa worms and jack rabbits; honeysuckle and snapdragons (which smelled like old cigar butts); by sunflowers and hollyhocks, raw sugar cane and baked yams; pigs' feet, chili and blue haw ice cream. By parades, public dances and jam sessions, Easter sunrise ceremonies and large funerals. By contests between fire-and-brimstone preachers and by presiding elders who got "laughing-happy" when moved by the spirit of God.

I was impressed by expert players of the "dozens" and certain notorious bootleggers of corn whiskey. By jazz musicians and fortunetellers and by men who did anything well; by strange sicknesses and by interesting brick or razor scars; by expert cursing vocabularies as well as by exalted praying and terrifying shouting, and by transcendent playing or singing of the blues. I was fascinated by old ladies, those who had seen slavery and those who were defiant of white folk and black alike; by the enticing walks of prostitutes and by the limping walks affected by Negro hustlers, especially those who wore Stetson hats, expensive shoes with well-starched overalls, usually with a diamond stickpin (when not in hock) in their tieless collars as their gambling uniforms.

And there were the blind men who preached on corners, and the blind men who sang the blues to the accompaniment of washboard and guitar; and the white junkmen who sang mountain music and the famous hucksters of fruit and vegetables.

And there was the Indian–Negro confusion. There were Negroes who were part Indian and who lived on reservations, and Indians who had children who lived in towns as Negroes, and Negroes who were Indians and traveled back and forth between the groups with no trouble. And Indians who were as wild as wild Negroes and others who were as solid and as steady as bankers. There were the teachers, too, inspiring teachers and villainous teachers who chased after the girl students, and certain female teachers who one wished would chase after young male students. And a handsome old principal of military bearing who had been blemished by his classmates at West Point when they discovered on the eve of graduation that he was a Negro. There were certain Jews, Mexicans, Chinese cooks, a German orchestra conductor and an English grocer who owned a Franklin touring car. And certain Negro mechanics—"Cadillac Slim," "Sticks" Walker, Buddy Bunn and Oscar Pitman—who had so assimilated the automobile that they seemed to be behind a steering wheel even as they walked the streets or danced with girls. And there were the whites who despised us and the others who shared our hardships and our joys.

There is much more, but this is sufficient to indicate some of what was present even in a segregated community to form the background of my work, my sense of life.

And now comes the next step. I went to Tuskegee to study music, hoping to become a composer of symphonies and there, during my second year, I read *The Waste Land* and that, although I was then unaware of it, was the real transition to writing.

Mrs. L. C. McFarland had taught us much of Negro history in grade school and from her I'd learned of the New Negro Movement of the twenties, of Langston Hughes, Countee Cullen, Claude McKay, James Weldon Johnson and the others. They had inspired pride and had given me a closer identification with poetry (by now, oddly enough, I seldom thought of my hidden name), but with music so much on my mind it never occurred to me to try to imitate them. Still I read their work and was excited by the glamour of the Harlem which emerged from their poems and it was good to know that there were Negro writers. —Then came *The Waste Land*.

I was much more under the spell of literature than I realized at the time. *Wuthering Heights* had caused me an agony of unexpressible emotion and the same was true of *Jude the Obscure*, but *The Waste Land* seized my mind. I was intrigued by its power to move me while eluding my understanding. Somehow its rhythms were often closer to those of jazz than were those of the Negro poets, and even though I could not understand then, its range of allusion was as mixed and as varied as that of Louis Armstrong. Yet there were its discontinuities, its changes of pace and its hidden system of organization which escaped me.

There was nothing to do but look up the references in the footnotes to the poem, and thus began my conscious education in literature.

For this, the library at Tuskegee was quite adequate and I used it. Soon I was reading a whole range of subjects drawn upon by the poet, and this led, in turn, to criticism and to Pound and Ford Madox Ford, Sherwood Anderson and Gertrude Stein, Hemingway and Fitzgerald and "round about 'til I was come" back to Melville and Twain—the writers who are taught and doubtlessly overtaught today. Perhaps it was my good luck that they were not taught at Tuskegee, I wouldn't know. But at the time I was playing, having an intellectually interesting good time.

Having given so much attention to the techniques of music, the process of learning something of the craft and intention of modern poetry and fiction seemed quite familiar. Besides, it was absolutely painless because it involved no deadlines or credits. Even then, however, a process which I described earlier had begun to operate. The more I learned of literature in this conscious way, the more the details of my background became transformed. I heard undertones in remembered conversations which had escaped me before, local customs took on a more universal meaning, values which I hadn't understood were revealed; some of the people whom I had known were diminished while others were elevated in stature. More important, I began to see my own possibilities with more objective, and in some ways, more hopeful eyes.

The following summer I went to New York seeking work,

which I did not find, and remained there, but the personal transformation continued. Reading had become a conscious process of growth and discovery, a method of reordering the world. And that world had widened considerably.

At Tuskegee I had handled manuscripts which Prokofiev had given to Hazel Harrison, a Negro concert pianist who taught there and who had known him in Europe, and through Miss Harrison I had become aware of Prokofiev's symphonies. I had also become aware of the radical movement in politics and art, and in New York had begun reading the work of André Malraux, not only the fiction but chapters published from his *Psychology of Art*. And in my search for an expression of modern sensibility in the works of Negro writers I discovered Richard Wright. Shortly thereafter I was to meet Wright, and it was at his suggestion that I wrote both my first book review and my first short story. These were fatal suggestions.

For although I had tried my hand at poetry while at Tuskegee, it hadn't occurred to me that I might write fiction, but once he suggested it, it seemed the most natural thing to try. Fortunately for me, Wright, then on the verge of his first success, was eager to talk with a beginner and I was able to save valuable time in searching out those works in which writing was discussed as a craft. He guided me to Henry James' prefaces, to Conrad, to Joseph Warren Beach and to the letters of Dostoievsky. There were other advisers and other books involved, of course, but what is important here is that I was consciously concerned with the art of fiction, that almost from the beginning I was grappling quite consciously with the art through which I wished to realize myself. And this was not done in isolation; the Spanish Civil War was now in progress and the Depression was still on. The world was being shaken up, and through one of those odd instances which occur to young provincials in New York, I was to hear Malraux make an appeal for the Spanish Loyalists at the same party where I first heard the folk singer Leadbelly perform. Wright and I were there seeking money for the magazine which he had come to New York to edit.

Art and politics; a great French novelist and a Negro folk singer; a young writer who was soon to publish *Uncle Tom's Children;* and I who had barely begun to study his craft. It is such accidents, such fortuitous meetings, which count for so much in our lives. I had never dreamed that I would be in the presence of Malraux, of whose work I became aware on my second day in Harlem when Langston Hughes suggested that I read *Man's Fate* and *Days of Wrath* before returning them to a friend of his. And it is this fortuitous circumstance which led to my selecting Malraux as a literary "ancestor," whom, unlike a relative, the artist is permitted to choose. There was in progress at the time all the agitation over the Scottsboro boys and the Herndon Case, and I was aware of both. I had to be; I myself had been taken off a freight train at Decatur, Alabama, only three years before while on my way to Tuskegee. But while I joined in the agitation for their release, my main energies went into learning to write.

I began to publish enough, and not too slowly, to justify my hopes for success, and as I continued, I made a most perplexing discovery; namely, that for all his conscious concern with technique, a writer did not so much create the novel as he was created *by* the novel. That is, one did not make an arbitrary gesture when one sought to write. And when I say that the novelist is created by the novel, I mean to remind you that fictional techniques are not a mere set of objective tools, but something much more intimate: a way of feeling, of seeing and of expressing one's sense of life. And the process of *acquiring* technique is a process of modifying one's responses, of learning to see and feel, to hear and observe, to evoke and evaluate the images of memory and of summoning up and directing the imagination; of learning to conceive of human values in the ways which have been established by the great writers who have developed and extended the art. And perhaps the writer's greatest freedom, as artist, lies precisely in his possession of technique; for it is through technique that he comes to possess and express the meaning of his life.

Perhaps at this point it would be useful to recapitulate the route—perhaps as mazelike as that of *Finnegan's Wake*—which I have been trying to describe; that which leads from the writer's discovery of a sense of purpose, which is that of becoming a writer, and then the involvement in the passionate struggle required to master a bit of technique, and then, as this begins to take shape, the disconcerting discovery that it is *technique* which transforms the individual before he is able in turn to transform it. And in that personal transformation he discovers somethings else: he discovers that he has taken on certain obligations, that he must not embarrass his chosen form, and that in order to avoid this he must develop taste. He learns—and this is most discouraging—that he is involved with values which turn in their *own* way, and not in the ways of politics, upon the central issues affecting his nation and his time. He learns that the American novel, from its first consciousness of itself as a literary form, has grappled with the meaning of the American experience; that it has been aware and has sought to define the nature of that experience by addressing itself to the specific details, the moods, the landscapes, the cityscapes, the tempo of American change. And that it has borne, at its best, the full weight of that burden of conscience and consciousness which Americans inherit as one of the results of the revolutionary circumstances of our national beginnings.

We began as a nation not through the accidents of race or religion or geography (Robert Penn Warren has dwelled on these circumstances) but when a group of men, *some* of them political philosophers, put down, upon what we now recognize as being quite sacred papers, their conception of the nation which they intended to establish on these shores. They described, as we know, the obligations of the state to the citizen, of the citizen to the state; they committed themselves to certain ideas of justice, just as they committed us to a system which would guarantee all of its citizens equality of opportunity.

I need not describe the problems which have arisen from these beginnings. I need only remind you that the contradiction between these noble ideals and the actualities of our conduct generated a guilt, an unease of spirit, from the very beginning, and that the American novel at its best has always been concerned with this basic moral predicament. During Melville's time and Twain's, it was an implicit aspect of their major themes; by the twentieth century and after the discouraging and traumatic effect of the Civil War and the Reconstruction it had gone underground, had become *understated*. Nevertheless it did not disappear completely and it is to be found operating in the work of Henry James as well as in that of Hemingway and Fitzgerald. And then (and as one who believes in the impelling moral function of the novel and who believes in the moral seriousness of the form) it pleases me no end that it comes into explicit statement again in the works of Richard Wright and William Faulkner, writers who lived close to moral and political problems which would not stay put underground.

I go into these details not to recapitulate the history of the American novel but to indicate the trend of thought which was set into motion when I began to discover the nature of that process with which I was actually involved. Whatever the opinions and decisions of critics, a novelist must arrive at his own conclusions as to the meaning and function of the form with which he is engaged, and these are, in all modesty, some of mine.

In order to orient myself I also began to learn that the American novel had long concerned itself with the puzzle of the one-and-the-many; the mystery of how each of us, despite his origin in diverse regions, with our diverse racial, cultural, religious backgrounds, speaking his own diverse idiom of the American in his own accent, is, nevertheless, American. And with this concern with the implicit pluralism of the country and with the composite nature of the ideal character called "the American," there goes a concern with gauging the health of the American promise, with depicting the extent to which it was being achieved, being made manifest in our daily conduct.

And with all of this there still remained the specific concerns of literature. Among these is the need to keep literary standards high, the necessity of exploring new possibilities of language which would allow it to retain that flexibility and fidelity to the common speech which has been its glory since Mark Twain. For me this meant learning to add to it the wonderful resources of Negro American speech and idiom and to bring into range as fully and eloquently as possible the complex reality of the American experience as it shaped and was shaped by the lives of my own people.

Notice that I stress as "fully" as possible, because I would no more strive to write great novels by leaving out the complexity of circumstances which go to make up the Negro experience and which alone go to make the obvious injustice bearable, than I would think of preparing myself to become President of the United States simply by studying Negro American history or confining myself to studying those laws affecting civil rights.

For it seems to me that one of the obligations I took on when I committed myself to the art and form of the novel was that of striving for the broadest range, the discovery and articulation of the most exalted values. And I must squeeze these from the life which I know best. (A highly truncated impression of that life I attempted to convey to you earlier.)

If all this sounds a bit heady, remember that I did not destroy that troublesome middle name of mine, I only suppressed it. Sometimes it reminds me of my obligations to the man who named me.

It is our fate as human beings always to give up some good things for other good things, to throw off certain bad circumstances only to create others. Thus there is a value for the writer in trying to give as thorough a report of social reality as possible. Only by doing so may we grasp and convey the cost of change. Only by considering the broadest accumulation of data may we make choices that are based upon our own hard-earned sense of reality. Speaking from my own special area of American culture, I feel that to embrace uncritically values which are extended to us by others is to reject the validity, even the sacredness, of our own experience. It is also to forget that the small share of reality which each of our diverse groups is able to snatch from the whirling chaos of history belongs not to the group alone, but to all of us. It is a property and a witness which can be ignored only to the danger of the entire nation.

I could suppress the name of my namesake out of respect for the achievements of its original bearer but I cannot escape the obligation of attempting to achieve some of the things which he asked of the American writer. As Henry James suggested, being an American is an arduous task, and for most of us, I suspect, the difficulty begins with the name.

Address sponsored by the Gertrude Clarke Whittall
Foundation, Library of Congress, January 6, 1964.

The Art of Fiction:
An Interview

RALPH ELLISON: Let me say right now that my book [*Invisible Man*] is not an autobiographical work.

INTERVIEWERS (ALFRED CHESTER, VILMA HOWARD) You weren't thrown out of school like the boy in your novel?

ELLISON: No. Though, like him, I went from one job to another.

INTERVIEWERS: Why did you give up music and begin writing?

ELLISON: I didn't give up music, but I became interested in writing through incessant reading. In 1935 I discovered Eliot's *The Waste Land*, which moved and intrigued me but defied my powers of analysis—such as they were—

and I wondered why I had never read anything of equal intensity and sensibility by an American Negro writer. Later on, in New York, I read a poem by Richard Wright, who, as luck would have it, came to town the next week. He was editing a magazine called *New Challenge* and asked me to try a book review of E. Waters Turpin's *These Low Grounds*. On the basis of this review Wright suggested that I try a short story, which I did. I tried to use my knowledge of riding freight trains. He liked the story well enough to accept it and it got as far as the galley proofs when it was bumped from the issue because there was too much material. Just after that the magazine failed.

INTERVIEWERS: But you went on writing—

ELLISON: With difficulty, because this was the Recession of 1937. I went to Dayton, Ohio, where my brother and I hunted and sold game to earn a living. At night I practiced writing and studied Joyce, Dostoievsky, Stein and Hemingway. Especially Hemingway; I read him to learn his sentence structure and how to organize a story. I guess many young writers were doing this, but I also used his description of hunting when I went into the fields the next day. I had been hunting since I was eleven, but no one had broken down the process of wing-shooting for me and it was from reading Hemingway that I learned to lead a bird. When he describes something in print, believe him; believe him even when he describes the process of art in terms of baseball or boxing; he's been there.

INTERVIEWERS: Were you affected by the social realism of the period?

ELLISON: I was seeking to learn and social realism was a highly regarded theory, though I didn't think too much of the so-called proletarian fiction even when I was most impressed by Marxism. I was intrigued by Malraux, who at that time was being claimed by the Communists. I noticed, however, that whenever the heroes of Man's Fate[1] regarded their condition during moments of heightened self-consciousness, their thinking was something other than Marxist. Actually they were more profoundly intellectual than their real-life counterparts. Of course, Malraux was more of a humanist than most of the Marxist writers of that period—and also much more of an artist. He was the artist-revolutionary rather than a politician when he wrote Man's Fate, and the book lives not because of a political position embraced at the time, but because of its larger concern with the tragic struggle of humanity. Most of the social realists of the period were concerned less with tragedy than with injustice. I wasn't, and am not, primarily concerned with injustice, but with art.

INTERVIEWERS: Then you consider your novel a purely literary work as opposed to one in the tradition of social protest.

ELLISON: Now mind! I recognize no dichotomy between art and protest. Dostoievsky's Notes from Underground is, among other things, a protest against the limitations of nineteenth-century rationalism; Don Quixote, Man's Fate, Œdipus Rex, The Trial—all these embody protest, even against the limitation of human life itself. If social protest is antithetical to art, what then shall we make of Goya, Dickens and Twain? One hears a lot of complaints about the so-called "protest novel," especially when written by Negroes; but it seems to me that the critics could more accurately complain about their lack of craftsmanship and their provincialism.

INTERVIEWERS: But isn't it going to be difficult for the Negro writer to escape provincialism when his literature is concerned with a minority?

---

[1] La Condition Humaine.

ELLISON: All novels are about certain minorities: the individual is a minority. The universal in the novel—and isn't that what we're all clamoring for these days?—is reached only through the depiction of the specific man in a specific circumstance.

INTERVIEWERS: But still, how is the Negro writer, in terms of what is expected of him by critics and readers, going to escape his particular need for social protest and reach the "universal" you speak of?

ELLISON: If the Negro, or any other writer, is going to do what is expected of him, he's lost the battle before he takes the field. I suspect that all the agony that goes into writing is borne precisely because the writer longs for acceptance —but it must be acceptance on his own terms. Perhaps, though, this thing cuts both ways: the Negro novelist draws his blackness too tightly around him when he sits down to write—that's what the anti-protest critics believe —but perhaps the white reader draws his whiteness around himself when he sits down to read. He doesn't want to identify himself with Negro characters in terms of our immediate racial and social situation, though on the deeper human level, identification can become compelling when the situation is revealed artistically. The white reader doesn't want to get too close, not even in an imaginary re-creation of society. Negro writers have felt this and it has led to much of our failure.

Too many books by Negro writers are addressed to a white audience. By doing this the authors run the risk of limiting themselves to the audience's presumptions of what a Negro is or should be; the tendency is to become involved in polemics, to plead the Negro's humanity. You know, many white people question that humanity but I don't think that Negroes can afford to indulge in such a false issue. For us the question should be, What are the specific *forms* of that humanity, and what in our background is worth preserving or abandoning. The clue to this can be found in folklore, which offers the first drawings of any group's character. It preserves mainly those situations which have repeated themselves again and again in the history of any given group. It describes those rites, manners, customs, and so forth, which insure the good life, or destroy it; and it describes those boundaries of feeling, thought and action which that particular group has found to be the limitation of the human condition. It projects this wisdom in symbols which express the group's will to survive; it embodies those values by which the group lives and dies. These drawings may be crude but they are nonetheless profound in that they represent the group's attempt to humanize the world. It's no accident that great literature, the products of individual artists, is erected upon this humble base. The hero of Dostoievsky's *Notes from Underground* and the hero of Gogol's *The Overcoat* appear in their rudimentary forms far back in Russian folklore. French literature has never ceased exploring the nature of the Frenchman . . . Or take Picasso—

INTERVIEWERS: How does Picasso fit into all this?

ELLISON: Why, he's the greatest wrestler with forms and techniques of them all. Just the same he's never abandoned the old symbolic forms of Spanish art: the guitar, the bull, daggers, women, shawls, veils, mirrors. Such symbols serve a dual function: they allow the artist to speak of complex experiences and to annihilate time with simple lines and curves; and they allow the viewer an orientation, both emotional and associative, which goes so deep that a total culture may resound in a simple rhythm, an image. It has been said that Escudero could recapitulate the history and spirit of the Spanish dance with a simple arabesque of his fingers.

INTERVIEWERS: But these are examples from homogeneous

cultures. How representative of the American nation would you say Negro folklore is?

ELLISON: The history of the American Negro is a most intimate part of American history. Through the very process of slavery came the building of the United States. Negro folklore, evolving within a larger culture which regarded it as inferior, was an especially courageous expression. It announced the Negro's willingness to trust his own experience, his own sensibilities as to the definition of reality, rather than allow his masters to define these crucial matters for him. His experience is that of America and the West, and is as rich a body of experience as one would find anywhere. We can view it narrowly as something exotic, folksy or "low-down," or we may identify ourselves with it and recognize it as an important segment of the larger American experience—not lying at the bottom of it, but intertwined, diffused in its very texture. I can't take this lightly or be impressed by those who cannot see its importance; it is important to *me*. One ironic witness to the beauty and the universality of this art is the fact that the descendants of the very men who enslaved us can now sing the spirituals and find in the singing an exaltation of their own humanity. Just take a look at some of the slave songs, blues, folk ballads; their possibilities for the writer are infinitely suggestive. Some of them have named human situations so well that a whole corps of writers could not exhaust their universality. For instance, here's an old slave verse:

> *Ole Aunt Dinah, she's just like me*
> *She work so hard she want to be free*
> *But old Aunt Dinah's gittin' kinda ole*
> *She's afraid to go to Canada on account of the cold.*
>
> *Ole Uncle Jack, now he's a mighty "good nigger"*
> *You tell him that you want to be free for a fac'*

*Next thing you know they done stripped the skin
off your back.*

*Now old Uncle Ned, he want to be free
He found his way north by the moss on the tree
He cross that river floating in a tub
The patateroller[2] give him a mighty close rub.*

It's crude, but in it you have three universal attitudes toward the problem of freedom. You can refine it and sketch in the psychological subtleties and historical and philosophical allusions, action and what not, but I don't think its basic definition can be exhausted. Perhaps some genius could do as much with it as Mann has done with the Joseph story.

INTERVIEWERS: Can you give us an example of the use of folklore in your own novel?

ELLISON: Well, there are certain themes, symbols and images which are based on folk material. For example, there is the old saying amongst Negroes: If you're black, stay back; if you're brown, stick around; if you're white, you're right. And there is the joke Negroes tell on themselves about their being so black they can't be seen in the dark. In my book this sort of thing was merged with the meanings which blackness and light have long had in Western mythology: evil and goodness, ignorance and knowledge, and so on. In my novel the narrator's development is one through blackness to light; that is, from ignorance to enlightenment: invisibility to visibility. He leaves the South and goes North; this, as you will notice in reading Negro folktales, is always the road to freedom—the movement upward. You have the same thing again when he leaves his underground cave for the open.

It took me a long time to learn how to adapt such examples of myth into my work—also ritual. The use of rit-

---

[2] Patroller.

ual is equally a vital part of the creative process. I learned a few things from Eliot, Joyce and Hemingway, but not how to adapt them. When I started writing, I knew that in both *The Waste Land* and *Ulysses* ancient myth and ritual were used to give form and significance to the material; but it took me a few years to realize that the myths and rites which we find functioning in our everyday lives could be used in the same way. In my first attempt at a novel—which I was unable to complete—I began by trying to manipulate the simple structural unities of *beginning, middle* and *end,* but when I attempted to deal with the psychological strata—the images, symbols and emotional configurations—of the experience at hand, I discovered that the unities were simply cool points of stability on which one could suspend the narrative line— but beneath the surface of apparently rational human relationships there seethed a chaos before which I was helpless. People rationalize what they shun or are incapable of dealing with; these superstitions and their rationalizations become ritual as they govern behavior. The rituals become social forms, and it is one of the functions of the artist to recognize them and raise them to the level of art.

I don't know whether I'm getting this over or not. Let's put it this way: Take the "Battle Royal" passage in my novel, where the boys are blindfolded and forced to fight each other for the amusement of the white observers. This is a vital part of behavior pattern in the South, which both Negroes and whites thoughtlessly accept. It is a ritual in preservation of caste lines, a keeping of taboo to appease the gods and ward off bad luck. It is also the initiation ritual to which all greenhorns are subjected. This passage which states what Negroes will see I did not have to invent; the patterns were already there in society, so that all I had to do was present them in a broader context of meaning. In any society there are many rituals of situation which, for the most part, go unquestioned. They can be simple or elaborate, but they are the connective tissue between the work of art and the audience.

INTERVIEWERS: Do you think a reader unacquainted with this folklore can properly understand your work?

ELLISON: Yes, I think so. It's like jazz; there's no inherent problem which prohibits understanding but the assumptions brought to it. We don't all dig Shakespeare uniformly, or even *Little Red Riding Hood*. The understanding of art depends finally upon one's willingness to extend one's humanity and one's knowledge of human life. I noticed, incidentally, that the Germans, having no special caste assumptions concerning American Negroes, dealt with my work simply as a novel. I think the Americans will come to view it that way in twenty years—if it's around that long.

INTERVIEWERS: Don't you think it will be?

ELLISON: I doubt it. It's not an important novel. I failed of eloquence, and many of the immediate issues are rapidly fading away. If it does last, it will be simply because there are things going on in its depth that are of more permanent interest than on its surface. I hope so, anyway.

INTERVIEWERS: Have the critics given you any constructive help in your writing, or changed in any way your aims in fiction?

ELLISON: No, except that I have a better idea of how the critics react, of what they see and fail to see, of how their sense of life differs with mine and mine with theirs. In some instances they were nice for the wrong reasons. In the United States—and I don't want this to sound like an apology for my own failures—some reviewers did not see what was before them because of this nonsense about protest.

INTERVIEWERS : Did the critics change your view of yourself as a writer?

ELLISON: I can't say that they did. I've been seeing by my own candle too long for that. The critics did give me a sharper sense of a larger audience, yes; and some convinced me that they were willing to judge me in terms of my writing rather than in terms of my racial identity. But there is one widely syndicated critical bankrupt who made liberal noises during the thirties and has been frightened ever since. He attacked my book as a "literary race riot." By and large, the critics and readers gave me an affirmed sense of my identity as a writer. You might know this within yourself, but to have it affirmed by others is of utmost importance. Writing is, after all, a form of communication.

INTERVIEWER: When did you begin *Invisible Man*?

ELLISON: In the summer of 1945. I had returned from the sea, ill, with advice to get some rest. Part of my illness was due, no doubt, to the fact that I had not been able to write a novel for which I'd received a Rosenwald Fellowship the previous winter. So on a farm in Vermont where I was reading *The Hero* by Lord Raglan and speculating on the nature of Negro leadership in the United States, I wrote the first paragraph of *Invisible Man*, and was soon involved in the struggle of creating the novel.

INTERVIEWERS: How long did it take you to write it?

ELLISON: Five years, with one year out for a short novel which was unsatisfactory, ill-conceived and never submitted for publication.

INTERVIEWERS: Did you have everything thought out before you began to write *Invisible Man*?

ELLISON: The symbols and their connections were known to me. I began it with a chart of the three-part division. It was a conceptual frame with most of the ideas and some incidents indicated. The three parts represent the narrator's movement from, using Kenneth Burke's terms, purpose to passion to perception. These three major sections are built up of smaller units of three which mark the course of the action and which depend for their development upon what I hoped was a consistent and developing motivation. However, you'll note that the maximum insight on the hero's part isn't reached until the final section. After all, it's a novel about innocence and human error, a struggle through illusion to reality. Each section begins with a sheet of paper; each piece of paper is exchanged for another and contains a definition of his identity, or the social role he is to play as defined for him by others. But all say essentially the same thing, "Keep this nigger boy running." Before he could have some voice in his own destiny he had to discard these old identities and illusions; his enlightenment couldn't come until then. Once he recognizes the hole of darkness into which these papers put him, he has to burn them. That's the plan and the intention; whether I achieved this is something else.

INTERVIEWERS: Would you say that the search for identity is primarily an American theme?

ELLISON: It is *the* American theme. The nature of our society is such that we are prevented from knowing who we are. It is still a young society, and this is an integral part of its development.

INTERVIEWERS: A common criticism of "first novels" is that the central incident is either omitted or weak. *Invisible Man* seems to suffer here; shouldn't we have been present at the scenes which are the dividing lines in the book —namely, when the Brotherhood organization moves the narrator downtown, then back uptown?

ELLISON: I think you missed the point. The major flaw in the hero's character is his unquestioning willingness to do what is required of him by others as a way to success, and this was the specific form of his "innocence." He goes where he is told to go; he does what he is told to do; he does not even choose his Brotherhood name. It is chosen for him and he accepts it. He has accepted party discipline and thus cannot be present at the scene since it is not the will of the Brotherhood leaders. What is important is not the scene but his failure to question their decision. There is also the fact that no single person can be everywhere at once, nor can a single consciousness be aware of all the nuances of a large social action. What happens uptown while he is downtown is part of his darkness, both symbolic and actual. No, I don't feel that any vital scenes have been left out.

INTERVIEWERS: Why did you find it necessary to shift styles throughout the book, particularly in the Prologue and Epilogue?

ELLISON: The Prologue was written afterwards, really—in terms of a shift in the hero's point of view. I wanted to throw the reader off balance—make him accept certain non-naturalistic effects. It was really a memoir written underground, and I wanted a foreshadowing through which I hoped the reader would view the actions which took place in the main body of the book. For another thing, the styles of life presented are different. In the South, where he was trying to fit into a traditional pattern and where his sense of certainty had not yet been challenged, I felt a more naturalistic treatment was adequate. The college Trustee's speech to the students is really an echo of a certain kind of Southern rhetoric and I enjoyed trying to re-create it. As the hero passes from the South to the North, from the relatively stable to the swiftly changing, his sense of certainty is lost and the style becomes expressionistic. Later on during his fall from grace in the Brotherhood it becomes somewhat surrealistic. The styles try to express both his state of consciousness and the state of society. The Epilogue was necessary to complete the action begun when he set out to write his memoirs.

INTERVIEWERS: After four hundred pages you still felt the Epilogue was necessary?

ELLISON: Yes. Look at it this way. The book is a series of reversals. It is the portrait of the artist as a rabble-rouser, thus the various mediums of expression. In the Epilogue the hero discovers what he had not discovered throughout the book: you have to make your own decisions; you have to think for yourself. The hero comes up from underground because the act of writing and thinking necessitated it. He could not stay down there.

INTERVIEWERS: You say that the book is "a series of reversals." It seemed to us that this was a weakness, that it was built on a series of provocative situations which were canceled by the calling up of conventional emotions—

ELLISON: I don't quite see what you mean.

INTERVIEWERS: Well, for one thing, you begin with a provocative situation of the American Negro's status in society. The responsibility for this is that of the white American citizen; that's where the guilt lies. Then you cancel it by introducing the Communist Party, or the Brotherhood, so that the reader tends to say to himself: "Ah, they're the guilty ones. They're the ones who mistreat him; not us."

ELLISON: I think that's a case of misreading. And I didn't identify the Brotherhood as the C.P., but since you do I'll remind you that they, too, are white. The hero's invisibility is not a matter of being seen, but a refusal to run the risk of his own humanity, which involves guilt. This is not an attack upon white society! It is what the hero refuses to do in each section which leads to further action. He must assert and achieve his own humanity; he cannot run with the pack and do this—this is the reason for all the reversals. The Epilogue is the most final reversal of all; therefore it is a necessary statement.

INTERVIEWERS: And the love affairs—or almost love affairs—

ELLISON: (*Laughing*) I'm glad you put it that way. The point is that when thrown into a situation which he thinks he wants, the hero is sometimes thrown at a loss; he doesn't know how to act. After he had made this speech about the Place of the Woman in Our Society, for example, and was approached by one of the women in the audience, he thought she wanted to talk about the Brotherhood and found that she wanted to talk about brother-*and*-*sisterhood*. Look, didn't you find the book at all *funny*? I felt that such a man as this character would have been incapable of a love affair; it would have been inconsistent with his personality.

INTERVIEWERS: Do you have any difficulty controlling your characters? E. M. Forster says that he sometimes finds a character running away with him.

ELLISON: No, because I find that a sense of the ritual understructure of the fiction helps to guide the creation of characters. Action is the thing. We are what we do and do not do. The problem for me is to get from A to B to C. My anxiety about transitions greatly prolonged the writing of my book. The naturalists stick to case histories and sociology and are willing to compete with the camera and the tape recorder. I despise concreteness in writing, but when reality is deranged in fiction, one must worry about the seams.

INTERVIEWERS: Do you have difficulty turning real characters into fiction?

ELLISON: Real characters are just a limitation. It's like turning your own life into fiction: you have to be hindered by chronology and fact. A number of the characters just jumped out, like Rinehart and Ras.

INTERVIEWERS: Isn't Ras based on Marcus Garvey? [3]

ELLISON: No. In 1950 my wife and I were staying at a vacation spot where we met some white liberals who thought the best way to be friendly was to tell us what it was like to be Negro. I got mad at hearing this from people who otherwise seemed very intelligent. I had already sketched Ras but the passion of his statement came out after I went upstairs that night feeling that we needed to have this thing out once and for all and get it done with; then we could go on living like people and individuals. No conscious reference to Garvey is intended.

INTERVIEWERS: What about Rinehart? Is he related to Rinehart in the blues tradition, or Django Rheinhardt, the jazz musician?

ELLISON: There is a peculiar set of circumstances connected with my choice of that name. My old Oklahoma friend, Jimmy Rushing, the blues singer, used to sing one with a refrain that went:

> *Rinehart, Rinehart,*
> *It's so lonesome up here*
> *On Beacon Hill . . .*

which haunted me, and as I was thinking of a character who was a master of disguise, of coincidence, this name with its suggestion of inner and outer came to my mind. Later I learned that it was a call used by Harvard students when they prepared to riot, a call to chaos. Which is very interesting, because it is not long after Rinehart appears in my novel that the riot breaks out in Harlem. Rinehart is my name for the personification of chaos. He is also intended to represent America and change. He has lived so long with chaos that he knows how to manipulate it. It is the old theme of *The Confidence Man*. He is a

---

[3] Marcus Garvey, Negro nationalist and founder of a "Back to Africa" movement in the U.S. during the early 1900's.

figure in a country with no solid past or stable class lines; therefore he is able to move about easily from one to the other. (*He pauses, thoughtfully*)

You know, I'm still thinking of your question about the use of Negro experience as material for fiction. One function of serious literature is to deal with the moral core of a given society. Well, in the United States the Negro and his status have always stood for that moral concern. He symbolizes among other things the human and social possibility of equality. This is the moral question raised in our two great nineteenth-century novels, *Moby Dick* and *Huckleberry Finn*. The very center of Twain's book revolves finally around the boy's relations with Nigger Jim and the question of what Huck should do about getting Jim free after the two scoundrels had sold him. There is a magic here worth conjuring, and that reaches to the very nerve of the American consciousness—so why should I abandon it? Our so-called race problem has now lined up with the world problems of colonialism and the struggle of the West to gain the allegiance of the remaining nonwhite people who have thus far remained outside the Communist sphere; thus its possibilities for art have increased rather than lessened. Looking at the novelist as manipulator and depictor of moral problems, I ask myself how much of the achievement of democratic ideals in the United States has been affected by the steady pressure of Negroes and those whites who were sensitive to the implications of our condition; and I know that without that pressure the position of our country before the world would be much more serious than it is even now. Here is part of the social dynamics of a great society. Perhaps the discomfort about protest in books by Negro authors comes because since the nineteenth century American literature has avoided profound moral searching. It was too painful, and besides, there were specific problems of language and form to which the writers could address themselves. They did wonderful things, but perhaps they left the real problems untouched. There are exceptions, of course, like Faulkner, who has been working the great moral theme all along, taking it up where Mark Twain put it down.

I feel that with my decision to devote myself to the novel I took on one of the responsibilities inherited by those who practice the craft in the United States: that of describing for all that fragment of the huge diverse American experience which I know best, and which offers me the possibility of contributing not only to the growth of the literature but to the shaping of the culture as I should like it to be. The American novel is in this sense a conquest of the frontier; as it describes our experience, it creates it.

—From *The Paris Review*, Spring 1955.

SOUND and the MAINSTREAM

Living with Music

In those days it was either live with music or die with noise, and we chose rather desperately to live. In the process our apartment—what with its booby-trappings of audio equipment, wires, discs and tapes—came to resemble the Collier mansion, but that was later. First there was the neighborhood, assorted drunks and a singer.

We were living at the time in a tiny ground-floor-rear apartment in which I was also trying to write. I say "trying" advisedly. To our right, separated by a thin wall, was a small restaurant with a juke box the size of the Roxy. To our left, a night-employed swing enthusiast who took his lullaby music so loud that every morning promptly at nine Basie's brasses started blasting my typewriter off its stand. Our living room looked out across a small back yard to a rough stone wall to an apartment building which, towering above, caught every passing thoroughfare sound and rifled it straight down to me.

There were also howling cats and barking dogs, none capable of music worth living with, so we'll pass them by.

But the court behind the wall, which on the far side came knee-high to a short Iroquois, was a forum for various singing and/or preaching drunks who wandered back from the corner bar. From these you sometimes heard a fair barbershop style "Bill Bailey," free-wheeling versions of "The Bastard King of England," the saga of Uncle Bud, or a deeply felt rendition of Leroy Carr's "How Long Blues." The preaching drunks took on any topic that came to mind: current events, the fate of the long-sunk *Titanic* or the relative merits of the Giants and the Dodgers. Naturally there was great argument and occasional fighting—none of it fatal but all of it loud.

I shouldn't complain, however, for these were rather entertaining drunks, who like the birds appeared in the spring and left with the first fall cold. A more dedicated fellow was there all the time, day and night, come rain, come shine. Up on the corner lived a drunk of legend, a true phenomenon, who could surely have qualified as the king of all the world's winos—not excluding the French. He was neither poetic like the others nor ambitious like the singer (to whom we'll presently come) but his drinking bouts were truly awe-inspiring and he was not without his sensitivity. In the throes of his passion he would shout to the whole wide world one concise command, "Shut up!" Which was disconcerting enough to all who heard (except, perhaps, the singer), but such were the labyrinthine acoustics of courtyards and areaways that he seemed to direct his command at me. The writer's block which this produced is indescribable. On one heroic occasion he yelled his obsessive command without one interruption longer than necessary to take another drink (and with no appreciable loss of volume, penetration or authority) for three long summer days and nights, and shortly afterwards he died. Just how many lines of agitated prose he cost me I'll never know, but in all that chaos of sound I sympathized with his obsession, for I, too, hungered and thirsted for quiet. Nor did he inspire me to a painful identification, and for that I was thankful. Identification, after all, involves feelings of guilt and responsibility, and since I could hardly hear my own typewriter keys I felt in no way accountable for his condition. We were simply fellow victims of the madding crowd. May he rest in peace.

No, these more involved feelings were aroused by a more intimate source of noise, one that got beneath the skin and worked into the very structure of one's consciousness—like the "fate" motif in Beethoven's Fifth or the knocking-at-the-gates scene in *Macbeth*. For at the top of our pyramid of noise there was a singer who lived directly above us; you might say we had a singer on our ceiling.

Now, I had learned from the jazz musicians I had known as a boy in Oklahoma City something of the discipline and devotion to his art required of the artist. Hence I knew something of what the singer faced. These jazzmen, many of them now world-famous, lived for and with music intensely. Their driving motivation was neither money nor fame, but the will to achieve the most eloquent expression of idea-emotions through the technical mastery of their instruments (which, incidentally, some of them wore as a priest wears the cross) and the give and take, the subtle rhythmical shaping and blending of idea, tone and imagination demanded of group improvisation. The delicate balance struck between strong individual personality and the group during those early jam sessions was a marvel of social organization. I had learned too that the end of all this discipline and technical mastery was the desire to express an affirmative way of life through its musical tradition and that this tradition insisted that each artist achieve his creativity within its frame. He must learn the best of the past, and add to it his personal vision. Life could be harsh, loud and wrong if it wished, but they lived it fully, and when they expressed their attitude toward the world it was with a fluid style that reduced the chaos of living to form.

The objectives of these jazzmen were not at all those of the singer on our ceiling, but though a purist committed to the mastery of the *bel canto* style, German *lieder*, modern French art songs and a few American slave songs sung as if *bel canto*, she was intensely devoted to her art. From morning to night she vocalized, regardless of the condition of her voice, the weather or my screaming nerves. There were times when her notes, sifting through her floor and my ceiling, bouncing down the walls and ricocheting off the building in the rear, whistled like tenpenny nails, buzzed like a saw, wheezed like the asthma of a Hercules, trumpeted like an enraged African elephant—and the squeaky pedal of her piano rested plumb center above my typing chair. After a year of non-co-operation from the neighbor on my left I became desperate enough to cool down the hot blast of his phongraph by calling the cops, but the singer presented a serious ethical problem: Could I, an aspiring artist, complain against the hard work and devotion to craft of another aspiring artist?

Then there was my sense of guilt. Each time I prepared to shatter the ceiling in protest I was restrained by the knowledge that I, too, during my boyhood, had tried to master a musical instrument and to the great distress of my neighbors—perhaps even greater than that which I now suffered. For while our singer was concerned basically with a single tradition and style, I had been caught actively between two: that of the Negro folk music, both sacred and profane, slave song and jazz, and that of Western classical music. It was most confusing; the folk tradition demanded that I play what I heard and felt around me, while those who were seeking to teach the classical tradition in the schools insisted that I play strictly according to the book and express that which I was *supposed* to feel. This sometimes led to heated clashes of wills. Once during a third-grade music appreciation class a friend of mine insisted that it was a large green snake he saw swimming down a quiet brook instead of the snowy bird the teacher felt that Saint-Saëns' *Carnival of the Animals* should evoke. The rest of us sat there and lied like little black, brown and yellow Trojans about that swan, but our stalwart classmate held firm to his snake. In the end he got himself spanked and reduced the teacher to tears, but truth, reality and our environment were redeemed. For we were all familiar with snakes, while a swan was simply something the Ugly Duckling of the story grew up to be. Fortunately some of us grew up with a genuine appreciation of classical music *despite* such teaching methods. But as an inspiring trumpeter I was to wallow in sin for years before being awakened to guilt by our singer.

Caught mid-range between my two traditions, where one attitude often clashed with the other and one technique of playing was by the other opposed, I caused whole blocks of people to suffer.

Indeed, I terrorized a good part of an entire city section. During summer vacation I blew sustained tones out of the window for hours, usually starting—especially on Sunday mornings—before breakfast. I sputtered whole days through M. Arban's (he's the great authority on the instrument) double- and triple-tonguing exercises—with an effect like that of a jackass hiccupping off a big meal of briars. During school-term mornings I practiced a truly exhibitionist "Reveille" before leaving for school, and in the evening I generously gave the ever-listening world a long, slow version of "Taps," ineptly played but throbbing with what I in my adolescent vagueness felt was a romantic sadness. For it was farewell to day and a love song to life and a peace-be-with-you to all the dead and dying.

On hot summer afternoons I tormented the ears of all not blessedly deaf with imitations of the latest hot solos of Hot

Lips Paige (then a local hero), the leaping right hand of Earl "Fatha" Hines, or the rowdy poetic flights of Louis Armstrong. Naturally I rehearsed also such school-band standbys as the *Light Cavalry* Overture, Sousa's "Stars and Stripes Forever," the *William Tell* Overture, and "Tiger Rag." (Not even an after-school job as office boy to a dentist could stop my efforts. Frequently, by way of encouraging my development in the proper cultural direction, the dentist asked me proudly to render Schubert's *Serenade* for some poor devil with his jaw propped open in the dental chair. When the drill got going, or the forceps bit deep, I blew real strong.)

Sometimes, inspired by the even then considerable virtuosity of the late Charlie Christian (who during our school days played marvelous riffs on a cigar box banjo), I'd give whole summer afternoons and the evening hours after heavy suppers of black-eyed peas and turnip greens, cracklin' bread and buttermilk, lemonade and sweet potato cobbler, to practicing hard-driving blues. Such food oversupplied me with bursting energy, and from listening to Ma Rainey, Ida Cox and Clara Smith, who made regular appearances in our town, I knew exactly how I wanted my horn to sound. But in the effort to make it do so (I was no embryo Joe Smith or Tricky Sam Nanton) I sustained the curses of both Christian and infidel—along with the encouragement of those more sympathetic citizens who understood the profound satisfaction to be found in expressing oneself in the blues.

Despite those who complained and cried to heaven for Gabriel to blow a chorus so heavenly sweet and so hellishly hot that I'd forever put down my horn, there were more tolerant ones who were willing to pay in present pain for future pride.

For who knew what skinny kid with his chops wrapped around a trumpet mouthpiece and a faraway look in his eyes might become the next Armstrong? Yes, and send you, at some big dance a few years hence, into an ecstasy of rhythm and memory and brassy affirmation of the goodness of being alive and part of the community? Someone had to; for it was part of the group tradition—though that was not how they said it.

"Let that boy blow," they'd say to the protesting ones. "He's got to talk baby talk on that thing before he can preach on it. Next thing you know he's liable to be up there with Duke Ellington. Sure, plenty Oklahoma boys are up there with the big bands. Son, let's hear you try those "Trouble in Mind Blues." Now try and make it sound like ole Ida Cox sings it."

And I'd draw in my breath and do Miss Cox great violence.

Thus the crimes and aspirations of my youth. It had been years since I had played the trumpet or irritated a single ear with other than the spoken or written word, but as far as my singing neighbor was concerned I had to hold my peace. I was forced to listen, and in listening I soon became involved to the point of identification. If she sang badly I'd hear my own futility in the windy sound; if well, I'd stare at my typewriter and despair that I should ever make my prose so sing. She left me neither night nor day, this singer on our ceiling, and as my writing languished I became more and more upset. Thus one desperate morning I decided that since I seemed doomed to live within a shrieking chaos I might as well contribute my share; perhaps if I fought noise with noise I'd attain some small peace. Then a miracle: I turned on my radio (an old Philco AM set connected to a small Pilot FM tuner) and I heard the words

> *Art thou troubled?*
> *Music will calm thee . . .*

I stopped as though struck by the voice of an angel. It was Kathleen Ferrier, that loveliest of singers, giving voice to the aria from Handel's *Rodelinda*. The voice was so completely expressive of words and music that I accepted it without question—what lover of the vocal art could resist her?

Yet it was ironic, for after giving up my trumpet for the typewriter I had avoided too close a contact with the very art which she recommended as balm. For I had started music early and lived with it daily, and when I broke I tried to break clean. Now in this magical moment all the old love, the old fascination with music superbly rendered, flooded back. When she finished I realized that with such music in my own apartment, the chaotic sounds from without and above had sunk, if not into silence, then well below the level where they mattered. Here was a way out. If I was to live and write in that apartment, it would be only through the grace of music. I had tuned in a Ferrier recital, and when it ended I rushed out for several of her records, certain that now deliverance was mine.

But not yet. Between the hi-fi record and the ear, I learned, there was a new electronic world. In that realization our apartment was well on its way toward becoming an audio booby trap. It was 1949 and I rushed to the Audio Fair. I have, I confess, as much gadget-resistance as the next American of my age, weight and slight income; but little did I dream of the test to which it would be put. I had hardly entered the fair before I heard David Sarser's and Mel Sprinkle's Musician's Amplifier, took a look at its schematic and, recalling a boyhood acquaintance with such matters, decided that I could build one. I did, several times before it measured within specifications. And still our system was lacking. Fortunately my wife shared my passion for music, so we went on to buy, piece by piece, a fine speaker system, a first-rate AM-FM tuner, a transcription turntable and a speaker cabinet. I built half a dozen or more preamplifiers and record compensators before finding a commercial one that satisfied my ear, and, finally, we acquired an arm, a magnetic cartridge and—glory of the house—a tape recorder. All this plunge into electronics, mind you, had as its simple end the enjoyment of recorded music as it was intended to be heard. I was obsessed with the idea of reproducing sound with such fidelity that even when using music as a defense behind which I could write, it would reach the unconscious levels of the mind with the least distortion. And it didn't come easily. There were wires and pieces of equipment all over the tiny apartment (I became a compulsive experimenter) and it was worth your life to move about without first taking careful bearings. Once we were almost crushed in our sleep by the tape machine, for which there was space only on a shelf at the head of our bed. But it was worth it.

For now when we played a recording on our system even the drunks on the wall could recognize its quality. I'm ashamed to admit, however, that I did not always restrict its use to the demands of pleasure or defense. Indeed, with such marvels of science at my control I lost my humility. My ethical consideration for the singer up above shriveled like a plant in too much sunlight. For instead of soothing, music seemed to release the beast in me. Now when jarred from my writer's reveries by some especially enthusiastic flourish of our singer, I'd rush to my music system with blood in my eyes and burst a few decibels in her direction. If she defied me with a few more pounds of pressure against her diaphragm, then a war of decibels was declared.

If, let us say, she were singing "*Depuis le Jour*" from *Louise*, I'd put on a tape of Bidu Sayão performing the same aria, and let the rafters ring. If it was some song by Mahler, I'd match her spitefully with Marian Anderson or Kathleen Ferrier; if she offended with something from *Der Rosenkavalier*, I'd attack her flank with Lotte Lehmann. If she brought me up from my desk with art songs by Ravel or Rachmaninoff, I'd defend myself with Maggie Teyte or Jen-

nie Tourel. If she polished a spiritual to a meaningless arti-
ness I'd play Bessie Smith to remind her of the earth out of
which we came. Once in a while I'd forget completely that I
was supposed to be a gentleman and blast her with Strauss'
Zarathustra, Bartók's *Concerto for Orchestra,* Ellington's
"Flaming Sword," the famous crescendo from *The Pines of
Rome,* or Satchmo scatting, "I'll be Glad When You're Dead"
(you rascal you!). Oh, I was living with music with a sweet
vengeance.

One might think that all this would have made me her
most hated enemy, but not at all. When I met her on the
stoop a few weeks after my rebellion, expecting her fully to
slap my face, she astonished me by complimenting our music
system. She even questioned me concerning the artists I had
used against her. After that, on days when the acoustics
were right, she'd stop singing until the piece was finished
and then applaud—not always, I guessed, without a justifi-
able touch of sarcasm. And although I was now getting on
with my writing, the unfairness of this business bore in upon
me. Aware that I could not have withstood a similar comparison with literary artists of like caliber, I grew remorseful. I
also came to admire the singer's courage and control, for
she was neither intimidated into silence nor goaded into un-
disciplined screaming; she persevered, she marked the
phrasing of the great singers I sent her way, she improved
her style.

Better still, she vocalized more softly, and I, in turn, used
music less and less as a weapon and more for its magic with
mood and memory. After a while a simple twirl of the volume
control up a few decibels and down again would bring a live-
and-let-live reduction of her volume. We have long since
moved from that apartment and that most interesting neighborhood and now the floors and walls of our present apartment are adequately thick and there is even a closet large
enough to house the audio system; the only wire visible is

that leading from the closet to the corner speaker system. Still we are indebted to the singer and the old environment for forcing us to discover one of the most deeply satisfying aspects of our living. Perhaps the enjoyment of music is always suffused with past experience; for me, at least, this is true.

It seems a long way and a long time from the glorious days of Oklahoma jazz dances, the jam sessions at Halley Richardson's place on Deep Second, from the phonographs shouting the blues in the back alleys I knew as a delivery boy, and from the days when watermelon men with voices like mellow bugles shouted their wares in time with the rhythm of their horses' hoofs and farther still from the washerwomen singing slave songs as they stirred sooty tubs in sunny yards; and a long time, too, from those intense, conflicting days when the school music program of Oklahoma City was tuning our earthy young ears to classical accents—with music appreciation classes and free musical instruments and basic instruction for any child who cared to learn and uniforms for all who made the band. There was a mistaken notion on the part of some of the teachers that classical music had nothing to do with the rhythms, relaxed or hectic, of daily living, and that one should crook the little finger when listening to such refined strains. And the blues and the spirituals—jazz—? they would have destroyed them and scattered the pieces. Nevertheless, we learned some of it all, for in the United States when traditions are juxtaposed they tend, regardless of what we do to prevent it, irresistibly to merge. Thus musically at least each child in our town was an heir of all the ages. One learns by moving from the familiar to the unfamiliar, and while it might sound incongruous at first, the step from the spirituality of the spirituals to that of the Beethoven of the symphonies or the Bach of the chorales is not as vast as it seems. Nor is the romanticism of a Brahms or Chopin completely unrelated to that of Louis Armstrong.

Those who know their native culture and love it unchauvinistically are never lost when encountering the unfamiliar.

Living with music today we find Mozart and Ellington, Kirsten Flagstad and Chippie Hill, William L. Dawson and Carl Orff all forming part of our regular fare. For all exalt life in rhythm and melody; all add to its significance. Perhaps in the swift change of American society in which the meanings of one's origin are so quickly lost, one of the chief values of living with music lies in its power to give us an orientation in time. In doing so, it gives significance to all those indefinable aspects of experience which nevertheless help to make us what we are. In the swift whirl of time music is a constant, reminding us of what we were and of that toward which we aspired. Art thou troubled? Music will not only calm, it will ennoble thee.

—From *High Fidelity*, December 1955.

The Golden Age, Time Past

> *That which we do is what we are. That which we remember is, more often than not, that which we would like to have been; or that which we hope to be. Thus our memory and our identity are ever at odds; our history ever a tall tale told by inattentive idealists.*

It has been a long time now, and not many remember how it was in the old days; not really. Not even those who were there to see and hear as it happened, who were pressed in the crowds beneath the dim rosy lights of the bar in the smoke-veiled room, and who shared, night after night, the mysterious spell created by the talk, the laughter, grease paint, powder, perfume, sweat, alcohol and food—all blended and simmering, like a stew on the restaurant range, and brought to a sustained moment of elusive meaning by the timbres and accents of musical instruments locked in passionate recitative. It has been too long now, some seventeen years.

Above the bandstand there later appeared a mural depicting a group of jazzmen holding a jam session in a narrow Harlem bedroom. While an exhausted girl with shapely legs sleeps on her stomach in a big brass bed, they bend to their music in a quiet concatenation of unheard sound: a trumpeter, a guitarist, a clarinetist, a drummer; their only audience a small, cock-eared dog. The clarinetist is white. The guitarist strums with an enigmatic smile. The trumpet is muted. The barefooted drummer, beating a folded newspaper with whisk-brooms in lieu of a drum, stirs the eye's ear like a blast of brasses in a midnight street. A bottle of port rests on a dresser, but it, like the girl, is ignored. The artist, Charles Graham, adds mystery to, as well as illumination within, the scene by having them play by the light of a kerosene lamp. The painting, executed in a harsh documentary style reminiscent of W.P.A. art, conveys a feeling of musical effort caught in timeless and unrhetorical suspension, the sad remoteness of a scene observed through a wall of crystal.

Except for the lamp, the room might well have been one in the Hotel Cecil, the building on 118th Street in which Minton's Playhouse is located, and although painted in 1946, some time after the revolutionary doings there had begun, the mural should help recall the old days vividly. But the décor of the place has been changed and now it is covered, most of the time, by draperies. These require a tricky skill of those who would draw them aside. And even then there will still only be the girl who must sleep forever unhearing, and the men who must forever gesture the same soundless tune. Besides, the time it celebrates is dead and gone and perhaps not even those who came when it was still fresh and new remember those days as they were.

Neither do those remember who knew Henry Minton, who gave the place his name. Nor those who shared in the noisy lostness of New York the rediscovered community of the feasts, evocative of home, of South, of good times, the best and most unself-conscious of times, created by the generous portions of Negro American cuisine—the hash, grits, fried chicken, the ham-seasoned vegetables, the hot biscuits and rolls and the free whiskey—with which, each Monday night, Teddy Hill honored the entire cast of current Apollo Theatre shows. They were gathered here from all parts of America and they broke bread together and there was a sense of good feeling and promise, but what shape the fulfilled promise would take they did not know, and few except the more restless of the younger musicians even questioned. Yet it was an exceptional moment and the world was swinging with change.

Most of them, black and white alike, were hardly aware of where they were or what time it was; nor did they wish to be. They thought of Minton's as a sanctuary, where in an atmosphere blended of nostalgia and a music-and-drink-lulled suspension of time they could retreat from the wartime tensions of the town. The meaning of time-present was not their concern; thus when they try to tell it now the meaning escapes them.

For they were caught up in events which made that time exceptionally and uniquely *then,* and which brought, among the other changes which have reshaped the world, a momentous modulation into a new key of musical sensibility; in brief, a revolution in culture.

So how *can* they remember? Even in swiftly changing America there are few such moments, and at best Americans give but a limited attention to history. Too much happens too rapidly, and before we can evaluate it, or exhaust its meaning or pleasure, there is something new to concern us. Ours is the tempo of the motion picture, not that of the still camera, and we waste experience as we wasted the forest. During the time it was happening the sociologists were concerned with the riots, unemployment and industrial tensions of the time, the historians with the onsweep of the war; and the critics and most serious students of culture found this area of our national life of little interest. So it was left to those who came to Minton's out of the needs of feeling, and when the moment was past no one retained more than a fragment of its happening. Afterward the very effort to put the fragments together transformed them—so that in place of true memory they now summon to mind pieces of legend. They retell the stories as they have been told and written, glamorized, inflated, made neat and smooth, with all incomprehensible details vanished along with most of the wonder —not how it was as they themselves knew it.

When asked how it was back then, back in the forties, they will smile, then, frowning with the puzzlement of one attempting to recall the details of a pleasant but elusive dream, they'll say: "Oh, man, it was a hell of a time! A wailing time! Things were jumping, you couldn't get in here for the people. The place was packed with celebrities. Park Avenue, man! Big people in show business, college professors along with the pimps and their women. And college boys and girls. Everybody came. You know how the old words to the 'Basin Street Blues' used to go before Sinatra got hold of it? *Basin Street is the street where the dark and the light folks meet* —that's what I'm talking about. That was Minton's, man. It was a place where everybody could come to be entertained because it was a place that was jumping with good times."

Or some will tell you that it was here that Dizzy Gillespie found his own trumpet voice; that here Kenny Clarke worked out the patterns of his drumming style; where Charlie Christian played out the last creative and truly satisfying moments of his brief life, his New York home; where Charlie Parker built the monument of his art; where Thelonius Monk formulated his contribution to the chordal progressions and the hide-and-seek melodic methods of modern jazz. And they'll call such famous names as Lester Young and Ben Webster, Coleman Hawkins; or Fats Waller, who came here in the after-hour stillness of the early morning to compose.

They'll tell you that Benny Goodman, Art Tatum, Count Basie and Lena Horne would drop in to join in the fun; that it was here that George Shearing played on his first night in the United States; or of Tony Scott's great love of the place; and they'll repeat all the stories of how, when and by whom the word "bebop" was coined here—but, withal, few actually remember, and these leave much unresolved.

Usually music gives resonance to memory (and Minton's was a hotbed of jazz), but not the music then in the making here. It was itself a texture of fragments, repetitive, nervous, not fully formed; its melodic lines underground, secret and taunting; its riffs jeering—"Salt peanuts! Salt peanuts!" Its timbres flat or shrill, with a minimum of thrilling vibrato. Its rhythms were out of stride and seemingly arbitrary, its drummers frozen-faced introverts dedicated to chaos. And in it the steady flow of memory, desire and defined experience summed up by the traditional jazz beat and blues mood seemed swept like a great river from its old, deep bed. We know better now, and recognize the old moods in the new sounds, but what we know is that which was then becoming. For most of those who gathered here, the enduring meaning of the great moment at Minton's took place off to the side, beyond the range of attention, like a death blow glimpsed from the corner of the eye, the revolutionary rumpus sounding like a series of flubbed notes blasting the talk with discord. So that the events which made Minton's *Minton's* arrived in conflict and ran their course—then the heat was gone and all that is left to mark its passage is the controlled fury of the music itself, sealed pure and irrevocable, banalities and excellencies alike, in the early recordings; or swept along by our restless quest for the new, to be diluted in more recent styles, the best of it absorbed like drops of fully distilled technique, mood and emotions into the great stream of jazz.

Left also to confuse our sense of what happened is the

word "bop," hardly more than a nonsense syllable, by which the music synthesized at Minton's came to be known. A most inadequate word which does little, really, to help us remember. A word which throws up its hands in clownish self-deprecation before all the complexity of sound and rhythm and self-assertive passion which it pretends to name; a mask-word for the charged ambiguities of the new sound, hiding the serious face of art.

Nor does it help that so much has come to pass in the meantime. There have been two hot wars and that which continues, called "cold." And the unknown young men who brought a new edge to the sound of jazz and who scrambled the rhythms of those who used the small clear space at Minton's for dancing are no longer so young or unknown; indeed, they are referred to now by nickname in even the remotest of places. And in Paris and Munich and Tokyo they'll tell you the details of how, after years of trying, "Dizzy" (meaning John Birks Gillespie) vanquished "Roy" (meaning Roy Eldridge) during a jam session at Minton's, to become thereby the new king of trumpeters. Or how, later, while jetting over the world on the blasts of his special tilt-belled horn, he jammed with a snake charmer in Pakistan. "Sent the bloody cobra, man," they'll tell you in London's Soho. So their subsequent fame has blurred the sharp, ugly lines of their rebellion even in the memories of those who found them most strange and distasteful.

What's more, our memory of some of the more brilliant young men has been touched by the aura of death, and we feel guilt that the fury of their passing was the price paid for the art they left us to enjoy unscathed: Charlie Christian, burned out by tuberculosis like a guitar consumed in a tenement fire; Fats Navarro, wrecked by the tensions and needling temptations of his orgiastic trade, a big man physically as well as musically, shrunken to nothingness; and, most notably of all, Charlie Parker, called "Bird," now deified, worshiped and studied and, like any fertility god, mangled by his admirers and imitators, who coughed up his life and died—as incredibly as the leopard which Hemingway tells us was found "dried and frozen" near the summit of Mount Kilimanjaro—in the hotel suite of a Baroness. (Nor has anyone explained what a "yardbird" was seeking at that social altitude, though we know that ideally anything is possible within a democracy, and we know quite well that upper-class Europeans were seriously interested in jazz long before Newport became hospitable.) All this is too much for memory; the dry facts are too easily lost in legend and glamour. (With jazz we are yet not in the age of history, but linger in that of folklore.) We know for certain only that the strange sounds which they and their fellows threw against the hum and buzz of vague signification that seethed in the drinking crowd at Minton's and which, like disgruntled conspirators meeting fatefully to assemble the random parts of a bomb, they joined here and beat and blew into a new jazz style—these sounds we know now to have become the clichés, the technical exercises and the standard of achievement not only for fledgling musicians all over the United States, but for Dutchmen and Swedes, Italians and Frenchmen, Germans and Belgians, and even Japanese. All these, in places which came to mind during the Minton days only as points where the war was in progress and where one might soon be sent to fight and die, are now spotted with young men who study the discs on which the revolution hatched in Minton's is preserved with all the intensity that young American painters bring to the works, say, of Kandinsky, Picasso and Klee. Surely this is an odd swing of the cultural tide. Yet Stravinsky, Webern and Berg notwithstanding, or, more recently, Boulez or Stockhausen—such young men (many of them excellent musicians in the highest European tradition) find in the music made articulate at Minton's some key to a fuller freedom of self-realization.

Indeed for many young Europeans the developments which took place here and the careers of those who brought it about have become the latest episodes in the great American epic. They collect the recordings and thrive on the legends as eagerly, perhaps, as young Americans.

Today the bartenders at Minton's will tell you how they come fresh off the ships or planes, bringing their brightly expectant and—in this Harlem atmosphere—startlingly innocent European faces, to buy drinks and stand looking about for the source of the mystery. They try to reconcile the quiet reality of the place with the events which fired, at such long range, their imaginations. They come as to a shrine; as we to the Louvre, Notre Dame or St. Peter's; as young Americans hurry to the Café Flore, the Deux Magots, the Rotonde or the Café du Dôme in Paris. For some years now they have been coming to ask, with all the solemnity of pilgrims inquiring of a sacred relic, to see the nicotine-stained amplifier which Teddy Hill provided for Charlie Christian's guitar. And this is quite proper, for every shrine should have its relic.

Perhaps Minton's has more meaning for European jazz fans than for Americans, even for those who regularly went there. Certainly it has a *different* meaning. For them it is associated with those continental cafés in which great changes, political and artistic, have been plotted; it is to modern jazz what the Café Voltaire in Zurich is to the Dadaist phase of modern literature and painting. Few of those who visited Harlem during the forties would associate it so, but there is a context of meaning in which Minton's and the musical activities which took place there can be meaningfully placed.

Jazz, for all the insistence of the legends, has been far more closely associated with cabarets and dance halls than with brothels, and it was these which provided both the employment for the musicians and an audience initiated and aware of the overtones of the music; which knew the language of riffs, the unstated meanings of the blues idiom, and the dance steps developed from, and complementary to, its rhythms. And in the beginning it was in the Negro dance hall and night club that jazz was most completely a part of a total cultural expression; and in which it was freest and most satisfying, both for the musicians and for those in whose lives it played a major role. As a night club in a Negro community then, Minton's was part of a national pattern.

But in the old days Minton's was far more than this; it was also a rendezvous for musicians. As such, and although it was not formally organized, it goes back historically to the first New York center of Negro musicians, the Clef Club. Organized in 1910, during the start of the great migration of Negroes northward, by James Reese Europe, the director whom Irene Castle credits with having invented the fox trot, the Clef Club was set up on West 53rd Street to serve as a meeting place and booking office for Negro musicians and entertainers. Here wage scales were regulated, musical styles and techniques worked out, and entertainment was supplied for such establishments as Rector's and Delmonico's, and for such producers as Florenz Ziegfeld and Oscar Hammerstein. Later, when Harlem evolved into a Negro section, a similar function was served by the Rhythm Club, located then in the old Lafayette Theatre building on 132nd Street and Seventh Avenue. Henry Minton, a former saxophonist and officer of the Rhythm Club, became the first Negro delegate to Local 802 of the American Federation of Musicians and was thus doubly aware of the needs, artistic as well as economic, of jazzmen. He was generous with loans, was fond of food himself and, as an old acquaintance recalled, "loved to put a pot on the range" to share with unemployed friends. Naturally when he opened Minton's Playhouse many musicians made it their own.

Henry Minton also provided, as did the Clef and Rhythm

clubs, a necessity more important to jazz musicians than food: a place in which to hold their interminable jam sessions. And it is here that Minton's becomes most important to the development of modern jazz. It is here, too, that it joins up with all the countless rooms, private and public, in which jazzmen have worked out the secrets of their craft. Today jam sessions are offered as entertainment by night clubs and on radio and television, and some are quite exciting; but what is seen and heard is only one aspect of the true jam session: the "cutting session," or contest of improvisational skill and physical endurance between two or more musicians. But the jam session is far more than this, and when carried out by musicians, in the privacy of small rooms (as in the mural at Minton's) or in such places as Halley Richardson's shoeshine parlor in Oklahoma City—where I first heard Lester Young jamming in a shine chair, his head thrown back, his horn even then outthrust, his feet working on the footrests, as he played with and against Lem Johnson, Ben Webster (this was 1929) and other members of the old Blue Devils Orchestra—or during the after hours in Piney Brown's old Sunset Club in Kansas City; in such places as these with only musicians and jazzmen present, then the jam session is revealed as the jazzman's true academy.

It is here that he learns tradition, group techniques and style. For although since the twenties many jazzmen have had conservatory training and were well grounded in formal theory and instrumental technique, when we approach jazz we are entering quite a different sphere of training. Here it is more meaningful to speak, not of courses of study, of grades and degrees, but of apprenticeship, ordeals, initiation ceremonies, of rebirth. For after the jazzman has learned the fundamentals of his instrument and the traditional techniques of jazz—the intonations, the mute work, manipulation of timbre, the body of traditional styles—he must then "find himself," must be reborn, must find, as it were, his soul. All this through achieving that subtle identification between his instrument and his deepest drives which will allow him to express his own unique ideas and his own unique voice. He must achieve, in short, his self-determined identity.

In this his instructors are his fellow musicians, especially the acknowledged masters, and his recognition of manhood depends upon their acceptance of his ability as having reached a standard which is all the more difficult for not having been rigidly codified. This does not depend upon his ability to simply hold a job but upon his power to express an individuality in tone. Nor is his status ever unquestioned, for the health of jazz and the unceasing attraction which it holds for the musicians themselves lies in the ceaseless warfare for mastery and recognition—not among the general public, though commercial success is not spurned, but among their artistic peers. And even the greatest can never rest on past accomplishments, for, as with the fast guns of the old West, there is always someone waiting in a jam session to blow him literally, not only down, but into shame and discouragement.

By making his club hospitable to jam sessions even to the point that customers who were not musicians were crowded out, Henry Minton provided a retreat, a homogeneous community where a collectivity of common experience could find continuity and meaningful expression. Thus the stage was set for the birth of bop.

In 1941 Mr. Minton handed over his management to Teddy Hill, the saxophonist and former band leader, and Hill turned the Playhouse into a musical dueling ground. Not only did he continue Minton's policies, he expanded them. It was Hill who established the Monday Celebrity Nights, the house band which included such members from his own disbanded orchestra as Kenny Clark, Dizzy Gillespie, along with Thelonius Monk, sometimes with Joe Guy, and, later, Charlie Christian and Charlie Parker; and it was Hill who allowed the musicians free rein to play whatever they liked. Perhaps no other club except Clarke Monroe's Uptown House was so permissive, and with the hospitality extended to musicians of all schools the news spread swiftly. Minton's became the focal point for musicians all over the country.

Herman Pritchard, who presided over the bar in the old days, tells us that every time they came, "Lester Young and Ben Webster used to tie up in battle like dogs in the road. They'd fight on those saxophones until they were tired out, then they'd put in long-distance calls to their mothers, both of whom lived in Kansas City, and tell them about it."

And most of the masters of jazz came either to observe or to participate and be influenced and listen to their own discoveries transformed; and the aspiring stars sought to win their approval, as the younger tenor men tried to win the esteem of Coleman Hawkins. Or they tried to vanquish them in jamming contests as Gillespie is said to have outblown his idol, Roy Eldridge. It was during this period that Eddie "Lockjaw" Davis underwent an ordeal of jeering rejection until finally he came through as an admired tenor man.

In the perspective of time we now see that what was happening at Minton's was a continuing symposium of jazz, a summation of all the styles, personal and traditional, of jazz. Here it was possible to hear its resources of technique, ideas, harmonic structure, melodic phrasing and rhythmical possibilities explored more thoroughly than was ever possible before. It was also possible to hear the first attempts toward a conscious statement of the sensibility of the younger generation of musicians as they worked out the techniques, structures and rhythmical patterns with which to express themselves. Part of this was arbitrary, a revolt of the younger against the established stylists; part of it was inevitable. For jazz had reached a crisis and new paths were certain to be searched for and found. An increasing number of the younger men were formally trained and the post-Depression developments in the country had made for quite a break between their experience and that of the older men. Many were even of a different physical build. Often they were quiet and of a reserve which contrasted sharply with the exuberant and outgoing lyricism of the older men, and they were intensely concerned that their identity as Negroes placed no restriction upon the music they played or the manner in which they used their talent. They were concerned, they said, with art, not entertainment. Especially were they resentful of Louis Armstrong, whom (confusing the spirit of his music with his clowning) they considered an Uncle Tom.

But they too, some of them, had their own myths and misconceptions: That theirs was the only generation of Negro musicians who listened to or enjoyed the classics; that to be truly free they must act exactly the opposite of what white people might believe, rightly or wrongly, a Negro to be; that the performing artist can be completely and absolutely free of the obligations of the entertainer, and that they could play jazz with dignity only by frowning and treating the audience with aggressive contempt; and that to be in control, artistically and personally, one must be so cool as to quench one's own human fire.

Nor should we overlook the despair which must have swept Minton's before the technical mastery, the tonal authenticity, the authority and the fecundity of imagination of such men as Hawkins, Young, Goodman, Tatum, Teagarden, Ellington and Waller. Despair, after all, is ever an important force in revolutions.

They were also responding to the non-musical pressures affecting jazz. It was a time of big bands, and the greatest prestige and economic returns were falling outside the Negro community—often to leaders whose popularity grew from the compositions and arrangements of Negroes—to white instrumentalists whose only originality lay in the enterprise with which they rushed to market with some Negro musician's hard-won style. Still there was no policy of racial discrimination at Minton's. Indeed, it was very much like those Negro cabarets of the twenties and thirties in which a megaphone was placed on the piano so that anyone with the urge could sing a blues. Nevertheless, the inside-dopesters will tell you that the "changes" or chord progressions and the melodic inversions worked out by the creators of bop sprang partially from their desire to create a jazz which could not be so easily imitated and exploited by white musicians to whom the market was more open simply *because* of their whiteness. They wished to receive credit for what they created, and besides, it was easier to "get rid of the trash" who crowded the bandstand with inept playing and thus make room for the real musicians, whether white or black. Nevertheless, white musicians like Tony Scott, Remo Palmieri and Al Haig who were part of the development at Minton's became so by passing a test of musicianship, sincerity and temperament. Later, it is said, the boppers became engrossed in solving the musical problems which they set themselves. Except for a few sympathetic older musicians it was they who best knew the promise of the Minton moment, and it was they, caught like the rest in all the complex forces of American life which comes to focus in jazz, who made the most of it. Now the tall tales told as history must feed on the results of their efforts.

—From *Esquire*, January 1959.

As the Spirit Moves Mahalia

There are certain women singers who possess, beyond all
the boundaries of our admiration for their art, an uncanny
power to evoke our love. We warm with pleasure at mere
mention of their names; their simplest songs sing in our
hearts like the remembered voices of old dear friends, and
when we are lost within the listening anonymity of darkened
concert halls, they seem to seek us out unerringly. Standing
regal within the bright isolation of the stage, their subtlest
effects seem meant for us and us alone; privately, as across
the intimate space of our own living rooms. And when we
encounter the simple dignity of their immediate presence,
we suddenly ponder the mystery of human greatness.

Perhaps this power springs from their dedication, their
having subjected themselves successfully to the demanding
discipline necessary to the mastery of their chosen art. Or,
perhaps, it is a quality with which they are born as some are

born with bright orange hair. Perhaps, though we think not, it is acquired, a technique of "presence." But whatever its source, it touches us as a rich abundance of human warmth and sympathy. Indeed, we feel that if the idea of aristocracy is more than mere class conceit, then these surely are our natural queens. For they enchant the eye as they caress the ear, and in their presence we sense the full, moony glory of womanhood in all its mystery—maid, matron and matriarch. They are the sincere ones whose humanity dominates the artifices of the art with which they stir us, and when they sing we have some notion of our better selves.

Lotte Lehmann is one of these, and Marian Anderson. Both Madame Ernestine Schumann-Heink and Kathleen Ferrier possessed it. Nor is it limited to these mistresses of high art. Pastoria Pavon, "La Niña de Los Peines," the great flamenco singer, is another and so is Mahalia Jackson, the subject of this piece, who reminds us that while not all great singers possess this quality, those who do, no matter how obscure their origin, are soon claimed by the world as its own.

Mahalia Jackson, a large, handsome brown-skinned woman in her middle forties, who began singing in her father's church at the age of five, is a Negro of the *American* Negroes, and is, as the Spanish say, a woman of much quality. Her early experience was typical of Negro women of a certain class in the South. Born in New Orleans, she left school in the eighth grade and went to work as a nursemaid. Later she worked in the cotton fields of Louisiana and as a domestic. Her main social life was centered in the Baptist Church. She grew up with the sound of jazz in her ears, and, being an admirer of Bessie Smith, was aware of the prizes and acclaim awaiting any mistress of the blues, but in her religious views the blues and jazz are profane forms and a temptation to be resisted. She also knew something of the painful experiences which go into the forging of a true singer of the blues.

In 1927, following the classical pattern of Negro migration, Mahalia went to Chicago, where she worked as a laundress and studied beauty culture. Here, too, her social and artistic life was in the Negro community, centered in the Greater Salem Baptist Church. Here she became a member of the choir and a soloist with a quintet which toured the churches affiliated with the National Baptist Convention. Up until the forties she operated within a world of music which was confined, for the most part, to Negro communities, and it was by her ability to move such audiences as are found here that her reputation grew. It was also such audiences which, by purchasing over two million copies of her famous "Move On Up a Little Higher," brought her to national attention.

When listening to such recordings as *Sweet Little Jesus Boy, Bless This House, Mahalia Jackson,* or *In the Upper Room,* it is impossible to escape the fact that Mahalia Jackson is possessed of a profound religious conviction. Nor can we escape the awareness that no singer living has a greater ability to move us—regardless of our own religious attitudes —with the projected emotion of a song. Perhaps with the interpretive artist the distinction so often made between popular and serious art is not so great as it seems. Perhaps what counts is the personal quality of the individual artist, the depth of his experience and his sense of life. Certainly Miss Jackson possesses a quality of dignity and the ability to project a sincerity of purpose which is characteristic of only the greatest of interpretive artists.

Nor should it be assumed that her singing is simply the expression of the Negro's "natural" ability as is held by the stereotype (would that it were only true!). For although its techniques are not taught formally, Miss Jackson is the master of an art of singing which is as complex and of an even older origin than that of jazz.

It is an art which was acquired during those years when she sang in the comparative obscurity of the Negro community, and which, with the inevitable dilutions, comes into our national song style usually through the singers of jazz and the blues. It is an art which depends upon the employment of the full expressive resources of the human voice— from the rough growls employed by blues singers, the intermediate sounds, half-cry, half-recitative, which are common to Eastern music; the shouts and hollers of American Negro folk cries; the rough-edged tones and broad vibratos, the high, shrill and grating tones which rasp one's ears like the agonized flourishes of flamenco, to the gut tones, which remind us of where the jazz trombone found its human source. It is an art which employs a broad rhythmic freedom and accents the lyric line to reinforce the emotional impact. It utilizes half-tones, glissandi, blue notes, humming and moaning. Or again, it calls upon the most lyrical, floating tones of which the voice is capable. Its diction ranges from the most precise to the near liquidation of word-meaning in the sound; a pronunciation which is almost of the academy one instant and of the broadest cotton-field dialect the next. And it is most eclectic in its use of other musical idiom; indeed, it borrows any effect which will aid in the arousing and control of emotion. Especially is it free in its use of the effects of jazz; its tempos (with the characteristic economy of Negro expression it shares a common rhythmic and harmonic base with jazz) are taken along with its intonations, and, in ensemble singing, its orchestral voicing. In Mahalia's own "Move On Up a Little Higher" there is a riff straight out of early Ellington. Most of all it is an art which swings, and in the South there are many crudely trained groups who use it naturally for the expression of religious feeling who could teach the jazz modernists quite a bit about polyrhythmics and polytonality.

Since the forties this type of vocal music, known loosely as "gospel singing," has become a big business, both within the Negro community and without. Negro producers have found it highly profitable to hold contests in which groups of gospel singers are pitted against one another, and the radio stations which cater to the Negro market give many hours of their air time to this music. Today there are groups who follow regular circuits just as the old Negro jazzmen, blues singers and vaudeville acts followed the old T.O.B.A. circuit through the Negro communities of the nation. Some form the troupes of traveling evangelists and move about the country with their organs, tambourines, bones and drums. Some are led by ex-jazzmen who have put on the cloth, either sincerely or in response to the steady employment and growing market. So popular has the music become that there is a growing tendency to exploit its generic relationship to jazz and so-called rock-and-roll.

Indeed, many who come upon it outside the context of the Negro community tend to think of it as just another form of jazz, and the same confusion is carried over to the art of Mahalia Jackson. There is a widely held belief that she is really a blues singer who refuses, out of religious superstitions perhaps, to sing the blues; a jazz singer who coyly rejects her rightful place before a swinging band. And it *is* ironically true that just as a visitor who comes to Harlem seeking out many of the theatres and movie houses of the twenties will find them converted into churches, those who seek today for a living idea of the rich and moving art of Bessie Smith must go not to the night clubs and variety houses where those who call themselves blues singers find their existence, but must seek out Mahalia Jackson in a Negro church. And I insist upon the church and not the concert hall, because for all her concert appearances about the world she is not primarily a concert singer but a high priestess in the religious ceremony of her church. As such she is as far from the secular existentialism of the blues as Sartre is from St. John of the Cross. And it is in the setting of the church that the full timbre of her sincerity sounds most distinctly.

Certainly there was good evidence of this last July at the Newport Jazz Festival, where one of the most widely anticipated events was Miss Jackson's appearance with the Ellington Orchestra. Ellington had supplied the "Come Sunday" movement of his *Black, Brown and Beige Suite* (which with its organ-like close had contained one of Johnny Hodges's most serenely moving solos, a superb evocation of Sunday peace) with lyrics for Mahalia to sing. To make way for her, three of the original movements were abandoned along with the Hodges solo, but in their place she was given words of such banality that for all the fervor of her singing and the band's excellent performance, that Sunday sun simply would not arise. Nor does the recorded version change our opinion that this was a most unfortunate marriage and an error of taste, and the rather unformed setting of the Twenty-third Psalm which completes the side does nothing to improve things. In fact, only the sound and certain of the transitions between movements are an improvement over the old version of the suite. Originally "Come Sunday" was Ellington's moving *impression* of Sunday peace and religious quiet, but he got little of this into the words. So little, in fact, that it was impossible for Mahalia to release that vast fund of emotion with which Southern Negroes have charged the scenes and symbols of the Gospels.

Only the fortunate few who braved the Sunday morning rain to attend the Afro-American Episcopal Church services heard Mahalia at her best at Newport. Many had doubtless been absent from church or synagogue for years, but here they saw her in her proper setting and the venture into the strangeness of the Negro church was worth the visit. Here they could see, to the extent we can visualize such a thing, the world which Mahalia summons up with her voice; the spiritual reality which infuses her song. Here it could be seen that the true function of her singing is not simply to entertain, but to prepare the congregation for the minister's message, to make it receptive to the spirit and, with effects of voice and rhythm, to evoke a shared community of experience.

As she herself put it while complaining of the length of the time allowed her during a recording session, "I'm used to singing in church, where they don't stop me until the Lord comes." By which she meant, not until she had created the spiritual and emotional climate in which the Word is made manifest; not until, and as the spirit moves her, the song of Mahalia the high priestess sings within the heart of the congregation as its own voice of faith.

When in possession of the words which embody her religious convictions Mahalia can dominate even the strongest jazz beat and instill it with her own fervor. *Bless This House* contains songs set to rumba, waltz and two-step but what she does to them provides a triumphal blending of popular dance movements with religious passion. In *Sweet Little Jesus Boy*, the song "The Holy Babe" is a Negro version of an old English count-rhyme, and while enumerating the gifts of the Christian God to man, Mahalia and Mildred Falls, her pianist, create a rhythmical drive such as is expected of the entire Basie band. It is all joy and exultation and swing, but it is nonetheless religious music. Many who are moved by Mahalia and her spirit have been so impressed by the emotional release of her music that they fail to see the frame within which she moves. But even *In the Upper Room* and *Mahalia Jackson*—in which she reminds us most poignantly of Bessie Smith, and in which the common singing techniques of the spirituals and the blues are most clearly to be heard—are directed toward the after life and thus are intensely religious. For those who cannot—or will not—visit Mahalia in her proper setting, these records are the next best thing.

—From *Saturday Review*, September 27, 1958.

On Bird, Bird-Watching, and Jazz

Bird: The Legend of Charlie Parker, a collection of anecdotes, testimonies and descriptions of the life of the famous jazz saxophonist, may be described as an attempt to define just what species of bird Bird really was. Introduced by Robert Reisner's description of his own turbulent friendship and business relations with Parker, it presents contributions by some eighty-three fellow Bird watchers, including a wife and his mother, Mrs. Addie Parker. There are also poems, photographs, descriptions of his funeral, memorial and estate, a chronology of his life, and an extensive discography by Erik Wiedemann.

One of the founders of postwar jazz, Parker had, as an improviser, as marked an influence upon jazz as Louis Armstrong, Coleman Hawkins or Johnny Hodges. He was also famous for his riotous living, which, heightened by alcohol and drugs, led many of his admirers to consider him a latter-day François Villon. Between the beginning of his fame at about 1945 and his death in 1955, he became the central figure of a cult which glorified in his escapades no less than in his music. The present volume is mainly concerned with the escapades, the circumstances behind them and their effect upon Bird's friends and family.

Oddly enough, while several explanations are advanced as to how Charles Parker, Jr., became known as "Bird" ("Yardbird," in an earlier metamorphosis), none is conclusive. There is, however, overpowering internal evidence that whatever the true circumstance of his ornithological designation, it had little to do with the chicken yard. Randy roosters and operatic hens are familiars to fans of the animated cartoons, but for all the pathetic comedy of his living—and despite the crabbed and constricted character of his style—Parker was a most inventive melodist; in bird-watcher's terminology, a true songster.

This failure in the exposition of Bird's legend is intriguing, for nicknames are indicative of a change from a given to an achieved identity, whether by rise or fall, and they tell us something of the nicknamed individual's interaction with his fellows. Thus, since we suspect that more of legend is involved in his renaming than Mr. Reisner's title indicates, let us at least consult Roger Tory Peterson's *Field Guide to the Birds* for a hint as to why, during a period when most jazzmen were labeled "cats," someone hung the bird on Charlie. Let us note too that "legend" originally meant "the story of a saint" and that saints were often identified with symbolic animals.

Two species won our immediate attention, the goldfinch and the mockingbird—the goldfinch because the beatnik phrase "Bird lives," which, following Parker's death, has been chalked endlessly on Village buildings and subway walls, reminds us that during the thirteenth and fourteenth centuries a symbolic goldfinch frequently appeared in European devotional paintings. An apocryphal story has it that upon being given a clay bird for a toy, the infant Jesus brought it miraculously to life as a goldfinch. Thus the small, tawny-brown bird with a bright red patch about the base of its bill and a broad yellow band across its wings became a representative of the soul, the Passion and the Sacrifice. In more worldly late-Renaissance art, the little bird became the ambiguous symbol of death and the soul's immortality. For our own purposes, however, its song poses a major problem: it is like that of a canary—which, soul or no soul, rules the goldfinch out.

The mockingbird, *Mimus polyglottos,* is more promising. Peterson informs us that its song consists of "long successions of notes and phrases of great variety, with each phrase repeated a half-dozen times before going on to the next," that the mockingbirds are "excellent mimics" who "adeptly imitate a score or more species found in the neighborhood," and that they frequently sing at night—a description which not only comes close to Parker's way with a saxophone but even hints at a trait of his character. For although he *usually* sang at night, his playing was characterized by velocity, by long-continued successions of notes and phrases, by swoops, bleats, echoes, rapidly repeated bebops—I mean rebopped bebops—by mocking mimicry of other jazzmen's styles, and by interpolations of motifs from extraneous melodies, all of which added up to a dazzling display of wit, satire, burlesque and pathos. Further, he was as expert at issuing his improvisations from the dense brush as from the extreme treetops of the harmonic landscape, and there was, without doubt, as irrepressible a mockery in his personal conduct as in his music.

Mimic thrushes, which include the catbird and brown thrasher, along with the mockingbird, are not only great virtuosi, they are the tricksters and con men of the bird world. Like Parker, who is described as a confidence man and a practical joker by several of the commentators, they take off on the songs of other birds, inflating, inverting and turning them wrong side out, and are capable of driving a prowling ("square") cat wild. Utterly irreverent and romantic, they are not beyond bugging human beings. Indeed, on summer nights in the South, when the moon hangs low, the mockingbirds sing as though determined to heat every drop of romance in the sleeping adolescent's heart to fever pitch. Their song thrills and swings the entire moon-struck night to arouse one's sense of the mystery, the promise and the frustration of being human, alive and hot in the blood. They are as delightful to eye as to ear, but sometimes a similarity of voice and appearance makes for a confusion with the shrikes, a species given to impaling insects and smaller songbirds on the points of thorns, and they are destroyed. They are fond of fruit, especially mulberries, and if there is a tree in your yard, there will be, along with the wonderful music, much chalky, blue-tinted evidence of their presence. Under such conditions be careful and heed Parker's warning to his friends—who sometimes were subjected to a shrike-like treatment—"you must pay your dues to Bird."

Though notes of bitterness sound through Mr. Reisner's book, he and his friends paid willingly for the delight and frustration which Parker brought into their lives. Thus their comments—which are quite unreliable as history—constitute less a collective biography than a celebration of his living and a lamentation of his dying, and are, in the ritual sense, his apotheosis or epiphany into the glory of those who have been reborn in legend.

Symbolic birds, myth and ritual—what strange metaphors to arise during the discussion of a book about a jazz musician! And yet, who knows very much of what jazz is really about? Or how shall we ever know until we are willing to confront anything and everything which it sweeps across our path? Consider that at least as early as T. S. Eliot's creation of a new aesthetic for poetry through the artful juxtapositioning of earlier styles, Louis Armstrong, way down the river in New Orleans, was working out a similar technique for jazz. This is not a matter of giving the music fine airs—it doesn't need them—but of saying that whatever touches our highly conscious creators of culture is apt to be reflected here.

The thrust toward respectability exhibited by the Negro jazzmen of Parker's generation drew much of its immediate fire from their understandable rejection of the traditional entertainer's role—a heritage from the minstrel tradition—exemplified by such an outstanding creative musician as Louis Armstrong. But when they fastened the epithet "Uncle Tom" upon Armstrong's music they confused artistic quality with questions of personal conduct, a confusion which would ultimately reduce their own music to the mere matter of race. By rejecting Armstrong they thought to rid themselves of the entertainer's role. And by way of getting rid of the role they demanded, in the name of their racial identity, a purity of status which by definition is impossible for the performing artist.

The result was a grim comedy of racial manners; with the musicians employing a calculated surliness and rudeness, treating the audience very much as many white merchants in poor Negro neighborhoods treat their customers, and the white audiences were shocked at first but learned quickly to accept such treatment as evidence of "artistic" temperament. Then comes a comic reversal. Today the white audience expects the rudeness as part of the entertainment. If it fails to appear the audience is disappointed. For the jazzmen it has become a proposition of the more you win, the more you lose. Certain older jazzmen possessed a clearer idea of the division between their identities as performers and as private individuals. Off stage and while playing in ensemble, they carried themselves like college professors or high church deacons; when soloing they donned the comic mask and went into frenzied pantomimes of hotness—even when playing "cool"—and when done, dropped the mask and returned to their chairs with dignity. Perhaps they realized that whatever his style, the performing artist remains an entertainer, even as Heifetz, Rubinstein or young Glenn Gould.

For all the revolutionary ardor of his style, Dizzy Gillespie, a co-founder with Parker of modern jazz and a man with a savage eye for the incongruous, is no less a clown than Louis, and his wide reputation rests as much upon his entertaining personality as upon his gifted musicianship. There is even a morbid entertainment value in watching the funereal posturing of the Modern Jazz Quartet, and doubtless, part of the tension created in their listeners arises from the anticipation that during some unguarded moment, the grinning visage of the traditional delight-maker (inferior because performing at the audience's command; superior because he can perform, effectively, through the magic of his art) will emerge from behind those bearded masks. In the United States, where each of us is a member of some minority group and where political power and entertainment alike are derived from viewing and manipulating the human predicaments of others, the maintenance of dignity is never a simple matter—even for those with highest credentials. Gossip is one of our largest industries, the President is fair game for caricaturists, and there is always someone around to set a symbolic midget upon J. P. Morgan's unwilling knee.

No jazzman, not even Miles Davis, struggled harder to escape the entertainer's role than Charlie Parker. The pathos of his life lies in the ironic reversal through which his struggles to escape what in Armstrong is basically a *make-believe* role of clown—which the irreverent poetry and triumphant sound of his trumpet makes even the squarest of squares aware of—resulted in Parker's becoming something far more "primitive": a sacrificial figure whose struggles against personal chaos, on stage and off, served as entertainment for a ravenous, sensation-starved, culturally disoriented public which had but the slightest notion of its real significance. While he slowly died (like a man dismembering himself with a dull razor on a spotlighted stage) from the ceaseless conflict from which issued both his art and his destruction, his public reacted as though he were doing much the same thing as those saxophonists who hoot and honk and roll on the floor. In the end he had no private life and his most tragic moments were drained of human significance.

Here, perhaps, is an explanation, beyond all questions of reason, drugs or whiskey, of the violent contradictions detailed in Mr. Reisner's book of Parker's public conduct. In attempting to escape the role, at once sub- and super-human, in which he found himself, he sought to outrage his public into an awareness of his most human pain. Instead, he made himself notorious and in the end became unsure whether his fans came to enjoy his art or to be entertained by the "world's greatest junky," the "supreme hipster."

Sensitive and thoroughly aware of the terrifying cost of his art and his public image, he had to bear not only the dismemberment occasioned by rival musicians who imitated every nuance of his style—often with far greater financial return—but the imitation of his every self-destructive excess of personal conduct by those who had in no sense earned the right of such license. Worse, it was these who formed his cult.

Parker operated in the underworld of American culture, on that turbulent level where human instincts conflict with social institutions; where contemporary civilized values and hypocrisies are challenged by the Dionysian urges of a between-wars youth born to prosperity, conditioned by the threat of world destruction, and inspired—when not seeking total anarchy—by a need to bring social reality and our social pretensions into a more meaningful balance. Significantly enough, race is an active factor here, though not in the usual sense. When the jazz drummer Art Blakey was asked about Parker's meaning for Negroes, he replied, "They never heard of him." Parker's artistic success and highly publicized death have changed all that today, but interestingly enough, Bird was indeed a "white" hero. His greatest significance was for the educated white middle-class youth whose reactions to the inconsistencies of American life was the stance of casting off its education, language, dress, manners and moral standards: a revolt, apolitical in nature, which finds its most dramatic instance in the figure of the so-called white hipster. And whatever its justification, it was, and is, a reaction to the chaos which many youth sense at the center of our society.

For the postwar jazznik, Parker was Bird, a suffering, psychically wounded, law-breaking, life-affirming hero. For them he possessed something of the aura of that figure common to certain contemporary novels, which R. W. B. Lewis describes as the "picaresque saint." He was an obsessed outsider—and Bird was thrice alienated: as Negro, as addict, as exponent of a new and disturbing development in jazz—whose tortured and in many ways criminal striving for personal and moral integration invokes a sense of tragic fellowship in those who saw in his agony a ritualization of their own fears, rebellions and hunger for creativity. One of the most significant features of Reisner's book lies, then, in his subtitle—even though he prefers to participate in the re-creation of Bird's legend rather than perform the critical function of analyzing it.

Reisner, a former art historian who chooses to write in the

barely articulate jargon of the hipster, no more than hints at this (though Ted Joans spins it out in a wild surrealist poem). But when we read through the gossip of the accounts we recognize the presence of a modern American version of the ancient myth of the birth and death of the hero. We are told of his birth, his early discovery of his vocation, his dedication to his art, of his wanderings and early defeats; we are told of his initiation into the mysteries revealed by his drug and the regions of terror to which it conveyed him; we are told of his obsessive identification with his art and his moment of revelation and metamorphosis. Here is Parker's own version:

> I remember one night I was jamming in a chili house (Dan Wall's) on Seventh Avenue between 139th and 140th. It was December, 1939 . . . I'd been getting bored with the stereotyped changes that were being used all the time, all the time, and I kept thinking there's bound to be something else. I could hear it sometimes but I couldn't play it. Well, that night, I was working over "Cherokee," and, as I did, I found that by using the higher intervals of a chord as a melody line and backing them with appropriately related changes, I could play the thing I'd been hearing. I came alive.

From then on he reigns as a recognized master, creating, recording, inspiring others, finding fame, beginning a family. Then comes his waning, suffering, disintegration and death.

Many of the bare facts of Parker's life are presented in the useful chronology, but it is the individual commentators' embellishments on the facts which create the mythic dimension. Bird was a most gifted innovator and evidently a most ingratiating and difficult man—one whose friends had no need for an enemy, and whose enemies had no difficulty in justifying their hate. According to his witnesses he stretched the limits of human contradiction beyond belief. He was lovable and hateful, considerate and callous; he stole from friends and benefactors and borrowed without conscience, often without repaying, and yet was generous to absurdity.

He could be most kind to younger musicians or utterly crushing in his contempt for their ineptitude. He was passive and yet quick to pull a knife and pick a fight. He knew the difficulties which are often the lot of jazz musicians, but as a leader he tried to con his sidemen out of their wages. He evidently loved the idea of having a family and being a good father and provider, but found it as difficult as being a good son to his devoted mother. He was given to extremes of sadism and masochism, capable of the most staggering excesses and the most exacting physical discipline and assertion of will. Indeed, one gets the image of such a character as Stavrogin in Dostoievsky's *The Possessed*, who while many things to many people seemed essentially devoid of a human center—except, and an important exception indeed, Parker was an artist who found his moments of sustained and meaningful integration through the reed and keys of the alto saxophone. It is the recordings of his flights of music which remain, and it is these which form the true substance of his myth.

Which brings us, finally, to a few words about Parker's style. For all its velocity, brilliance and imagination there is in it a great deal of loneliness, self-deprecation and self-pity. With this there is a quality which seems to issue from its vibratoless tone: a sound of amateurish ineffectuality, as though he could never quite make it. It is this amateurish-sounding aspect which promises so much to the members of a do-it-yourself culture; it sounds with an assurance that you too can create your own do-it-yourself jazz. Dream stuff, of course, but there is a relationship between the Parker *sound* and the impossible genre of teen-age music which has developed since his death. Nevertheless, he captured something of the discordancies, the yearning, romance and cunning of the age and ordered it into a haunting art. He was not the god they see in him but for once the beatniks are correct: Bird lives—perhaps because his tradition and his art blew him to the meaningful center of things.

But what kind of bird was Parker? Back during the thirties members of the old Blue Devils Orchestra celebrated a certain robin by playing a lugubrious little tune called "They Picked Poor Robin." It was a jazz community joke, musically an extended "signifying riff" or melodic naming of a recurring human situation, and was played to satirize some betrayal of faith or loss of love observed from the bandstand. Sometimes it was played as the purple-fezzed musicians returned from the burial of an Elk, whereupon reaching the Negro business and entertainment district the late Walter Page would announce the melody dolefully on his tuba; then poor robin would transport the mourners from their somber mood to the spirit-lifting beat of "Oh, didn't he ramble" or some other happy tune. Parker, who studied with Buster Smith and jammed with other members of the disbanded Devils in Kansas City, might well have known the verse which Walter Page supplied to the tune:

> *Oh, they picked poor robin clean*
> *(repeat)*
> *They tied poor robin to a stump*
> *Lord, they picked all the feathers*
> *Round from robin's rump*
> *Oh, they picked poor robin clean.*

Poor robin was picked again and again and his pluckers were ever unnamed and mysterious. Yet the tune was inevitably productive of laughter—even when we ourselves were its object. For each of us recognized that his fate was somehow our own. Our defeats and failures—even our final defeat by death—were loaded upon his back and given ironic significance and thus made more bearable. Perhaps Charlie was poor robin come to New York and here to be sacrificed to the need for entertainment and for the creation of a new jazz style and awaits even now in death a meaning-making plucking by perceptive critics. The effectiveness of any sacrifice depends upon our identification with the agony of the hero-victim; to those who would still insist that Charlie was a mere yardbird, our reply can only be, "Aint nobody *here* but us chickens, boss!"

—From *Saturday Review*, July 28, 1962.

The Charlie Christian Story

Jazz, like the country which gave it birth, is fecund in its inventiveness, swift and traumatic in its developments and terribly wasteful of its resources. It is an orgiastic art which demands great physical stamina of its practitioners, and many of its most talented creators die young. More often than not (and this is especially true of its Negro exponents) its heroes remain local figures known only to small-town dance halls, and whose reputations are limited to the radius of a few hundred miles.

A case in point, and a compelling argument for closer study of roots and causes, is a recording devoted to the art of Charlie Christian, probably the greatest of jazz guitarists. He died in 1942 after a brief, spectacular career with the Benny Goodman Sextet. Had he not come from Oklahoma City in 1939, at the instigation of John Hammond, he might have shared the fate of many we knew in the period when Christian was growing up (and I doubt that it has changed very much today).

Some of the most brilliant of jazzmen made no records; their names appeared in print only in announcements of some local dance or remote "battles of music" against equally uncelebrated bands. Being devoted to an art which traditionally thrives on improvisation, these unrecorded artists very often have their most original ideas enter the public domain almost as rapidly as they are conceived to be quickly absorbed into the thought and technique of their fellows. Thus the riffs which swung the dancers and the band on some transcendent evening, and which inspired others to competitive flights of invention, become all too swiftly a part of the general style, leaving the originator as anonymous as the creators of the architecture called Gothic.

There is in this a cruel contradiction implicit in the art form itself. For true jazz is an art of individual assertion within and against the group. Each true jazz moment (as distinct from the uninspired commercial performance) springs from a contest in which each artist challenges all the rest; each solo flight, or improvisation, represents (like the successive canvases of a painter) a definition of his identity: as individual, as member of the collectivity and as a link in the chain of tradition. Thus, because jazz finds its very life in an endless improvisation upon traditional materials, the jazzman must lose his identity even as he finds it—how often do we see even the most famous of jazz artists being devoured alive by their imitators, and, shamelessly, in the public spotlight?

So at best the musical contributions of these local, unrecorded heroes of jazz are enjoyed by a few fellow musicians and by a few dancers who admire them and afford them the meager economic return which allows them to keep playing, but very often they live beyond the period of youthful dedication, hoping in vain that some visiting big-band leader will provide the opportunity to break through to the wider spheres of jazz. Indeed, to escape these fates the artists must be very talented, very individual, as restlessly inventive as Picasso, and very lucky.

Charles Christian, when Hammond brought him to the attention of Goodman, was for most of his life such a local jazz hero. Nor do I use the term loosely, for having known him since 1923, when he and my younger brother were members of the same first-grade class, I can recall no time when he was not admired for his skillful playing of stringed instruments. Indeed, a great part of his time in the manual-training department of Douglass School was spent constructing guitars from cigar boxes, instruments upon which both he and his older brother, Clarence, were dazzlingly adept. Incidentally, in their excellent notes to the album Al Avakian and Bob Prince are mistaken when they assume that Christian was innocent of contact with musical forms more sophisticated than the blues, and it would be well that here I offer a correction. Before Charlie was big enough to handle a guitar himself he served as a guide for his father, a blind guitarist and singer. Later he joined with his father, his brothers Clarence and Edward (an arranger, pianist, violinist and performer on the string bass and tuba), and made his contribution to the family income by strolling with them through the white middle-class sections of Oklahoma City, where they played serenades on request. Their repertory included the light classics as well as the blues, and there was no doubt in the minds of those who heard them that the musical value they gave was worth far more than the money they received. Later on Edward, who took leading roles in the standard operettas performed by members of the high-school chorus, led his own band and played gigs from time to time with such musicians as "Hot Lips" Paige, Walter Page, Sammy Price, Lem C. Johnson (to mention a few), all members at some point of the Blue Devils Orchestra, which later merged with the Benny Moten group to become the famous Count Basie Band. I need only mention that Oklahoma City was a regular stopping point for Kansas City-based orchestras, or that a number of the local musicians were conservatory-trained and were capable of sight-reading the hodgepodge scores which during the "million-dollar production" stage of the silent movies were furnished the stands of pit orchestras.

The facts in these matters are always more intriguing than the legends. In the school which we attended harmony was taught from the ninth through the twelfth grades; there was an extensive and compulsory music-appreciation program, and, though Charles was never a member, a concert band and orchestra and several vocal organizations. In brief, both in his home and in the community Charles Christian was subjected to many diverse musical influences. It was the era of radio, and for a while a local newspaper gave away cheap plastic recordings of such orchestras as Jean Goldkette's along with subscriptions. The big media of communication were active for better or worse, even then, and the Negro community was never completely isolated from their influence.

However, perhaps the most stimulating influence upon Christian, and one with whom he was later to be identified, was that of a tall, intense young musician who arrived in Oklahoma City sometime in 1929 and who, with his heavy white sweater, blue stocking cap and up-and-out-thrust silver saxophone, left absolutely no reed player and few young players of any instrument unstirred by the wild, excitingly original flights of his imagination. Who else but Lester Young, who with his battered horn upset the entire Negro section of the town. One of our friends gave up his valved instrument for the tenor saxophone and soon ran away from home to carry the new message to Baltimore, while a good part of the efforts of the rest was spent trying to absorb and transform the Youngian style. Indeed, only one other young musician created anything like the excitement attending Young's stay in the town. This was Carlton George, who had played with Earl Hines and whose trumpet style was shaped after the excursions of Hines's right hand. He, however, was a minor influence, having arrived during the national ascendancy of Louis Armstrong and during the local reign of Oran ("Hot Lips") Paige.

When we consider the stylistic development of Charles Christian we are reminded how little we actually know of the origins of even the most recent of jazz styles, or of when and where they actually started; or of the tensions, personal, sociological, or technical, out of which such an original artist achieves his stylistic identity. For while there is now a rather extensive history of discography and recording sessions there is but the bare beginnings of a historiography of jazz. We know much of jazz as entertainment, but a mere handful of clichés constitutes our knowledge of jazz as experience. Worse, it is this which is frequently taken for all there is, and we get the impression that jazz styles are created in some club on some particular occasion and there and then codified according to the preconceptions of the jazz publicists in an atmosphere as grave and traditional, say, as that attending the deliberations of the Academie Française. It is this which leads to the notion that jazz was invented in a particular house of ill fame by "Jelly Roll" Morton, who admitted the crime himself; that swing was invented by Goodman about 1935; that T. Monk, K. Clarke, and J. B. "D" Gillespie invented "progressive" jazz at Minton's Playhouse in Harlem about 1941.

This is, of course, convenient but only relatively true, and the effort to let the history of jazz as entertainment stand for the whole of jazz ignores the most fundamental knowledge of the dynamics of stylistic growth which has been acquired from studies in other branches of music and from our knowledge of the growth of other art forms. The jazz artist who becomes nationally known is written about as though he came into existence only upon his arrival in New York. His career in the big cities, where jazz is more of a commercial entertainment than part of a total way of life, is stressed at the expense of his life in the South, the Southwest and the Midwest, where most Negro musicians at least found their early development. Thus we are left with an impression of mysterious rootlessness, and the true and often annoying complexity of American cultural experience is oversimplified.

With jazz this has made for the phenomena of an art form existing in a curious state of history and pre-history simultaneously. Not that it isn't recognized that it is an art with deep roots in the past, but that the nature of its deep connection with social conditions here and now is slighted. Charlie Christian is a case in point. He flowered from a background with roots not only in a tradition of music, but in a deep division in the Negro community as well. He spent much of his life in a slum in which all the forms of disintegration attending the urbanization of rural Negroes ran riot. Although he himself was from a respectable family, the wooden tenement in which he grew up was full of poverty, crime and sickness. It was also alive and exciting, and I enjoyed visiting there, for the people both lived and sang the blues. Nonetheless, it was doubtless here that he developed the tuberculosis from which he died.

More important, jazz was regarded by most of the respectable Negroes of the town as a backward, low-class form of expression, and there was a marked difference between those who accepted and lived close to their folk experience and those whose status strivings led them to reject and deny it. Charlie rejected this attitude in turn, along with those who held it—even to the point of not participating in the musical activities of the school. Like Jimmy Rushing, whose father was a businessman and whose mother was active in church affairs, he had heard the voice of jazz and would hear no other. Ironically, what was perhaps his greatest social triumph came in death, when the respectable Negro middle-class not only joined in the public mourning, but acclaimed him hero and took credit for his development. The attention which the sheer quality of his music should have secured him was won only by his big-town success.

Fortunately for us, Charles concentrated on the guitar and left the school band to his brother Edward, and his decision was a major part of his luck. For although it is seldom recognized, there is a conflict between what the Negro American musician feels in the community around him and the given (or classical) techniques of his instrument. He feels a tension between his desire to master the classical style of playing and his compulsion to express those sounds which form a musical definition of Negro American experience. In early jazz these sounds found their fullest expression in the timbre of the blues voice, and the use of mutes, water glasses and derbies on the bells of their horns arose out of an attempt to imitate this sound. Among the younger musicians of the thirties, especially those who contributed to the growth of bop, this desire to master the classical technique was linked with the struggle for recognition in the larger society, and with a desire to throw off those non-musical features which came into jazz from the minstrel tradition. Actually, it was for this reason that Louis Armstrong (who is not only a great performing artist but a clown in the Elizabethan sense of the word) became their scapegoat. What was not always understood was that there were actually two separate bodies of instrumental techniques: the one classic and widely recognized and "correct"; and the other eclectic, partly unconscious, and "jazzy." And it was the tension between these two bodies of technique which led to many of the technical discoveries of jazz. Further, we are now aware of the existence of a fully developed and endlessly flexible technique of jazz expression, which has become quite independent of the social environment in which it developed if not of its spirit.

Interestingly enough, the guitar (long regarded as a traditional instrument of Southern Negroes) was subjected to little of this conflict between techniques and ways of experiencing the world. Its role in the jazz orchestra was important but unobtrusive, and before Christian little had been done to explore its full potentialities for jazz. Thus Christian was able to experiment with the least influence from either traditional or contemporary sources. Starting long before he was aware of his mission—as would seem to be the way with important innovators in the arts—he taught himself to voice the guitar as a solo instrument, a development made possible through the perfecting of the electronically amplified instrument—and the rest is history.

With Christian the guitar found its jazz voice. With his entry into the jazz circles his musical intelligence was able to exert its influence upon his peers and to affect the course of the future development of jazz. This album of his work—so irresistible and danceable in its swing, so intellectually stimulating in its ideas—is important not only for its contribution to our knowledge of the evolution of contemporary jazz style; it also offers one of the best arguments for bringing more serious critical intelligence to this branch of our national culture.

—From *Saturday Review*, May 17, 1958.

Remembering Jimmy

In the old days the voice was high and clear and poignantly
lyrical. Steel-bright in its upper range and, at its best, silky
smooth, it was possessed of a purity somehow impervious to
both the stress of singing above a twelve-piece band and the
urgency of Rushing's own blazing fervor. On dance nights,
when you stood on the rise of the school grounds two blocks
to the east, you could hear it jetting from the dance hall like
a blue flame in the dark; now soaring high above the trumpets and trombones, now skimming the froth of reeds and
rhythm as it called some woman's anguished name—or demanded in a high, thin, passionately lyrical line, "Baaaaay-
bay, Bay-aaaay-bay! Tell me what's the matter now!"—above
the shouting of the swinging band.

Nor was there need for the by now famous signature line:
"If anybody asks you who sang this song/ Tell 'em/ it was
little Jimmy Rushing/ he's been here and gone"—for every-

one on Oklahoma City's "East Side" knew that sweet, high-floating sound. "Deep Second" was our fond nickname for the block in which Rushing worked and lived, and where most Negro business and entertainment were found, and before he went to cheer a wider world his voice evoked the festive spirit of the place. Indeed, he was the natural herald of its blues-romance, his song the singing essence of its joy. For Jimmy Rushing was not simply a local entertainer, he expressed a value, an attitude about the world for which our lives afforded no other definition. We had a Negro church and a segregated school, a few lodges and fraternal organizations, and beyond these there was all the great white world. We were pushed off to what seemed to be the least desirable side of the city (but which some years later was found to contain one of the state's richest pools of oil), and our system of justice was based upon Texas law, yet there was an optimism within the Negro community and a sense of possibility which, despite our awareness of limitation (dramatized so brutally in the Tulsa riot of 1921), transcended all of this; and it was this rock-bottom sense of reality, coupled with our sense of the possibility of rising above it, which sounded in Rushing's voice.

And how it carried! In those days I lived near the Rock Island roundhouse, where, with a steady clanging of bells and a great groaning of wheels along the rails, switch engines made up trains of freight unceasingly. Yet often in the late-spring night I could hear Rushing as I lay four blocks away in bed, carrying to me as clear as a full-bored riff on "Hot Lips" Paige's horn. Heard thus, across the dark blocks lined with locust trees, through the night throbbing with the natural aural imagery of the blues, with high-balling trains, departing bells, lonesome guitar chords simmering up from a shack in the alley—it was easy to imagine the voice as setting the pattern to which the instruments of the Blue Devils Orchestra and all the random sounds of night arose, affirming, as it were, some ideal native to the time and to the land. When we were still too young to attend night dances, but yet old enough to gather beneath the corner street lamp on summer evenings, anyone might halt the conversation to exclaim "Listen, they're raising hell down at Slaughter's Hall," and we'd turn our heads westward to hear Jimmy's voice soar up the hill and down, as pure and as miraculously unhindered by distance and earthbound things as is the body in youthful dreams of flying.

"Now, that's the Right Reverend Jimmy Rushing preaching now, man," someone would say. And rising to the cue another would answer, "Yeah, and that's old Elder 'Hot Lips' signifying along with him; urging him on, man." And, keeping it building, "Huh, but though you can't hear him out this far, Ole Deacon Big-un [the late Walter Page] is up there patting his foot and slapping on his big belly [the bass viol] to keep those fools in line." And we might go on to name all the members of the band as though they were the Biblical four-and-twenty elders, while laughing at the impious wit of applying church titles to a form of music which all the preachers assured us was the devil's potent tool.

Our wit was true, for Jimmy Rushing, along with the other jazz musicians whom we knew, had made a choice, had dedicated himself to a mode of expression and a way of life no less "righteously" than others dedicated themselves to the church. Jazz and the blues did not fit into the scheme of things as spelled out by our two main institutions, the church and the school, but they gave expression to attitudes which found no place in these and helped to give our lives some semblance of wholeness. Jazz and the public jazz dance was a third institution in our lives, and a vital one; and though Jimmy was far from being a preacher, he was, as official floor manager or master-of-the-dance at Slaughter's Hall, the leader of a public rite.

He was no Mr. Five-by-five in those days, but a compact,

debonair young man who dressed with an easy elegance. Much later, during theatre appearances with Basie's famous band, he sometimes cut an old step from slavery days called "falling off the log" for the sheer humor provided by the rapid, and apparently precarious, shifting of his great bulk, but in the Oklahoma days he was capable of an amazing grace of movement. A nineteenth-century formality still clung to public dances at the time, and there was quite a variety of steps. Jimmy danced them all, gliding before the crowd over the polished floor, sometimes with a girl, sometimes with a huge megaphone held chest-high before him as he swayed. The evenings began with the more formal steps, to popular and semi-classical music, and proceeded to become more expressive as the spirit of jazz and the blues became dominant. It was when Jimmy's voice began to soar with the spirit of the blues that the dancers—and the musicians—achieved that feeling of communion which was the true meaning of the public jazz dance. The blues, the singer, the band and the dancers formed the vital whole of jazz as an institutional form, and even today neither part is quite complete without the rest. The thinness of much of the so-called "modern jazz" is especially reflective of this loss of wholeness, and it is quite possible that Rushing retains his vitality simply because he has kept close to the small Negro public dance.

The occasion for this shamelessly nostalgic outburst is provided by a series of Rushing recordings issued over the past few years: Vanguard's *Jazz Showcase;* Columbia's *Goin' to Chicago, Listen to the Blues with Jimmy Rushing, If This Ain't the Blues, The Jazz Odyssey of James Rushing, Esq.,* and *Little Jimmy Rushing and the Big Brass.* An older recording, Decca's *Kansas City Jazz,* contains Rushing's best version of his classic "Good Morning Blues," and offers a vivid idea of the styles and combinations of musicians which made up the milieu in which Rushing found his early development. These discs form a valuable introduction to the art of Jimmy Rushing in all its fervor and variety.

Rushing is known today primarily as a blues singer, but not so in those days. He began as a singer of ballads, bringing to them a sincerity and a feeling for dramatizing the lyrics in the musical phrase which charged the banal lines with the mysterious potentiality of meaning which haunts the blues. And it was, perhaps, Rushing's beginning as a ballad singer which gives his blues interpretations their special quality. For one of the significant aspects of his art is the imposition of a romantic lyricism upon the blues tradition (compare his version of "See See Rider" with that of Ma Rainey); a lyricism which is not of the Deep South, but of the Southwest: a romanticism native to the frontier, imposed upon the violent rawness of a part of the nation which only thirteen years before Rushing's birth was still Indian territory. Thus there is an optimism in it which echoes the spirit of those Negroes who, like Rushing's father, had come to Oklahoma in search of a more human way of life.

Rushing is one of the first singers to sing the blues before a big band, and even today he seldom comes across as a blues "shouter," but maintains the lyricism which has always been his way with the blues. Indeed, when we listen to his handling of lyrics we become aware of that quality which makes for the mysteriousness of the blues: their ability to imply far more than they state outright and their capacity to make the details of sex convey meanings which touch upon the metaphysical. For, indeed, they always find poetry in the limits of the Negro vocabulary. Perhaps because he is more educated and came from a family already well on its rise into what is called the "Negro middle class," Jimmy has always shown a concern for the correctness of language, and out of the tension between the traditional folk pronunciation and his training in school, he has worked out a flexibility of enunciation and a rhythmical agility with words which make us constantly aware of the meanings which shimmer just beyond the limits of the lyrics. The blues is an art of ambiguity, an assertion of the irrepressibly human over all circumstance whether created by others or by one's own human failings. They are the only consistent art in the United States which constantly remind us of our limitations while encouraging us to see how far we can actually go. When understood in their more profound implication, they are a corrective, an attempt to draw a line upon man's own limitless assertion.

Significantly, Jimmy Rushing was able to spread the appeal of the blues to a wider American audience after the Depression had made us a bit more circumspect about the human cost of living of our "American way of life." It seems especially fitting now, when circumstance and its own position of leadership has forced the nation once more to examine its actions and its intentions, that the blues are once more becoming popular. There is great demand for Rushing in Europe, from which he has just returned with the Goodman band. And I think we need him more here at home. Certainly this collection of discs will make us aware that there is emotional continuity in American life, and that the abiding moods expressed in our most vital popular art form are not simply a matter of entertainment; they also tell us who and where we are.

—From *Saturday Review*, July 12, 1958.

Blues People

In his Introduction to *Blues People* LeRoi Jones advises us to approach the work as

> . . . a strictly theoretical endeavor. Theoretical, in that none of the questions it poses can be said to have been answered definitely or for all time (sic!), etc. In fact, the whole book proposes more questions than it will answer. The only questions it will properly move to answer have, I think, been answered already within the patterns of American life. We need only give these patterns serious scrutiny and draw certain permissible conclusions.

It is a useful warning and one hopes that it will be regarded by those jazz publicists who have the quite irresponsible habit of sweeping up any novel pronouncement written about jazz and slapping it upon the first available record liner as the latest insight into the mysteries of American Negro expression.

/ 247

Jones would take his subject seriously—as the best of jazz critics have always done—and he himself should be so taken. He has attempted to place the blues within the context of a total culture and to see this native art form through the disciplines of sociology, anthropology and (though he seriously underrates its importance in the creating of a viable theory) history, and he spells out explicitly his assumptions concerning the relation between the blues, the people who created them and the larger American culture. Although I find several of his assumptions questionable, this is valuable in itself. It would be well if all jazz critics did likewise; not only would it expose those who have no business in the field, but it would sharpen the thinking of the few who have something enlightening to contribute. *Blues People,* like much that is written by Negro Americans at the present moment, takes on an inevitable resonance from the Freedom Movement, but it is in itself characterized by a straining for a note of militancy which is, to say the least, distracting. Its introductory mood of scholarly analysis frequently shatters into a dissonance of accusation, and one gets the impression that while Jones wants to perform a crucial task which he feels *someone* should take on—as indeed someone should—he is frustrated by the restraint demanded of the critical pen and would like to pick up a club.

Perhaps this explains why Jones, who is also a poet and editor of a poetry magazine, gives little attention to the blues as lyric, as a form of poetry. He appears to be attracted to the blues for what he believes they tell us of the sociology of Negro American identity and attitude. Thus, after beginning with the circumstances in which he sees their origin, he considers the ultimate values of American society:

The Negro as slave is one thing. The Negro as American is quite another. But the *path* the slave took to "citizenship" is what I want to look at. And I make my analogy through the slave citizen's music—through the music that is most closely associated with him: blues and a later, but parallel, development, jazz. And it seems to me that if the Negro represents, or is symbolic of, something in and about the nature of American culture, this certainly should be revealed by his characteristic music. . . . I am saying that if the music of the Negro in America, in all its permutations, is subjected to a socio-anthropological as well as musical scrutiny, something about the essential nature of the Negro's existence in this country ought to be revealed, as well as something about the essential nature of this country, i.e., society as a whole. . . .

The tremendous burden of sociology which Jones would place upon this body of music is enough to give even the blues the blues. At one point he tells us that "the one peculiar reference to the drastic change in the Negro from slavery to 'citizenship' is in his music." And later with more precision, he states:

. . . The point I want to make most evident here is that I cite the beginning of the blues as one beginning of American Negroes. Or, let me say, the reaction and subsequent relation of the Negro's experience in this country in *his* English is one beginning of the Negro's conscious appearance on the American scene.

No one could quarrel with Mr. Jones's stress upon beginnings. In 1833, two hundred and fourteen years after the first Africans were brought to these shores as slaves, a certain Mrs. Lydia Maria Child, a leading member of the American Anti-Slavery Society, published a paper entitled: *An Appeal in Favor of that Class of Americans Called Africans.* I am uncertain to what extent it actually reveals Mrs. Child's ideas concerning the complex relationship between time, place, cultural and/or national identity and race, but her title sounds like a fine bit of contemporary ironic *signifying* —"signifying" here meaning, in the unwritten dictionary of American Negro usage, "rhetorical understatements." It tells us much of the thinking of her opposition, and it reminds us that as late as the 1890s, a time when Negro composers, singers, dancers and comedians dominated the American musical stage, popular Negro songs (including James Weldon Johnson's "Under the Bamboo Tree," now immortalized by T. S. Eliot) were commonly referred to as "Ethiopian Airs."

Perhaps more than any other people, Americans have been locked in a deadly struggle with time, with history. We've fled the past and trained ourselves to suppress, if not forget, troublesome details of the national memory, and a great part of our optimism, like our progress, has been bought at the cost of ignoring the processes through which we've arrived at any given moment in our national existence. We've fought continuously with one another over who and what we are, and, with the exception of the Negro, over who and what is American. Jones is aware of this and, although he embarrasses his own argument, his emphasis is to the point.

For it would seem that while Negroes have been undergoing a process of "Americanization" from a time preceding the birth of this nation—including the fusing of their blood lines with other non-African strains, there has persisted a stubborn confusion as to their American identity. Somehow it was assumed that the Negroes, of all the diverse American peoples, would remain unaffected by the climate, the weather, the political circumstances—from which not even slaves were exempt—the social structures, the national manners, the modes of production and the tides of the market, the national ideals, the conflicts of values, the rising and falling of national morale, or the complex give and take of acculturalization which was undergone by all others who found their existence within the American democracy. This confusion still persists and it is Mr. Jones's concern with it which gives *Blues People* a claim upon our attention.

Mr. Jones sees the American Negro as the product of a

series of transformations, starting with the enslaved African, who became Afro-American slave, who became the American slave, who became, in turn, the highly qualified "citizen" whom we know today. The slave began by regarding himself as enslaved African, during the time when he still spoke his native language, or remembered it, practiced such aspects of his native religion as were possible and expressed himself musically in modes which were essentially African. These cultural traits became transmuted as the African lost consciousness of his African background, and his music, his religion, his language and his speech gradually became that of the American Negro. His sacred music became the spirituals, his work songs and dance music became the blues and primitive jazz, and his religion became a form of Afro-American Christianity. With the end of slavery Jones sees the development of jazz and the blues as results of the more varied forms of experience made available to the freedman. By the twentieth century the blues divided and became, on the one hand, a professionalized form of entertainment, while remaining, on the other, a form of folklore.

By which I suppose he means that some Negroes remained in the country and sang a crude form of the blues, while others went to the city, became more sophisticated, and paid to hear Ma Rainey, Bessie, or some of the other Smith girls sing them in night clubs or theatres. Jones gets this mixed up with ideas of social class—middle-class Negroes, whatever that term actually means, and light-skinned Negroes, or those Negroes corrupted by what Jones calls "White" culture—preferring the "classic" blues, and black, uncorrupted, country Negroes preferring "country blues."

For as with his music, so with the Negro. As Negroes became "middle-class" they rejected their tradition and themselves. ". . . they wanted any self which the mainstream dictated, and the mainstream *always* dictated. And this black middle class, in turn, tried always to dictate that self, or this image of a whiter Negro, to the poorer, blacker Negroes."

One would get the impression that there was a rigid correlation between color, education, income and the Negro's preference in music. But what are we to say of a white-skinned Negro with brown freckles who owns sixteen oil wells sunk in a piece of Texas land once farmed by his ex-slave parents who were a blue-eyed, white-skinned, red-headed (kinky) Negro woman from Virginia and a blue-gummed, black-skinned, curly-haired Negro male from Mississippi, and who not only sang bass in a Holy Roller church, played the market and voted Republican but collected blues recordings and was a walking depository of blues tradition? Jones's theory no more allows for the existence of such a Negro than it allows for himself; but that "concord of sensibilities" which has been defined as the meaning of culture, allows for much more variety than Jones would admit.

Much the same could be said of Jones's treatment of the jazz during the thirties, when he claims its broader acceptance (i.e., its economic "success" as entertainment) led to a dilution, to the loss of much of its "black" character which caused a certain group of rebellious Negro musicians to create the "anti-mainstream" jazz style called bebop.

Jones sees bop as a conscious gesture of separatism, ignoring the fact that the creators of the style were seeking, whatever their musical intentions—and they were the least political of men—a fresh form of entertainment which would allow them their fair share of the entertainment market, which had been dominated by whites during the swing era. And although the boppers were reacting, at least in part, to the high artistic achievement of Armstrong, Hawkins, Basie and Ellington (all Negroes, all masters of the blues-jazz tradition), Jones sees their music as a recognition of his contention "that when you are black in a society where black is an extreme liability [it] is one thing, but to understand that it is the society which is lacking and is impossibly deformed because of this lack, and not *yourself*, isolates you even more from that society."

Perhaps. But today nothing succeeds like rebellion (which Jones as a "beat" poet should know) and while a few boppers went to Europe to escape, or became Muslims, others took the usual tours for the State Department. Whether this makes *them* "middle class" in Jones's eyes I can't say, but his assertions—which are fine as personal statement—are not in keeping with the facts; his theory flounders before that complex of human motives which makes human history, and which is so characteristic of the American Negro.

Read as a record of an earnest young man's attempt to come to grips with his predicament as Negro American during a most turbulent period of our history, *Blues People* may be worth the reader's time. Taken as a theory of American Negro culture, it can only contribute more confusion than clarity. For Jones has stumbled over that ironic obstacle which lies in the path of any who would fashion a theory of American Negro culture while ignoring the intricate network of connections which binds Negroes to the larger society. To do so is to attempt a delicate brain surgery with a switch-blade. And it is possible that any viable theory of Negro American culture obligates us to fashion a more adequate theory of American culture as a whole. The heel bone is, after all, connected, through its various linkages, to the head bone. Attempt a serious evaluation of our national morality and up jumps the so-called Negro problem. Attempt to discuss jazz as a hermetic expression of Negro sensibility and immediately we must consider what the "mainstream" of American music really is.

Here political categories are apt to confuse, for while Negro slaves were socially, politically and economically separate (but only in a special sense even here), they were, in a cultural sense, much closer than Jones's theory allows him to admit.

"A slave," writes Jones, "cannot be a man." But what, one might ask, of those moments when he feels his metabolism aroused by the rising of the sap in spring? What of his identity among other slaves? With his wife? And isn't it closer to the truth that far from considering themselves only in terms of that abstraction, "a slave," the enslaved really thought of themselves as *men* who had been unjustly enslaved? And isn't the true answer to Mr. Jones's question, "What are you going to be when you grow up?" not, as he gives it, "a slave" but most probably a coachman, a teamster, a cook, the best damned steward on the Mississippi, the best jockey in Kentucky, a butler, a farmer, a stud, or, hopefully, a free man! Slavery was a most vicious system and those who endured and survived it a tough people, but it was *not* (and this is important for Negroes to remember for the sake of their own sense of who and what their grandparents were) a state of absolute repression.

A slave was, to the extent that he was a *musician,* one who expressed himself in music, a man who realized himself in the world of sound. Thus, while he might stand in awe before the superior technical ability of a white musician, and while he was forced to recognize a superior social status, he would never feel awed before the music which the technique of the white musician made available. His attitude as "musician" would lead him to seek to possess the music expressed through the technique, but until he could do so he would hum, whistle, sing or play the tunes to the best of his ability on any available instrument. And it was, indeed, out of the tension between desire and ability that the techniques of jazz emerged. This was likewise true of American Negro choral singing. For this, no literary explanation, no cultural analyses, no political slogans—indeed, not even a high degree of social or political freedom—was required. For the art—the blues, the spirituals, the jazz, the dance—was what we had in place of freedom.

Technique was then, as today, the key to creative freedom, but before this came a will toward expression. Thus, Jones's theory to the contrary. Negro musicians have never, as a group, felt alienated from any music sounded within their hearing, and it is my theory that it would be impossible to pinpoint the time when they were not shaping what Jones calls the mainstream of American music. Indeed, what group of musicians has made more of the sound of the American experience? Nor am I confining my statement to the sound of the slave experience, but am saying that the most authoritative rendering of America in music is that of American Negroes.

For as I see it, from the days of their introduction into the colonies, Negroes have taken, with the ruthlessness of those without articulate investments in cultural styles, whatever they could of European music, making of it that which would, when blended with the cultural tendencies inherited from Africa, express their own sense of life—while rejecting the rest. Perhaps this is only another way of saying that whatever the degree of injustice and inequality sustained by the slaves, American culture was, even before the official founding of the nation, pluralistic; and it was the African's origin in cultures in which art was highly functional which gave him an edge in shaping the music and dance of this nation.

The question of social and cultural snobbery is important here. The effectiveness of Negro music and dance is first recorded in the journals and letters of travelers but it is important to remember that they saw and understood only that which they were prepared to accept. Thus a Negro dancing a courtly dance appeared comic from the outside simply because the dancer was a slave. But to the Negro dancing it—
—and there is ample evidence that he danced it well—

burlesque or satire might have been the point, which might have been difficult for a white observer to even imagine. During the 1870s Lafcadio Hearn reports that the best singers of Irish songs, in Irish dialect, were Negro dock workers in Cincinnati, and advertisements from slavery days described escaped slaves who spoke in Scottish dialect. The master artisans of the South were slaves, and white Americans have been walking Negro walks, talking Negro flavored talk (and prizing it when spoken by Southern belles), dancing Negro dances and singing Negro melodies far too long to talk of a "mainstream" of American culture to which they're alien.

Jones attempts to impose an ideology upon this cultural complexity, and this might be useful if he knew enough of the related subjects to make it interesting. But his version of the blues lacks a sense of the excitement and surprise of men living in the world—of enslaved and politically weak men successfully imposing their values upon a powerful society through song and dance.

The blues speak to us simultaneously of the tragic and the comic aspects of the human condition and they express a profound sense of life shared by many Negro Americans precisely because their lives have combined these modes. This has been the heritage of a people who for hundreds of years could not celebrate birth or dignify death and whose need to live despite the dehumanizing pressures of slavery developed an endless capacity for laughing at their painful experiences. This is a group experience shared by many Negroes, and any effective study of the blues would treat them first as poetry and as ritual. Jones makes a distinction between classic and country blues, the one being entertainment and the other folklore. But the distinction is false. Classic blues were both entertainment *and* a form of folklore. When they were sung professionally in theatres, they were entertainment; when danced to in the form of recordings or used as a means of transmitting the traditional verses and their wisdom, they were folklore. There are levels of time and function involved here, and the blues which might be used in one place as entertainment (as gospel music is now being used in night clubs and on theatre stages) might be put to a ritual use in another. Bessie Smith might have been a "blues queen" to the society at large, but within the tighter Negro community where the blues were part of a total way of life, and a major expression of an attitude toward life, she was a priestess, a celebrant who affirmed the values of the group and man's ability to deal with chaos.

It is unfortunate that Jones thought it necessary to ignore the aesthetic nature of the blues in order to make his ideological point, for he might have come much closer had he considered the blues not as politics but as art. This would have still required the disciplines of anthropology and sociology—but as practiced by Constance Rourke, who was well aware of how much of American cultural expression is Negro. And he could learn much from the Cambridge School's discoveries of the connection between poetry, drama and ritual as a means of analyzing how the blues function in their proper environment. Simple taste should have led Jones to Stanley Edgar Hyman's work on the blues instead of Paul Oliver's sadly misdirected effort.

For the blues are not primarily concerned with civil rights or obvious political protest; they are an art form and thus a transcendence of those conditions created within the Negro community by the denial of social justice. As such they are one of the techniques through which Negroes have survived and kept their courage during that long period when many whites assumed, as some still assume, they were afraid.

Much has been made of the fact that *Blues People* is one of the few books by a Negro to treat the subject. Unfortunately for those who expect that Negroes would have a special insight into this mysterious art, this is not enough. Here, too, the critical intelligence must perform the difficult task which only it can perform.

—From *The New York Review,*
February 6, 1964.

III

The SHADOW
and the ACT

Some Questions and
Some Answers

What do you understand today by "Negro culture"?

What I understand by the term "Negro culture" is so vague as to be meaningless. Indeed, I find the term "Negro" vague even in its racial connotations, for in Africa there are several non-white racial strains and one suspects that the term came into usage as a means of obliterating cultural differences between the various African peoples. In this way the ruthless disruption of highly developed cultures raised no troubling moral questions. The term, used mainly by whites, represented a "trained incapacity" to make or feel moral distinctions where black men were concerned.

As for the term "culture," used in this connection, I know of no valid demonstration that culture is transmitted through the genes.

In Africa the blacks identify themselves by their tribal names, thus it is significant that it is only in the United States that the term "Negro" has acquired specific cultural content. Spelled with a capital "N" by most publications (one of the important early victories of my own people in their fight for self-definition), the term describes a people whose origin began with the introduction of African slaves to the American colonies in 1619, and which today represents the fusing with the original African strains of many racial blood lines—among them English, Irish, Scotch, French, Spanish and American Indian. Although the American Civil War brought an end to the importation of African peoples into the United States, this mixture of bloods has by no means ceased —not even in the South where the whites are obsessed with racial purity—so that today the anthropologists tell us that very few American Negroes are of pure African blood. It occurs to me that in the light of this, even if culture were transmitted through the blood stream we would encounter quite a problem in explaining just how the genes bearing "Negro" culture could so overpower those bearing French or English culture, which in all other ways are assumed to be superior.

But to continue, the American Negro people is North American in origin and has evolved under specifically American conditions: climatic, nutritional, historical, political and social. It takes its character from the experience of American slavery and the struggle for, and the achievement of, emancipation; from the dynamics of American race and caste discrimination, and from living in a highly industrialized and highly mobile society possessing a relatively high standard of living and an explicitly stated equalitarian concept of freedom. Its spiritual outlook is basically Protestant, its system of kinship is Western, its time and historical sense are American (United States), and its secular values are those professed, ideally at least, by all of the people of the United States.

Culturally this people represents one of the many subcultures which make up that great amalgam of European and native American cultures which is the culture of the United States. This "American Negro culture" is expressed in a body of folklore, in the musical forms of the spirituals, the blues and jazz; an idiomatic version of American speech (especially in the Southern United States); a cuisine; a body of dance forms and even a dramaturgy which is generally unrecognized as such because still tied to the more folkish Negro churches. Some Negro preachers are great showmen.

It must, however, be pointed out that due to the close links which Negro Americans have with the rest of the nation these cultural expressions are constantly influencing the larger body of American culture and are in turn influenced by them. Nor should the existence of a specifically "Negro" idiom in any way be confused with the vague, racist terms "white culture" or "black culture"; rather it is a matter of diversity within unity. One could indeed go further and say that, in this sense, there is no other "Negro" culture. Haitians, for instance, are an "American" people and predominantly dark but their culture is an expression of Haitian conditions: it reflects the influence of French culture and the fusion of Catholic and native Haitian religious outlooks. Thus, since most so-called "Negro cultures" outside Africa are necessarily amalgams, it would seem more profitable to stress the term "culture" and leave the term "Negro" out of the discussion. It is not culture which binds the peoples who are of partially African origin now scattered throughout the world, but an identity of passions. We share a hatred for the alienation forced upon us by Europeans during the process of colonization and empire and we are bound by our common suffering more than by our pigmentation. But even this identification is shared by most non-white peoples, and while it has political value of great potency, its cultural value is almost nil.

In your opinion was there before the arrival of Europeans a single Negro culture that all Negroes shared, or was it the case, as among the whites, that there had been many different cultures, such as Judeo–Christianity, Brahmanism, etc. . . .?

Before the arrival of Europeans there were many African cultures.

What is the role of modern industrial evolution on the spiritual crisis of the Negro people of our times? Does industrial progress (capitalist or socialist) endanger the future of a genuine Negro culture?

The role of modern industrial evolution in the spiritual crisis of those whom you refer to as "Negro" peoples seems to me to be as ambiguous as its role in the lives of peoples of any racial identity: it depends upon how much human suffering must go into the achievement of industrialization, upon who operates the industries, upon how the products and profits are shared and upon the wisdom used in imposing technology upon the institutions and traditions of each particular society. Ironically, black men with the status of slaves contributed much of the brute labor which helped get the industrial revolution under way; in this process they were exploited, their natural resources were ravaged and their institutions and their cultures were devastated, and in most instances they were denied anything like participation in the European cultures which flowered as a result of the transformation of civilization under the growth of technology. But now it is precisely technology which promises them release from the brutalizing effects of over three hundred years of racism and European domination. Men cannot unmake history, thus it is not a question of reincarnating those cultural traditions which were destroyed, but a matter of using industrialization, modern medicine, modern science generally, to work in the interest of these peoples rather than against them. Nor is the disruption of continuity with the past necessarily a totally negative phenomenon; sometimes it makes possible a modulation of a people's way of life which allows for a more creative use of its energies. The United States is ample proof of this, and though we suffer much from the rupture of tradition, great good has come to the world through those achievements which were made possible. One thing seems clear, certain possibilities of culture are achievable only through the presence of industrial techniques.

It is not industrial progress per se which damages peoples or cultures, it is the exploitation of peoples in order to keep the machines fed with raw materials. It seems to me that the whole world is moving toward some new cultural synthesis, and partially through the discipline imposed by technology. There is, I believe, a threat when industrialism is linked to a political doctrine which has as its goal the subjugation of the world.

Is the birth of various religions in the present Negro societies progressive or regressive as far as culture is concerned?

I an unacquainted with the religious movements in the societies to which you refer. If the Mau Mau is one of these, then I must say that for all my disgust for those who provoked the natives to such obscene extremes, I feel it to be regressive indeed.

Several Negro poets from Africa explain that they write in French or English because the ancient languages are not adequate to express their feeling any longer. What do you think about this?

When it comes to the poet the vagueness of the term "Negro" becomes truly appalling, for if there is a "Negro" language I am unacquainted with it. Are these people Bantu, Sudanese, Nigerian, Watusi or what? As for the poets in question, it seems to me that in a general way they are faced by the problem confronted by the Irish, who for all their efforts to keep their language vital have had nevertheless their greatest poets expressing themselves in English, as in the case of Shaw, Yeats, Joyce and O'Casey. Perhaps the poet's true language is that in which he dreams. At any rate, it is true that for some time now poets throughout the world have drawn freely from all the world's tongues in order to create their vocabularies. One uses whatever one needs, to best express one's vision of the human predicament.

Another way of approaching the matter is to view the poem as a medium of communication—to whom do these poets wish to speak? Each poet creates his own language from that which he finds around him. Thus if these poets find the language of Shakespeare or Racine inadequate to reach their own peoples, then the other choice is to re-create their original language to the point where they may express their complex emotions. This is the manner in which the poet makes his contribution to literature, and the greatest literary creation of any culture is its language. Further, language is most alive when it is capable of dealing with the realities in which it operates. In the myth, God gave man the task of naming the objects of the world, thus one of the functions of the poet is to insist upon a correspondence between words and ever-changing reality, between ideals and actualities. The domain of the unstated, the undefined is his to conquer.

In my own case, having inherited the language of Shakespeare and Melville, Mark Twain and Lincoln and no other, I try to do my part in keeping the American language alive and rich by using in my work the music and idiom of American Negro speech, and by insisting that the words of that language correspond with the reality of American life as seen by my own people. Perhaps if I were a member of a bilingual society I would approach my task differently, but my work is addressed primarily to those who have my immediate group experience, for I am not protesting, nor pleading, my humanity; I am trying to communicate, to articulate and define a group experience.

What do you think of the present level of Negro sculpture? What future do you see for it?

I know little of current work in sculpture by Africans, but that which I have seen appears to possess little of that high artistic excellence characteristic of ancient African art. American Negro sculpture is, of course, simply American sculpture done by Negroes. Some is good, some bad. I don't see any possibility of work by these artists being created in a vacuum outside of those influences, national and international, individual and abstract, which influence any other American artist. When African sculpture is one influence it comes to them through the Cubists just as it did to most contemporary artists. That phenomenon which Malraux calls the "Imaginary Museum" draws no color line.

As for the future of African sculpture, it depends upon the future role which art will play in African societies which are now struggling into being. I doubt, however, that sculpture will ever play the same role that the so-called primitive art played, because the tribal societies which called this art into being have either been shattered or are being rapidly transformed. And if the influence of the primitive sculptures are to be seen in European art wherever one turns, so have the influences of modern Western art found their way into Africa. This process is more likely to increase rather than lessen. To the extent that art is an expression of transcendent values, the role of sculpture in these societies will depend upon the values of those societies.

What do you think of the future of "Negro music"?

I know only American Negro music, in this sense of the term. This music consists of jazz and the spirituals, but as with all things cultural in the United States these forms have been and are still being subjected to a constant process of assimilation. Thus, although it was the specific experience of Negroes which gave rise to these forms, they expressed and gave significance to feelings and sounds so characteristically American that both spirituals and jazz have been absorbed into the musical language of the culture as a whole. On the other hand, American Negro music was never created in a vacuum; it was the shaping of musical elements found in the culture—European, American Indian, the Afro-American rhythmical sense, the sound of the Negro voice—to the needs of a particular group. Today jazz is a national art form, but for me personally the source of the purist stream of this music is the Negro community, wherein the commercial motive in popular music is weaker, and where jazz remains vital because it is still linked with the Saturday night or the Sunday morning breakfast dance, which are still among the living social forms functioning within the Negro community.

Nor does this in any way contradict the fact that some of the leaders in the modern jazz movement are Negroes; we still move from the folk community to a highly conscious acquaintance with the twelve-tone composers and their methods in less time than it takes to complete a course in counterpoint, and these modern methods are quickly absorbed into the body of classical jazz. A man like Duke Ellington remains a vital and imaginative composer precisely because he has never severed his tie with the Negro dance and because his approach to the world's musical speech is eclectic.

Nevertheless there is the danger that the rapid absorption of Negro American musical forms by the commercial interests and their rapid vulgarization and dissemination through the mass media will corrupt the Negro's own taste, just as in Mexico the demand for modern designs in silver jewelry for export is leading to a dying away of native design. Thus I say that so much of the future depends upon the self-acceptance of the Negro composer and his integrity toward his musical tradition. Nor do I exclude the so-called serious composer; all are faced with the humanist American necessity of finding the balance between progress and continuity; between tradition and experimentation. For the jazz artist there is some insurance in continuing to play for dance audiences, for here the criticism is unspoiled by status-directed theories; Negroes simply won't accept shoddy dance music, thus the artist has a vital criticism danced out in the ritual of the dance.

Since the spirituals are religious music it would seem that their future is assured by the revitalization of the Negro American churches as is demonstrated in the leadership which these churches are giving in the struggle for civil rights. The old songs play quite a part in this and they in turn throb with new emotion flowing from the black American's revaluation of his experience. Negroes are no longer ashamed of their slave past but see in it sources of strength, and it is now generally recognized that the spirituals bespoke their birth as a people and asserted and defined their humanity. The desegregation struggle is only the socio-political manifestation of this process. Commercial rock-and-roll music is a brutalization of one stream of contemporary Negro church music, but I do not believe that even this obscene looting of a cultural expression can permanently damage the vital source—not for racial reasons but because for some time to come Negroes will live close to their traditional cultural patterns. Nor do I believe that as we win our struggle for full participation in American life we will abandon our group expression. Too much living and aspiration have gone into it, so that drained of its elements of defensiveness and alienation it will become even more precious to us, for we will see it ever clearer as a transcendent value. What we have counterpoised against the necessary rage for progress in American life (and which we share with other Americans) will have been proved to be at least as valuable as all our triumphs of technology. In spilling out his heart's blood in his contest with the machine, John Henry was asserting a national value as well as a Negro value.

What do you think of the attempt of Brazilian and American Negroes to adopt "White values" in place of "Negro values"? Is this only an illusion on their part, or will it be a source of creative development?

I am unqualified to speak of Brazil, but in the United States, the values of my own people are neither "white" nor "black," they are American. Nor can I see how they could be anything else, since we are a people who are involved in the texture of the American experience. And indeed, today the most dramatic fight for American ideals is being sparked by black Americans. Significantly, we are the only black peoples who are not fighting for separation from the "whites," but for a fuller participation in the society which we share with "whites." And it is of further significance that we pursue our goals precisely in terms of American Constitutionalism. If there is anything in this which points to "black values" it must lie in the circumstance that we really believe that all men are created equal and that they should be given a chance to achieve their highest potentialities, regardless of race, creed, color or past condition of servitude.

The terms in which the question is couched serve to obscure the cultural fact that the dynamism of American life is as much a part of the Negro American's personality as it is of the white American's. We differ from certain white Americans in that we have no reason to assume that race has a positive value, and in that we reject race thinking wherever we find it. And even this attitude is shared by millions of whites. Nor are we interested in being anything other than *Negro* Americans. One's racial identity is, after all, accidental, but the United States is an international country and its conscious character makes it possible for us to abandon the mistakes of the past. The point of our struggle is to be both Negro and American and to bring about that condition in American society in which this would be possible. In brief, there is an American Negro idiom, a style and a way of life, but none of this is inseparable from the conditions of American society, nor from its general modes or culture— mass distribution, race and intra-national conflicts, the radio, television, its system of education, its politics. If general American values influence us; we in turn influence them— speech, concept of liberty, justice, economic distribution, international outlook, our current attitude toward colonialism, our national image of ourselves as a nation. And this despite the fact that nothing which black Americans have won as a people has been won without struggle. For *no* group within the United States achieves anything without asserting its claims against the counterclaims of other groups. Thus as Americans we have accepted this conscious and ceaseless struggle as a condition of our freedom, and we are aware that each of our victories increases the area of freedom for all Americans, regardless of color. When we finally achieve the right of full participation in American life, what we make of it will depend upon our sense of cultural values, and our creative use of freedom, not upon our racial identification. I see no reason why the heritage of world culture— which represents a continuum—should be confused with the notion of race. Japan erected a highly efficient modern technology upon a religious culture which viewed the Em-

peror as a god. The Germany which produced Beethoven
and Hegel and Mann turned its science and technology to
the monstrous task of genocide; one hopes that when what
are known as the "Negro" societies are in full possession of
the world's knowledge and in control of their destinies, they
will bring to an end all those savageries which for centuries
have been committed in the name of race. From what we
are witnessing in certain parts of the world today, however, there is no guarantee that simply being non-white offers any guarantee of this. The demands of state policy are
apt to be more influential than morality. I would like to see
a qualified Negro as President of the United States. But I
suspect that even if this were today possible, the necessities
of the office would shape his actions far more than his racial
identity.

Would that we could but put the correct questions in these
matters, perhaps then great worlds of human energy could
be saved—especially by those of us who would be free.

—From *Preuves*, May 1958.

The Shadow and the Act

Faulkner has given us a metaphor. When, in the film *Intruder in the Dust*, the young Mississipian Chick Mallison falls into an ice-coated creek on a Negro's farm, he finds that he has plunged into the depth of a reality which constantly reveals itself as the reverse of what it had appeared before his plunge. Here the ice—white, brittle and eggshell-thin— symbolizes Chick's inherited views of the world, especially his Southern conception of Negroes. Emerging more shocked by the air than by the water, he finds himself locked in a moral struggle with the owner of the land, Lucas Beauchamp, the son of a slave, who, while aiding the boy, angers him by refusing to act toward him as Southern Negroes are expected to act.

To Lucas, Chick is not only a child but his guest. Thus he not only dries the boy's clothes, he insists that he eat the only food in the house, Lucas's own dinner. When Chick (whose

white standards won't allow him to accept the hospitality of
a Negro) attempts to pay him, Lucas refuses to accept the
money. What follows is one of the most sharply amusing
studies of Southern racial ethics to be seen anywhere. Asserting his whiteness, Chick throws the money on the floor,
ordering Lucas to pick it up; Lucas, disdaining to quarrel
with a child, has Chick's young Negro companion, Aleck
Sander, return the coins.

Defeated but still determined, Chick later seeks to dis-
charge his debt by sending Lucas and his wife a gift. Lucas
replies by sending Chick a gallon of molasses by—outrage
of all Southern Negro outrages!—a white boy on a mule.
He is too much, and from that moment it becomes Chick's
passion to repay his debt and to see Lucas for once "act like
a nigger." The opportunity has come, he thinks, when Lucas
is charged with shooting a white man in the back. But instead of humbling himself, Lucas (from his cell) tells, almost orders, Chick to prove him innocent by violating the
white man's grave.

In the end we see Chick recognizing Lucas as the representative of those virtues of courage, pride, independence
and patience that are usually attributed only to white men
—and, in his uncle's words, accepting the Negro as "the
keeper of our [the whites'] consciences." This bit of dialogue, coming after the real murderer is revealed as the
slain man's own brother, is, when viewed historically, about
the most remarkable concerning a Negro ever to come out
of Hollywood.

With this conversation, the falling into creeks, the digging
up of corpses and the confronting of lynch mobs that mark
the plot, all take on a new significance: Not only have we
been watching the consciousness of a young Southerner
grow through the stages of a superb mystery drama, we have
participated in a process by which the role of Negroes in

American life has been given what, for the movies, is a startling new definition.

To appreciate fully the significance of *Intruder in the Dust* in the history of Hollywood we must go back to the film that is regarded as the archetype of the modern American motion picture, *The Birth of a Nation.*

Originally entitled *The Clansman,* the film was inspired by another Southern novel, the Reverend Thomas Dixon's work of that title, which also inspired Joseph Simmons to found the Knights of the Ku Klux Klan. (What a role these malignant clergymen have played in our lives!) Re-entitled *The Birth of a Nation* as an afterthought, it was this film that forged the twin screen image of the Negro as bestial rapist and grinning, eye-rolling clown—stereotypes that are still with us today. Released during 1915, it resulted in controversy, riots, heavy profits and the growth of the Klan. Of it Terry Ramsaye, a historian of the American motion-picture industry writes: "The picture . . . and the K.K.K. secret society, which was the afterbirth of a nation, were sprouted from the same root. In subsequent years they reacted upon each other to the large profit of both. The film presented predigested dramatic experience and thrills. The society made the customers all actors in costume."

Usually *The Birth of a Nation* is discussed in terms of its contributions to cinema technique, but, as with every other technical advance since the oceanic sailing ship, it became a further instrument in the dehumanization of the Negro. And while few films have gone so far in projecting Negroes in a malignant light, few before the 1940s showed any concern with depicting their humanity. Just the opposite. In the struggle against Negro freedom, motion pictures have been one of the strongest instruments for justifying some white Americans' anti-Negro attitudes and practices. Thus the

South, through D. W. Griffith's genius, captured the enormous myth-making potential of the film form almost from the beginning. While the Negro stereotypes by no means made all white men Klansmen the cinema did to the extent that audiences accepted its image of Negroes, make them participants in the South's racial ritual of keeping the Negro "in his place."

After Reconstruction the political question of what was to be done with Negroes, "solved" by the Hayes-Tilden deal of 1876, came down to the psychological question: "How can the Negro's humanity be evaded?" The problem, arising in a democracy that holds all men as created equal, was a highly moral one: democratic ideals had to be squared with anti-Negro practices. One answer was to *deny* the Negro's humanity—a pattern set long before 1915. But with the release of *The Birth of a Nation* the propagation of subhuman images of Negroes became financially and dramatically profitable. The Negro as scapegoat could be sold as entertainment, could even be exported. If the film became the main manipulator of the American dream, for Negroes that dream contained a strong dose of such stuff as nightmares are made of.

We are recalling all this not so much as a means of indicting Hollywood as by way of placing *Intruder in the Dust,* and such recent films as *Home of the Brave, Lost Boundaries* and *Pinky,* in perspective. To direct an attack upon Hollywood would indeed be to confuse portrayal with action, image with reality. In the beginning was not the shadow, but the act, and the province of Hollywood is not action, but illusion. Actually, the anti-Negro images of the films were (and are) acceptable because of the existence throughout the United States of an audience obsessed with an inner psychological need to view Negroes as less than men. Thus, psychologically and ethically, these negative images constitute justifications for all those acts, legal, emotional, economic and political, which we label Jim Crow. The anti-Negro image is thus a ritual object of which Hollywood is not the creator, but the manipulator. Its role has been that of justifying the widely held myth of Negro unhumanness and inferiority by offering entertaining rituals through which that myth could be reaffirmed.

The great significance of the definition of Lucas Beauchamp's role in *Intruder in the Dust* is that it makes explicit the nature of Hollywood's changed attitude toward Negroes. Form being, in the words of Kenneth Burke, "the psychology of the audience," what is taking place in the American movie patron's mind? Why these new attempts to redefine the Negro's role? What has happened to the audience's mode of thinking?

For one thing there was the war; for another there is the fact that the United States' position as a leader in world affairs is shaken by its treatment of Negroes. Thus the thinking of white Americans is undergoing a process of change, and reflecting that change, we find that each of the films mentioned above deals with some basic and unusually negative assumption about Negroes: Are Negroes cowardly soldiers? (*Home of the Brave*); are Negroes the real polluters of the South? (*Intruder in the Dust*); have mulatto Negroes the right to pass as white, at the risk of having black babies, or if they have white-skinned children, of having to kill off their "white" identities by revealing to them that they are, alas, Negroes? (*Lost Boundaries*); and, finally, should Negro girls marry white men or—wonderful non sequitur—should they help their race? (*Pinky*).

Obviously these films are not *about* Negroes at all; they are about what whites think and feel about Negroes. And if they are taken as accurate reflectors of that thinking, it becomes apparent that there is much confusion. To make use of Faulkner's metaphor again, the film makers fell upon the eggshell ice but, unlike the child, weren't heavy enough to break it.

And, being unable to break it, they were unable to discover the real direction of their film narratives. In varying degree, they were unwilling to dig into the grave to expose the culprit, and thus we find them using ingenious devices for evading the full human rights of their Negroes. The result represents a defeat not only of drama, but of purpose.

In *Home of the Brave,* for instance, a psychiatrist tells the Negro soldier that his hysterical paralysis is like that of any other soldier who has lived when his friends have died; and we hear the soldier pronounced cured; indeed, we see him walk away prepared to open a bar and restaurant with a white veteran. But here there is an evasion (and by *evasion* I refer to the manipulation of the audience's attention away from reality to focus it upon false issues), because the guilt from which the Negro is supposed to suffer springs from an incident in which, immediately after his friend has called him a "yellowbelly nigger," he has wished the friend dead— only to see the wish granted by a sniper's bullet.

What happens to this racial element in the motivation of his guilt? The psychiatrist ignores it, and becomes a sleight-of-hand artist who makes it vanish by repeating again that the Negro is like everybody else. Nor, I believe, is this accidental, for it is here exactly that we come to the question of whether Negroes can rightfully be expected to risk their lives in an army in which they are slandered and discriminated against. Psychiatry is not, I'm afraid, the answer. The soldier suffers from concrete acts, not hallucinations.

And so with the others. In *Lost Boundaries* the question evaded is whether a mulatto Negro has the right to practice the old American pragmatic philosophy of capitalizing upon one's assets. For after all, whiteness *has* been given an economic and social value in our culture; and for the doctor upon whose life the film is based "passing" was the quickest and most certain means to success.

Yet Hollywood is uncertain about his right to do this. The

film does not render the true circumstances. In real life Dr. Albert Johnson, the Negro doctor who "passed" as white, purchased the thriving practice of a deceased physician in Gorham, New Hampshire, for a thousand dollars. Instead, a fiction is introduced in the film wherein Dr. Carter's initial motivation for "passing" arises after he is refused an internship by dark Negroes in an Atlanta hospital—because of his color! It just isn't real, since there are thousands of mulattoes living as Negroes in the South, many of them Negro leaders. The only functional purpose served by this fiction is to gain sympathy for Carter by placing part of the blame for his predicament upon black Negroes. Nor should the irony be missed that part of the sentiment evoked when the Carters are welcomed back into the community is gained by painting Negro life as horrible, a fate worse than a living death. It would seem that in the eyes of Hollywood, it is only "white" Negroes who ever suffer—or is it merely the "white" corpuscles of their blood?

Pinky, for instance, is the story of another suffering mulatto, and the suffering grows out of a confusion between race and love. If we attempt to reduce the heroine's problem to sentence form we'd get something like this: "Should white-skinned Negro girls marry white men, or should they inherit the plantations of old white artistocrats (provided they can find any old aristocrats to will them their plantations) or should they live in the South and open nursery schools for black Negroes?" It doesn't follow, but neither does the action. After sitting through a film concerned with interracial marriage, we see it suddenly become a courtroom battle over whether Negroes have the right to inherit property.

Pinky wins the plantation, and her lover, who has read of the fight in the Negro press, arrives and still loves her, race be hanged. But now Pinky decides that to marry him would "violate the race" and that she had better remain a

Negro. Ironically, nothing is said about the fact that her racial integrity, whatever that is, was violated before she was born. Her parents are never mentioned in the film. Following the will of the white aristocrat, who, before dying, advises her to "be true to herself," she opens a school for darker Negroes.

But in real life the choice is not between loving or denying one's race. Many couples manage to intermarry without violating their integrity, and indeed their marriage becomes the concrete expression of their integrity. In the film Jeanne Crain floats about like a sleepwalker, which seems to me to be exactly the way a girl so full of unreality would act. One thing is certain: no one is apt to mistake her for a Negro, not even a white one.

And yet, despite the absurdities with which these films are laden, they are all worth seeing, and if seen, capable of involving us emotionally. That they do is testimony to the deep centers of American emotion that they touch. Dealing with matters which, over the years, have been slowly charging up with guilt, they all display a vitality which escapes their slickest devices. And, naturally enough, one of the most interesting experiences connected with viewing them in predominantly white audiences is the profuse flow of tears and the sighs of profound emotional catharsis heard on all sides. It is as though there were some deep relief to be gained merely from seeing these subjects projected upon the screen.

It is here precisely that a danger lies. For the temptation toward self-congratulation which comes from seeing these films and sharing in their emotional release is apt to blind us to the true nature of what is unfolding—or failing to unfold—before our eyes. As an antidote to the sentimentality of these films, I suggest that they be seen in predominantly Negro audiences. For here, when the action goes phony, one will hear derisive laughter, not sobs. (Perhaps this is what Faulkner means about Negroes keeping the white man's conscience.) Seriously, *Intruder in the Dust* is the only film that could be shown in Harlem without arousing unintended laughter. For it is the only one of the four in which Negroes can make complete identification with their screen image. Interestingly, the factors that make this identification possible lie in its depiction not of racial but of human qualities.

Yet in the end, turning from art to life, we must even break with the definition of the Negro's role given us by Faulkner. For when it comes to conscience, we know that in this world each of us, black and white alike, must become the keeper of his own. This, in the deepest sense, is what these four films, taken as a group, should help us realize.

Faulkner himself seems to realize it. In the book *Intruder in the Dust*, Lucas attempts not so much to be the keeper of anyone else's conscience as to preserve his own life. Chick, in aiding Lucas, achieves that view of truth on which his own conscience depends.

—From *The Reporter*, December 6, 1949.

The Way It Is

The boy looked at me through the cracked door and stood staring with his large eyes until his mother came and invited me in. It was an average Harlem apartment, cool now with the shift in the fall weather. The room was clean and furnished with the old-fashioned furniture found so often up our way, two old upholstered chairs and a divan upon a faded blue and red rug. It was painfully clean, and the furniture crowded the narrow room.

"Sit right there, sir," the woman said. "It's where Wilbur use to sit before he went to camp, it's pretty comfortable."

I watched her ease herself tiredly upon the divan, the light from the large red lamp reflected upon her face from the top of a mirrored side table.

She must have been fifty, her hair slightly graying. The portrait of a young soldier smiled back from the top of a radio cabinet beside her.

She pointed. "That's my boy Wilbur right there," she said proudly. "He's a sergeant."

"Wilbur's got a medal for shooting so good," the boy said.

"You just be quiet and go eat your supper," she said. "All you can think about is guns and shooting." She spoke with the harsh tenderness so often used by Negro mothers.

The boy went, reluctantly opening the door. The odor of peas and rice and pork chops drifted through.

"Who was it, Tommy?" shrilled a voice on the other side.

"You two be quiet in there and eat your supper now," Mrs. Jackson called. "Them two just keeps my hands full. They just get into something *all* the time. I was coming up the street the other day and like to got the fright of my life. There was Tommy hanging on the back of a streetcar! But didn't I tan his bottom! I bet he won't even *look* at a streetcar for a long, long time. It ain't really that he's a *bad* child, it's just that he tries to do what he sees the other boys do. I wanted to send both him and his sister away to camp for the summer, but things was so tight this year that I couldn't do it. Raising kids in Harlem nowadays is more than a notion."

As is true so often in Negro American life, Mrs. Jackson, the mother, is the head of her family. Her husband had died several years ago; the smaller children were babies. She had kept going by doing domestic work and had kept the family together with the help of the older boy.

There is a quiet courage about Mrs. Jackson. And yet now and then the clenching and unclenching of her work-hardened fingers betray an anxiety that does not register in her face. I offer to wait until after she has eaten, but she says no, that she is too tired right now and she would rather talk than eat.

"You finding the writing business any better since the war?" she asked.

"I'm afraid not," I said.

"Is that so? Well, I don't know nothing about the writing

business. I just know that don't many colored go in for it. But I guess like everything else, some folks is doing good while others ain't. The other day I was over on 126th Street and saw them dispossessing a lawyer! Yes, sir, it was like back in the thirties. Things piled all over the sidewalk, the Negroes a-hanging out of the windows, and the poor man rushing around trying to get his stuff off the streets before it got dark, and everything."

I remembered the incident myself, having passed through the street that afternoon. Files, chest of drawers, bedsteads, tables and barrels had been piled along the sidewalk; with pink, blue and white mattresses and bundles of table linen and bedclothing piled on top. And the crowd had been as she described: some indignant, some curious, and all talking in subdued tones so as not to offend the evicted family. Law books had been piled upon the sidewalk near where a black and white kitten—and these are no writer's details—played games with itself in the coils of an upright bedspring. I told her I had seen the incident.

"Lord," she said. "And did you see all those law books he had? Looks like to me that anybody with all those books of law oughtn't to never get dispossessed.

"I was dispossessed, myself, back in thirty-seven, when we were all out of work. And they threatened me once since Wilbur's been in the Army. But I stood up for my rights and when the government sent the check we pulled through. Anybody's liable to get dispossessed though." She said it defensively.

"Just how do you find it otherwise?" I asked.

"Things is mighty tight, son . . . You'll have to excuse me for calling you 'son,' because I suspect you must be just about Wilbur's age."

She sat back abruptly. "How come you not in the Army?" she asked.

"I've a wife and dependents," I said.

"I see," She pondered. "Wilbur would have got married too, but he was helping me with the kids."

"That's the way it goes," I said.

"Things is tight," she said again. "With food so high and everything I sometimes don't know what's going to happen. Then, too, with Wilbur in the Army we naturally misses the money he use to bring in."

She regarded me shrewdly. "So you want to know about how we're doing? Don't you live in Harlem?"

"Oh, yes, but I want to know what *you* think about it."

"So's you can write it up?"

"Some of it, sure. But I won't use your name."

"Oh I don't care 'bout that. I *want* them to know how I feel."

She became silent. Then, "You didn't tell me where you live, you know," she said cagily. I had to laugh and she laughed too.

"I live up near Amsterdam Avenue," I said.

"You telling me the truth?"

"Honest."

"And is your place a nice one?"

"Just average. You know how they go," I said.

"I bet you live up there on Sugar Hill."

"Not me," I said.

"And you're sure you're not one of these investigators?"

"Of course not."

"I bet you are too." She smiled.

I shook my head and she laughed.

"They always starting something new," she said. "You can't keep up with them."

But now she seemed reassured and settled down to talk, her hands clasped loosely in her lap against the checkered design of her dress.

"Well, we're carrying on somehow. I'm still working and I manage to keep the young uns in school, and I pays the rent too. I guess maybe it would be a little better if the government would send the checks on time . . ."

She paused and pointed across the room to the picture of a young woman. "And it would be even better if Mary, that's my next oldest after Wilbur—if she could get some of that defense training so she could get a job what pays decent money. But don't look like she's going to get anything. She was out to the Western Electric plant in Kearney, New Jersey, the other day and they give her some kind of test, but that was the end of that."

"Did she pass the test?" I asked.

"Sure she passed. But they just put her name down on a card and told her they would keep her in mind. They always do that. They ask her a lot of questions, then they want to know if she ever had any experience in running machines, and when she says she ain't, they just take down her name. Now where is a colored girl going to get any experience in running all these kinds of machines they never even seen before?"

When I could not answer she threw up her hands.

"Well, there you have it, they got you any which way you turn. A few gets jobs, but most don't."

"Things are much better outside of New York," I said.

"So I hear," she said. "Guess if I was younger I'd take the kids and move to Jersey or up to Connecticut, where I hear there's some jobs for colored. Or even down South. Only I keep hearing about the trouble they're having down there. And I don't want the kids to grow up down there nohow. Had enough of that when I was a kid . . ."

"Have any of your friends gotten work through the F.E.P.C.?"

She thought for a moment.

"No, son. It seems to me that that committee is doing something everywhere but here in New York. Maybe that's why it's so bad for us—and you know it's bad 'cause you're colored yourself."

As I heard the clatter of dishes coming from the kitchen, her face suddenly assumed an outraged expression.

"Now you take my sister's boy, William. God bless his poor soul. William went to the trade schools and learned all about machines. He got so he could take any kind of machine apart and fix it and put it together again. He was machine-crazy! But he was a smart boy and a good boy. He got good marks in school too. But when he went to get a job in one of those factories where they make war machines of some kind, they wouldn't take him 'cause he was colored—*and they told him so!*"

She paused for breath, a red flush dyeing her skin. The tinted portrait of a brown mother holding a brown, shiny-haired baby posed madonna-like from a calendar above her head.

"Well, when they wouldn't take him some of the folks over to the church told him to take his case to the F.E.P.C., and he did. But they had so many cases and it took so long that William got discouraged and joined up in the Merchant Marine. That poor boy was just so disgusted that he said that he would have enlisted in the Army, only that his mamma's got two little ones like I have. So he went out on that boat 'cause it paid good money and a good bonus. It was real good money and he helped his mamma a heap. But it didn't last long before one of those submarines sunk the boat."

Her eyes strayed to the window, where a line of potted plants crowded the sill; a profusion of green things, slowly becoming silhouettes in the fading light. Snake plants, English ivy, and others, a potato plant in a glass jar, its vines twining around a cross of wood and its thousand thread-fine roots pushing hungrily against the wall of glass. A single red bloom pushed above the rest, and in one corner a corn plant threatened to touch the ceiling from the floor with its blade-like leaves.

The light was fading and her voice had slipped into the intense detachment of recent grief. "It was just about four months yesterday," she said. "He was such a fine boy. Everybody liked William."

She shook her head silently, her fingers gripping her folded arms as she swallowed tensely.

"It hurts to think about it," she said, getting up and snapping on another light, revealing a child's airplane model beneath the table. "Well, the folks from his union is being very nice to my sister, the whites as well as the colored. And you know," she added, leaning toward me, "it really makes you feel a little better when they come round—the white ones, I mean—and really tries to help. Like some of these ole relief investigators who come in wanting to run your life for you, but really like they interested in you. Something like colored folks in a way. We used to get after William for being with white folks so much, but these sure have shown themselves to be real friends."

She stared at me as though it was a fact which she deeply feared to accept.

"Some of them is going to try and see that my sister gets some sort of defense work. But what I'm trying to tell you is that it's a sin and a shame that a fine boy like William had to go fooling round on them ships when ever since he was a little ole boy he'd been crazy about machines."

"But don't you think that the Merchant Marine is helping to win the war?" I said. "It takes brave men to go out there, and they've done a lot."

"Sure they have," she said. "Sure they have. But I'm not talking about that. Anybody could do what they had him doing on that boat. Anybody can wait tables who's got sense enough to keep his fingernails clean! Waiting tables, when he could *make* things on a machine!

"You see that radio there? Well, William made that radio. It ain't no store set, no, sir, even though it looks like one. William made it for the kids. Made everything but the cabinet, and you can hear way down to Cuba and Mexico with it. And to think of that boy! Oh, it makes me so mad I don't know what to do! He ought to be here right now helping his mamma and lil brother and sister. But what can you do? You educated, son, you one of our educated Negroes that's been to college and everything. Now you tell me, *what can we do?*" She paused. "I'm a colored woman, and colored women can take it. I can hit the chillies to the subway every morning and stand in the white folks' kitchen all day long, but so much is happening in the world that I don't know which way to turn. First it's my sister's boy and then they sends my own boy down to Fort Bragg. I tells you I'm even afraid to open Wilbur's letters, some of the things he tells is so awful. I'm even afraid to open letters that the *government* sends sometimes about his insurance or something like that, 'cause I'm afraid it might be a message that Wilbur's been beaten up or killed by some of those white folks down there. Then I gets so mad I don't know what to do. I use to pray, but praying don't do no good. And too, like the union folks was telling us when we was so broken up about William, we got to fight the big Hitler over yonder even with all the little Hitlers over here. I wish they'd hurry up and send Wilbur on out of the country 'cause then maybe my mind would know some ease. Lord!" she sighed. "If it wasn't so serious I'd break down and laugh at my ownself."

She smiled now and the tension eased from her face and she leaned back against the divan and laughed. Then she became serious again.

"But, son, you really can't laugh about it. Not honestly laugh like you can about some things. It reminds me of that crazy man what's always running up and down the streets up here. You know, the one who's always hollering at the cars and making out like he's throwing bombs?"

"Of course, I've seen him often," I said.

"Sure you have. Well, I use to laugh at that poor man when he'd start acting the fool—you know how it is, you feel sorry for him but you can't help but laugh. They say he got that way in the last war. Well, I can understand him better now. Course I ain't had no bombs bursting in my ears like he had. But yet and still, with things pulling me thisaway and thataway, I sometimes feel that I'm going to go screaming up and down the streets just like that poor fellow does."

"He's shell-shocked," I said. "Sometimes I've seen him talking and acting just as normal as anyone."

"Is that so?" she said. "I always thought it was funny he never got hit by a car. I've seen them almost hit him, but he goes right back. One day I heard a man say, Lord, if that crazy fellow really had some bombs he'd get rid of every car in Harlem!"

We laughed and I prepared to go.

"Sorry you found me so gloomy today, son. But you know, things have a way of just piling up these days and I just had to talk about them. Anyway, you asked for me to tell you what I thought."

She walked with me to the door. Street lamps glowed on the avenue, lighting the early dark. The after-school cries of children drifted dimly in from the sidewalk.

She shivered close beside me.

"It's getting chilly already," she said. "I'm wondering what's going to happen this winter about the oil and coal situation. These ole holes we have to live in can get mighty cold. Now can't they though?"

I agreed.

"A friend of mine that moved up on Amsterdam Avenue about a month ago wanted to know why I don't move out of

Harlem. So I told her it wouldn't do no good to move 'cause anywhere they let us go gets to be Harlem right on. I done moved round too much not to know that. Oh yes!"

She shook her head knowingly.

"Harlem's like that old song says:

> *It's so high you can't get over it*
> *So low, you can't get under it,*
> *And so wide, you can't get round it . . .*

"That's the way it really is," she said. "Well, good-bye, son."

And as I went down the dimmed-out street the verse completed itself in my mind, *You must come through by the living gate . . .*

So there you have Mrs. Jackson. And that's the way "it really is" for her and many like her who are searching for that gate of freedom. In the very texture of their lives there is confusion, war-made confusion. And the problem is to get around, over, under and through this confusion. They do not ask for a lighter share of necessary war sacrifices than other Americans have to bear. But they do ask for equal reasons to believe that their sacrifices are worth-while, and they *do* want to be rid of the heavy resentment and bitterness which has been theirs for long before the war.

Forced in normal times to live at standards much lower than those the war has brought to the United States generally, they find it emotionally dificult to give their attention to the war. The struggle for existence constitutes a war in itself. The Mrs. Jacksons of Harlem offer one of the best arguments for the stabilization of prices and the freezing of rents. For twenty-five percent of those still on relief come from our five percent of New York's population. Mrs. Jackson finds it increasingly difficult to feed her children. She must pay six cents more on the dollar for food than do the mothers of similar-income sections of the city. And with the prospect of a heatless winter, Harlem, with its poor housing and high tuberculosis death rate, will know an increase of hardship.

It is an old story. Touch any phase of urban living in our democracy and its worst aspects are to be found in Harlem. Our housing is the poorest, and our rents the highest. Our people are the sickest, and Harlem Hospital the most over-crowded and understaffed. Our unemployment is the greatest, and our cost of food the most exorbitant. Our crime the most understandable and easily corrected, but the policemen sent among us the most brutal. Our desire to rid the world of fascism the most burning, and the obstacles placed in our way the most frustrating. Our need to see the war as a struggle between democracy and fascism the most intense and our temptation to interpret it as a "color" war the most compelling. Our need to believe in the age of the "common man" the most hope-inspiring, and our reasons to doubt that it will include us the most disheartening (this is no Whitmanesque catalogue of democratic exultations, while more than anything else we wish that it could be). And that's the way it is.

Many of Mrs. Jackson's neighbors are joining in the fight to freeze rents and for the broadening of the F.E.P.C., for Negroes and all other Americans. Their very lives demand that they back the President's stabilization program. That they must be victorious is one of the necessities upon which our democratic freedom rests. The Mrs. Jacksons cannot make the sacrifices necessary to participate in a total war if the conditions under which they live, the very ground on which they must fight, continues its offensive against them. Nor is this something to be solved by propaganda. Morale grows out of realities, not out of words alone. Only concrete action will be effective—lest irritation and confusion turn into exasperation, and exasperation change to disgust and finally into anti-war sentiment (and there is such a danger). Mrs. Jackson's reality must be democratized so that she may clarify her thinking and her emotions. And that's the way it really is.

—From *New Masses*, October 20, 1942.

Harlem Is Nowhere

One must descend to the basement and move along a confusing mazelike hall to reach it. Twice the passage seems to lead
against a blank wall; then at last one enters the brightly
lighted auditorium. And here, finally, are the social workers
at the reception desks; and there, waiting upon the benches
rowed beneath the pipes carrying warmth and water to the
floors above, are the patients. One sees white-jacketed psychiatrists carrying charts appear and vanish behind screens
that form the improvised interviewing cubicles. All is an
atmosphere of hurried efficiency; and the concerned faces
of the patients are brightened by the friendly smiles and
low-pitched voices of the expert workers. One has entered
the Lafargue Psychiatric Clinic.

This clinic (whose staff receives no salary and whose fee
is only twenty-five cents—to those who can afford it) is perhaps the most successful attempt in the nation to provide

psychotherapy for the underprivileged. Certainly it has become in two years one of Harlem's most important institutions. Not only is it the sole mental clinic in the section, it is the only center in the city wherein both Negroes and whites may receive extended psychiatric care. Thus its importance transcends even its great value as a center for psychotherapy: it represents an underground extension of democracy.

As one of the few institutions dedicated to recognizing the total implication of Negro life in the United States, the Lafargue Clinic rejects all stereotypes, and may be said to concern itself with any possible variations between the three basic social factors shaping an American Negro's personality: he is viewed as a member of a racial and cultural minority; as an American citizen caught in certain political and economic relationships; and as a modern man living in a revolutionary world. Accordingly, each patient, whether white or black, is approached dynamically as a being possessing a cultural and biological past who seeks to make his way toward the future in a world wherein each discovery about himself must be made in the here and now at the expense of hope, pain and fear—a being who in responding to the complex forces of America has become confused.

Leaving the Lafargue Clinic for a while, what are some of the forces which generate this confusion? Who is this total Negro whom the clinic seeks to know; what is the psychological character of the scene in which he dwells; how describe the past which he drags into this scene, and what is the future toward which he stumbles and becomes confused? Let us begin with the scene: Harlem.

To live in Harlem is to dwell in the very bowels of the city; it is to pass a labyrinthine existence among streets that explode monotonously skyward with the spires and crosses of churches and clutter under foot with garbage and decay. Harlem is a ruin—many of its ordinary aspects (its crimes, its casual violence, its crumbling buildings with littered area-ways, ill-smelling halls and vermin-invaded rooms) are in-distinguishable from the distorted images that appear in dreams, and which, like muggers haunting a lonely hall, quiver in the waking mind with hidden and threatening sig-nificance. Yet this is no dream but the reality of well over four hundred thousand Americans; a reality which for many defines and colors the world. Overcrowded and exploited politically and economically, Harlem is the scene and sym-bol of the Negro's perpetual alienation in the land of his birth.

But much has been written about the social and eco-nomic aspects of Harlem; we are here interested in its psy-chological character—a character that arises from the im-pact between urban slum conditions and folk sensibilities. Historically, American Negroes are caught in a vast process of change that has swept them from slavery to the condition of industrial man in a space of time so telescoped (a bare eighty-five years) that it is possible literally for them to step from feudalism into the vortex of industrialism simply by moving across the Mason-Dixon line.

This abruptness of change and the resulting clash of cul-tural factors within Negro personality account for some of the extreme contrasts found in Harlem, for both its negative and its positive characteristics. For if Harlem is the scene of the folk-Negro's death agony, it is also the setting of his transcendence. Here it is possible for talented youths to leap through the development of decades in a brief twenty years, while beside them white-haired adults crawl in the feudal darkness of their childhood. Here a former cotton picker develops the sensitive hands of a surgeon, and men whose grandparents still believe in magic prepare optimistically to become atomic scientists. Here the grandchildren of those who possessed no written literature examine their lives through the eyes of Freud and Marx, Kierkegaard and Kafka, Malraux and Sartre. It explains the nature of a world so fluid and shifting that often within the mind the real and the unreal merge, and the marvelous beckons from behind the same sordid reality that denies its existence.

Hence the most surreal fantasies are acted out upon the streets of Harlem; a man ducks in and out of traffic shouting and throwing imaginary grenades that actually exploded during World War I; a boy participates in the rape-robbery of his mother; a man beating his wife in a park uses boxing "science" and observes Marquess of Queensberry rules (no rabbit punching, no blows beneath the belt); two men hold a third while a lesbian slashes him to death with a razor blade; boy gangsters wielding homemade pistols (which in the South of their origin are but toy symbols of adolescent yearning for manhood) shoot down their young rivals. Life becomes a masquerade, exotic costumes are worn every day. Those who cannot afford to hire a horse wear riding habits; others who could not afford a hunting trip or who seldom attend sporting events carry shooting sticks.

For this is a world in which the major energy of the imagination goes not into creating works of art, but to overcome the frustrations of social discrimination. Not quite citizens and yet Americans, full of the tensions of modern man but regarded as primitives, Negro Americans are in desperate search for an identity. Rejecting the second-class status assigned them, they feel alienated and their whole lives have become a search for answers to the questions: Who am I, What am I, Why am I, and Where? Significantly, in Harlem the reply to the greeting, "How are you?" is very often, "Oh, man, I'm *nowhere*"—a phrase revealing an attitude so common that it has been reduced to a gesture, a seemingly trivial word. Indeed, Negroes are not unaware that the conditions of their lives demand new definitions of terms like *primitive* and *modern, ethical* and *unethical, moral* and *immoral, patriotism* and *treason, tragedy* and *comedy, sanity* and *insanity.*

But for a long time now—despite songs like the "Blow Top Blues" and the eruption of expressions like *frantic, buggy* and *mad* into Harlem's popular speech, doubtless a word-magic against the states they name—calm in face of the unreality of Negro life becomes increasingly difficult. And while some seek relief in strange hysterical forms of religion, in alcohol and drugs, and others learn to analyze the causes for their predicament and join with others to correct them, an increasing number have found their way to the Lafargue Psychiatric Clinic.

In relation to their Southern background, the cultural history of Negroes in the North reads like the legend of some tragic people out of mythology, a people which aspired to escape from its own unhappy homeland to the apparent peace of a distant mountain; but which, in migrating, made some fatal error of judgment and fell into a great chasm of mazelike passages that promise ever to lead to the mountain but end ever against a wall. Not that a Negro is worse off in the North than in the South, but that in the North he surrenders and does not replace certain important supports to his personality. He leaves a relatively static social order in which, having experienced its brutality for hundreds of years—indeed, having been formed within it and by it—he has developed those techniques of survival to which Faulkner refers as "endurance," and an ease of movement within explosive situations which makes Hemingway's definition of courage, "grace under pressure," appear mere swagger. He surrenders the protection of his peasant cynicism—his refusal to hope for the fulfillment of hopeless hopes—and his sense of being "at home in the world" gained from confronting and accepting (for day-to-day living, at least) the obscene absurdity of his predicament. Further, he leaves a still authoritative religion which gives his life a semblance of metaphysical wholeness; a family structure which is relatively stable; and a body of folklore—tested in life-and-death terms against his daily experience with nature and the Southern white man—that serves him as a guide to action.

These are the supports of Southern Negro rationality (and, to an extent, of the internal peace of the United States); humble, but of inestimable psychological value,[1] they allow Southern Negroes to maintain their almost mystical hope for a future of full democracy—a hope accompanied by an irrepressible belief in some Mecca of equality, located in the North and identified by the magic place names New York, Chicago, Detroit. A belief sustained (as all myth is sustained by ritual) by identifying themselves ritually with the successes of Negro celebrities, by reciting their exploits and enumerating their dollars, and by recounting the swiftness with which they spiral from humble birth to headline fame. And doubtless the blasting of this dream is as damaging to Negro personality as the slum scenes of filth, disorder and crumbling masonry in which it flies apart.

When Negroes are barred from participating in the main institutional life of society they lose far more than economic privileges or the satisfaction of saluting the flag with unmixed emotions. They lose one of the bulwarks which men place between themselves and the constant threat of chaos. For whatever the assigned function of social institutions, their psychological function is to protect the citizen against the irrational, incalculable forces that hover about the edges of human life like cosmic destruction lurking within an atomic stockpile.

And it is precisely the denial of this support through segregation and discrimination that leaves the most balanced Negro open to anxiety.

---

[1] Its political and economic value is the measure of both the positive and negative characteristics of American democracy.

Though caught not only in the tensions arising from his own swift history, but in those conflicts created in modern man by a revolutionary world, he cannot participate fully in the therapy which the white American achieves through patriotic ceremonies and by identifying himself with American wealth and power. Instead, he is thrown back upon his own "slum-shocked" institutions.

But these, like his folk personality, are caught in a process of chaotic change. His family disintegrates, his church splinters; his folk wisdom is discarded in the mistaken notion that it in no way applies to urban living; and his formal education (never really his own) provides him with neither scientific description nor rounded philosophical interpretation of the profound forces that are transforming his total being. Yet even his art is transformed; the lyrical ritual elements of folk jazz—that artistic projection of the only real individuality possible for him in the South, that embodiment of a superior democracy in which each individual cultivated his uniqueness and yet did not clash with his neighbors—have given way to the near-themeless technical virtuosity of bebop a further triumph of technology over humanism. His speech hardens; his movements are geared to the time clock; his diet changes; his sensibilities quicken and his intelligence expands. But without institutions to give him direction, and lacking a clear explanation of his predicament—the religious ones being inadequate, and those offered by political and labor leaders obviously incomplete and opportunistic—the individual feels that his world and his personality are out of key. The phrase "I'm nowhere" expresses the feeling borne in upon many Negroes that they have no stable, recognized place in society. One's identity drifts in a capricious reality in which even the most commonly held assumptions are questionable. One "is" literally, but one is nowhere; one wanders dazed in a ghetto maze, a "displaced person" of American democracy.

And as though all this were not enough of a strain on a people's sense of the rational, the conditions under which it lives are seized upon as proof of its inferiority. Thus the frustrations of Negro life (many of them the frustrations of *all* life during this historical moment) permeate the atmosphere of Harlem with what Dr. Frederick Wertham, Director of the Lafargue Clinic, terms "free-floating hostility," a hostility that bombards the individual from so many directions that he is often unable to identify it with any specific object. Some feel it the punishment of some racial or personal guilt and pray to God; others (called "evil Negroes" in Harlem) become enraged with the world. Sometimes it provokes dramatic mass responses, and the results are the spontaneous outbreaks called the "Harlem riots" of 1935 and 1943.

And why have these explosive matters—which are now a problem of our foreign policy—been ignored? Because there is an argument in progress between black men and white men as to the true nature of American reality. Following their own interests, whites impose interpretations upon Negro experience that are not only false but, in effect, a denial of Negro humanity (witness the shock when A. Philip Randolph questions, on the basis of Negro experience, the meaning of *treason*). Too weak to shout down these interpretations, Negroes live nevertheless as they have to live, and the concrete conditions of their lives are more real than white men's arguments

And it is here exactly that lies the importance of the Lafargue Psychiatric Clinic—both as a scientific laboratory and as an expression of forthright democratic action in its scientific willingness to dispense with preconceived notions and accept the realities of Negro, i.e., *American* life. It recognizes that the personality damage that brought it into being represents not the disintegration of a people's fiber, but the failure of a way of life. For not only is it an antidote to this failure, it represents a victory over another of its aspects.

For ten years, while heading various psychiatric institutions, Dr. Wertham had fought for a psychiatric center in which Negroes could receive treatment. But whether he approached politicians, city agencies or philanthropists, all gave excuses for not acting. The agencies were complacent, the politicians accused him of harboring political rather than humanitarian motives; certain liberal middlemen, who stand between Negroes and philanthropic dollars, accused him of trying to establish a segregated institution. Finally it was decided to establish the clinic without money or official recognition. The results were electric. When his fellow psychiatrists were asked to contribute their services, Dr. Wertham was overwhelmed with offers. These physicians, all of whom hold jobs in institutions which discriminate against Negroes, were eager to overcome this frustration to their science; and like some Southern Negroes who consider that part of themselves best which they hide beneath their servility, they consider their most important work that which is carried out in a Harlem ' asement.

Here, in the basement, a frustrated s̶ ̶ ̶e goes to find its true object: the confused of mind who se̶ reality. Both find the source of their frustrations in the sickness of the social order. As such, and in spite of the very fine work it is doing, a thousand Lafargue clinics could not dispel the sense of unreality that haunts Harlem. Knowing this, Dr. Wertham and his interracial staff seek a modest achievement: to give each bewildered patient an insight into the relation between his problems and his environment, and out of this understanding to reforge the will to endure in a hostile world.

—Unpublished. Written for *Magazine of the Year*, 1948.

An American Dilemma:
A Review

Gunnar Myrdal's *An American Dilemma* is not an easy book for an American Negro to review. Not because he might be overawed by its broad comprehensiveness; nor because of the sense of alienation and embarrassment that the book might arouse by reminding him that it is necessary in our democracy for a European scientist to affirm the American Negro's humanity; not even because it is an implied criticism of his own Negro social scientists' failure to define the problem as clearly. Instead, it is difficult because the book—as a study of a social ambiguity—is itself so nearly ambiguous that in order to appreciate it fully and yet protect his own humanity, the Negro must, while joining in the chorus of "Yeas" which the book has so deservedly evoked, utter a lusty and simultaneous "Nay."

In our society it is not unusual for a Negro to experience a sensation that he does not exist in the real world at all. He seems rather to exist in the nightmarish fantasy of the white American mind as a phantom that the white mind seeks unceasingly, by means both crude and subtle, to lay. Myrdal proves this no idle Negro fancy. He locates the Negro problem "in the heart of the [white] American . . . the conflict between his moral valuations on various levels of consciousness and generality." Indeed, the main virtue of *An American Dilemma* lies in its demonstration of how the mechanism of prejudice operates to disguise the moral conflict in the minds of whites produced by the clash on the social level between the American Creed and anti-Negro practices. There is, however, a danger in this very virtue.

For the solution of the problem of the American Negro and democracy lies only partially in the white man's free will. Its full solution will lie in the creation of a democracy in which the Negro will be free to define himself for what he is and, within the large framework of that democracy, for what he desires to be. Let this not be misunderstood. For one is apt, in welcoming *An American Dilemma*'s democratic contribution, to forget that all great democratic documents—and there is a certain greatness here—contain a strong charge of anti-democratic elements. Perhaps the wisest attitude for democrats is not to deplore the ambiguous element of democratic writings but to seek to understand them. For it is by making use of the positive contributions of such documents and rejecting their negative elements that democracy can be kept dynamic.

Since its inception, American social science has been closely bound with American Negro destiny. Even before the Civil War the Southern ruling class had inspired a pseudo-scientific literature attempting to prove the Negro inhuman and thus beyond any moral objections to human slavery. Sociology did not become closely concerned with the Negro, however, until after Emancipation gave the slaves the status—on paper at least—of nominal citizens. And if the end of the slave system created for this science the pragmatic problem of adjusting our society to include the new citizens, the compromise between the Northern and Southern ruling classes created the moral problem which Myrdal terms the American Dilemma.

This was a period, the 1870s, wherein scientific method, with its supposed objectivity and neutrality to values, was thought to be the answer to all problems. There is no better example of the confusion and opportunism springing from this false assumption than the relation of American social science to the Negro problem. And let us make no easy distinctions here between Northern and Southern social scientists; both groups used their graphs, charts and other paraphernalia to prove the Negro's biological, psychological, intellectual and moral inferiority; one group to justify the South's exploitation of Negroes and the other to justify the North's refusal to do anything basic about it.

Here was a science whose role, beneath its illusionary non-concern with values, was to reconcile the practical morality of American capitalism with the ideal morality of the American Creed.

Now, the task of reconciling moralities is usually the function of religion and philosophy, of art and psychoanalysis— all of which find myth-making indispensable. And in this, American sociological literature rivals all three: its mythmaking consisting of its "scientific" justification of antidemocratic and unscientific racial attitudes and practices. If Myrdal has done nothing else, he has used his science to discredit all of the vicious non-scientific nonsense that has cluttered our sociological literature. He has, in short, shorn it of its mythology.

It is rewarding to trace the connection between social science and the Negro a bit further. Usually when the condition of Negroes is discussed we get a Morality Play explanation in which the North is given the role of Good and the South that of Evil. This oversimplifies a complex matter. For at the end of the Civil War, the North lost interest in the Negro. The conditions for the growth of industrial capitalism had been won and the Negro "stood in the way of a return to national solidarity and a development of trade relations" between the North and the South. This problem was not easy to solve. Groups of Negroes had discovered the effectiveness of protest and what Myrdal shows to be the Negro's strongest weapon in pressing his claims: his hold upon the moral consciousness of Northern whites.

In order to deal with this problem the North did four things: it promoted Negro education in the South; it controlled his economic and political destiny, or allowed the South to do so; it built Booker T. Washington into a national spokesman of Negroes with Tuskegee Institute as his seat of power; and it organized social science as an instrumentality to sanction its methods.

It might be said that this explanation sounds too cynical, that much of the North's interest in Negro education grew out of a philanthropic impulse, and that it ignores the real contribution to the understanding of Negroes made by social science. But philanthropy on the psychological level is often guilt-motivated—even when most unconscious. And here, again, we have the moral conflict. When we look at the connection between Tuskegee and our most influential school of sociology, the Universtiy of Chicago, we are inclined to see more than an unconscious connection between economic interests and philanthropy, Negroes and social science.

But if on the black side of the color line Washington's "Tuskegee Machine" served to deflect Negro energy away from direct political action, on the white side of the line the moral problem nevertheless remained. It does not, therefore, seem quite accidental that the man responsible for inflating Tuskegee into a national symbol, and who is sometimes spoken of as the "power behind Washington's throne," was none other than Dr. Robert E. Park, co-founder of the University of Chicago School of Sociology.

The positive contributions of Dr. Park and those men connected with him are well established. American Negroes have benefited greatly from their research; and some of the most brilliant of Negro scholars have been connected with them. Perhaps the most just charge to be made against them is that of timidity. They have been, in the negative sense, victims of the imposed limitations of bourgeois science. Because certainly their recent works have moved closer and closer toward the conclusions made by Myrdal. Indeed, without their active participation, *An American Dilemma* would have been far less effective. Nevertheless, it was Myrdal who made the most of their findings. Perhaps it took the rise of fascism to free American social science of its timidity. Certainly it was necessary to clear it of some of the anti-Negro assumptions with which it started.

Dr. Robert E. Park was both a greater scientist and, in his attitude toward Negroes, a greater democrat than William Graham Sumner. (It will perhaps pain many to see these names in juxtaposition.) In our world, however, extremes quickly meet. Sumner believed it "the greatest folly of which man can be capable to sit down with a slate and pencil and plan out a new social world"; a point of view containing little hope for the underdog. But for all his good works, some of Park's assumptions were little better. The Negro, he felt "has always been interested rather in expression than in action; interested in life itself rather than in its reconstruction or reformation. The Negro is, by natural disposition, neither an intellectual nor an idealist, like the

Jew; nor a brooding introspective, like the East Indian; nor a pioneer and frontiersman, like the Anglo-Saxon. He is primarily an artist, loving life for its own sake. His *métier* is expression rather than action. He is, so to speak, the lady among the races."

Park's descriptive metaphor is so pregnant with mixed motives as to birth a thousand compromises and indecisions. Imagine the effect such teachings have had upon Negro students alone! Thus what started as part of a democratic attitude, ends not only uncomfortably close to the preachings of Sumner, but to those of Dr. Goebbels as well.

One becomes impatient with those critics who accuse American capitalism of neglecting social planning. Actually its planning lay in having the loosest plan possible. And when it was economically expedient to change plans it has been able to do so. During the Abolitionist period the moral nature of the Negro problem was generally recognized. But with the passing of the Reconsctruction the moral aspect was forced out of consciousness. Significantly, Booker T. Washington wrote a biography in which he deliberately gave the *coup de grâce* to the memory of Frederick Douglass, the Negro leader who, in his aggressive career, united the moral and political factions for the anti-slavery struggle.

Following World War I, under the war-stimulated revival of democracy, there was a brief moment when the moral nature of the problem threatened to come alive in the minds of white Americans. This time it was rationalized by projecting into popular fiction the stereotype of the Negro as an exotic primitive; while social science, under the pressure of war production needs, was devoted to proving that Negroes were not so inferior as a few decades before. It was during this period that some of the most scientifically valid concepts for understanding the Negro were advanced. But social science did not have the courage of its own research.

Following its vital Jamesian influence it began to discover the questionable values it supported and, until Myrdal arrived, timidly held its breath.

Why, then, should Myrdal be brought into the country in 1937 by the Carnegie Foundation to prepare this study and not before? Why this sudden junking of ideological fixtures?

According to F. P. Keppel, who writes the Foreword for the trustees of the Carnegie Corporation: "The underlying purpose of these studies is to contribute to the general advancement and diffusion of knowledge and understanding." There was, Mr. Keppel admits, another reason, namely, "the need of the foundation itself for fuller light in the formulation and development of its own program." Former Secretary of War, Newton D. Baker, target of much Negro discontent over the treatment of Negro soldiers during the last war, suggested the study; and the board agreed with him that "more knowledge and better organized and interrelated knowledge [of the Negro problem] were essential before the Corporation could intelligently distribute its own funds." And that "the gathering and digestion of the material might well have a usefulness far beyond our own needs."

These, we must admit, are all good reasons, although a bit vague. One thing, however, is clear: a need was felt for a new ideological approach to the Negro problem. This need was general, and if we look for a moment at those two groups —the left-wing parties and the New Deal—that showed the greatest concern with the Negro problem during the period between the Depression and the outbreak of the war, we are able to see how the need expressed itself.

Both the Left and the New Deal showed a far less restrained approach to the Negro than any groups since the Abolitionists. The Left brought the world-view of Marxism into the Negro community, introduced new techniques of organization and struggle, and included the Negro in its program on a basis of equality. Within its far more rigid framework the New Deal moved in the same democratic direction. Nevertheless, for all their activity, both groups neglected sharp ideological planning where the Negro was concerned. Both, it might be said, went about solving the Negro problem without defining the nature of the problem beyond its economic and narrowly political aspects. Which is not unusual for politicians—only here both groups consistently professed and demonstrated far more social vision than the average political party.

The most striking example of this failure is to be seen in the New Deal Administration's perpetuation of a Jim Crow Army, and the shamefaced support of it given by the Communists. It would be easy—on the basis of some of the slogans attributed to Negro people by the Communists, from time to time, and the New Deal's frequent retreats on Negro issues—to question the sincerity of these two groups. Or, in the case of the New Deal, attribute its failure to its desire to hold power in a concrete political situation; while the failure of the Communists could be laid to "Red perfidy." But this would be silly. Sincerity is not a quality that one expects of political parties, not even revolutionary ones. To question their sincerity makes room for the old idea of paternalism, and the corny notion that these groups have an obligation to "do something *for* the Negro."

The only sincerity to be expected of political parties is that flexible variety whereby they are enabled to put their own programs into effect. Regardless of their long-range intentions, on the practical level they are guided not by humanism so much as by expediencies of power. Thus if there is any insincerity here, it lies in the failure of these groups to make the best of their own interests by basing their alliances with Negroes upon a more scientific knowledge of the subtleties of Negro–White relations.

Dismissing the New Deal point of view as the eclectic creation of a capitalism in momentary retreat, what was influencing the Communists who emphasized the unity of theory and practice? This, we believe, sprang from their inheritance of the American Dilemma (which, incidentally disproves the red-baiters' charge that left-wingers are alien). Despite its projection of a morality based upon Marxist internationalism, it had inherited the moral problem centering upon the Negro which Myrdal finds in the very tissue of American thinking. And while we disagree with Myrdal's assumption that the psychological barrier between black and white workers is relatively rigid—their co-operation in unions and war plants disproves this—he has done the Left a service in pointing out that there *is* a psychological problem which, in this country, requires special attention.

For in our culture the problem of the irrational, that blind spot in our knowledge of society where Marx cries out for Freud and Freud for Marx, but where approaching, both grow wary and shout insults lest they actually meet, has taken the form of the Negro problem.

In Europe it was the fascists who made the manipulation of myth and symbol a vital part of their political technology. But here at home, as we have shown, it was only the Southern ruling class that showed a similar skill for psychology and ideological manipulation. By contrast, the planning of the Northern ruling groups in relation to the South and the Negro has always presented itself as non-planning and philanthropy on the surface, and as sociological theory underneath. Until the Depression the industrial and social isolationism of the South was felt to offer the broadest possibility for business exploitation. But attempts at national economic recovery proved this idea outdated; Northern capital could no longer turn its head while the Southern ruling group went its regressive way. Hence the New Deal's assault upon the ignorance and backwardness of the Southern "one-third of a nation." There was a vague recognition that the necessity of the economic base of American capitalism had become dislocated from its ideological superstructure. However, the nation, so technologically advanced and scientifically alert, showed itself amazingly backward in creating or borrowing techniques to bring these two aspects of social reality into focus. Not that the nature of the problem was not understood. Writers ranging from Earl Browder, through Max Lerner, to the New Deal Braintrusters had a lot to say about it. And Lerner especially emphasized the technological and psychological nature of the problem, stressed the neutrality of techniques and suggested learning even from the Nazi, if necessary. But for the most part, both New Deal and the official Left concentrated more upon the economic aspects of the problem—important though they were—rather than upon those points where economic and psychological pressures conflicted.

There is a certain ironic fittingness about the fact that these volumes, prepared with the streamlined thoroughness of a *Fortune* Magazine survey, and offering the most detailed documentation of the American Negro's humanity yet to appear, should come sponsored by a leading capitalist group. I say this grudgingly, for here the profit motive of the Right—clothed it is true in the guilt-dress of philanthropy—has proven more resourceful, imaginative and aware of its own best interests than the overcautious socialism of the Left. Not that we expect the Left to have resource to the funds—some $300,000—that went into the preparation of this elaborate study. But that it has failed even to *state* the problem in such broadly human terms, or with that cultural sophistication and social insight springing from Marxist theory, which, backed by passion and courage, has allowed the Left in other countries to deal more creatively with reality than the Right, and to overcome the Right's advantages of institutionalized power and erudition.

The reviewers have made much of Dr. Myrdal's being a foreigner, imported to do the study as one who had no emotional stake in the American Dilemma. And while this had undoubtedly aided his objectivity, the extent of it is apt to be overplayed.

The whole setting is dramatic. A young scholar-scientist of international reputation, a banker, economic adviser to the Swedish Government and a member of the Swedish Senate, is invited by one of the wealthiest groups in the United States to come in and publicly air its soiled democratic linen. Bearing this set of circumstances in mind while we consider the writing problem faced by Myrdal, we can see how the various social and economic factors which we have discussed come to bear upon his book.

First, Myrdal had to delve into those areas of the American mind most charged with emotion; he had to question his hosts' motivation and present his findings in such a way that his hosts would not be too offended. He had also to tell the South some unpleasant things about itself; he had to present facts unacceptable to certain reactionary sections of the capitalist class; and, in the words of Mr. Keppel, he had, "since the emotional factor affects Negroes no less than whites," to present his material in such a manner as not to "lessen the confidence of the Negroes in the United States."

And when we consider the great ideological struggle raging since the Depression, between the Left and the Right, we see an even further problem for the author: a problem of style—which fades over into a problem of interpretation. It also points to the real motivation for the work: An American Dilemma *is the blueprint for a more effective exploitation of the South's natural, industrial and human resources.* We use the term "exploitation" in both the positive and negative sense. In the positive sense it is the key to a more democratic and fruitful usage of the South's natural and human resources; and in the negative, it is the plan for a more

efficient and subtle manipulation of black and white relations—especially in the South.

In interpreting the results of this five-year study, Myrdal
found it confirming many of the social and economic assumptions of the Left, and throughout the book he has felt it
necessary to carry on a running battle with Marxism. Especially irritating to him has been the concept of class struggle
and the economic motivation of anti-Negro prejudice which
to an increasing number of Negro intellectuals correctly
analyzes their situation:

> As we look upon the problem of dynamic social causation,
> this approach is unrealistic and narrow. We do not, of
> course, deny that the conditions under which Negroes are
> allowed to earn a living are tremendously important for
> their welfare. But these conditions are closely interrelated
> to all other conditions of Negro life. When studying the
> variegated causes of discrimination in the labor market, it
> is, indeed, difficult to perceive what precisely is meant by
> "the economic factor. . . ." In an interdependent system of
> dynamic causation there is no "primary cause" but every-
> thing is cause *to* everything else."

To which one might answer "only if you throw out the class
struggle." All this, of course, avoids the question of power
and the question of who manipulates that power. Which to
us seems more of a stylistic maneuver than a scientific judgment.

For those concepts Myrdal substitutes what he terms a
"cumulative principle" or "vicious circle." And like Ezekiel's
wheels in the Negro spiritual, one of which ran "by faith"
and the other "by the grace of God," this vicious circle has no
earthly prime mover. It "just turns."

L. D. Reddick has pointed out that Myrdal tends to use
history simply as background and not as a functioning force
in current society. And we see this as one with Myrdal's refusal to locate the American *ethos* in terms of its material

manifestations, or to point out how it is manipulated—although he makes it the basis of his stylistic appeal. It is unlikely in this mechanist-minded culture that such a powerful force would go "unused."

Myrdal's stylistic method is admirable. In presenting his findings he uses the American *ethos* brilliantly to disarm all American social groupings, by appealing to their stake in the American Creed, and to locate the psychological barriers between them. But he also uses it to deny the existence of an American class struggle, and with facile economy it allows him to avoid admitting that actually there exist *two* American moralities, kept in balance by social science.

The limitations of Myrdal's vision of American democracy do not lie vague and misty beyond the horizon of history. They can be easily discerned through the Negro perspective.

Myrdal's study of the Negro is, in comparison with others, microscopic. Here, to name only a few aspects, we find analyses of Negro institutions, class groupings, family organization, economic problems, race theories and prejudices, the Negro press, church and leadership. Some of the insights are brilliant, especially those through which he demonstrated how many Negro personality traits, said to be "innate," are socially conditioned—even to types of Negro laughter and vocal intonation. But with all this he can only conclude that "the Negro's entire life and, consequently, also his opinions on the Negro problem are, in the main, to be considered as secondary reactions to more primary pressures from the side of the dominant white majority."

But can a people (its faith in an idealized American Creed notwithstanding) live and develop for over three hundred years simply by *reacting*? Are American Negroes simply the creation of white men, or have they at least helped to create themselves out of what they found around them? Men have made a way of life in caves and upon cliffs, why cannot Negroes have made a life upon the horns of the white man's dilemma?

Myrdal sees Negro culture and personality simply as the product of a "social pathology." Thus he assumes that "it is to the advantage of American Negroes as individuals and as a group to become assimilated into American culture, to acquire the traits held in esteem by the dominant white Americans." This, he admits, contains the value premise that *"here in America,* American culture is 'highest' in the pragmatic sense. . . ." Which aside from implying that Negro culture is not also American, assumes that Negroes should desire nothing better than what whites consider highest. But in the "pragmatic sense" lynching and Hollywood, fadism and radio advertising are products of the "higher" culture, and the Negro might ask, "Why, if my culture is pathological, must I exchange it for these?"

It does not occur to Myrdal that many of the Negro cultural manifestations which he considers merely reflective might also embody a *rejection* of what he considers "higher values." There is a dualism at work here. It is only partially true that Negroes turn away from white patterns because they are refused participation. There is nothing like distance to create objectivity, and exclusion gives rise to counter values. Men, as Dostoievsky observed, cannot live in revolt. Nor can they live in a state of "reacting." It will take a deeper science than Myrdal's—deep as that might be—to analyze what is happening among the masses of Negroes. Much of it is inarticulate, and Negro scholars have, for the most part, ignored it through clinging, as does Myrdal, to the sterile concept of "race."

Much of Negro culture might be negative, but there is also much of great value, of richness, which, because it has been secreted by living and has made their lives more meaningful, Negroes will not willingly disregard.

What is needed in our country is not an exchange of pathologies, but a change of the basis of society. This is a job which both Negroes and whites must perform together. In Negro culture there is much of value for America as a whole. What is needed are Negroes to take it and create of it "the uncreated consciousness of their race." In doing so they will do far more, they'll help create a more human American.

Certainly it would be unfair to expect Dr. Myrdal to see what Negro scholars and most American social scientists have failed to see. After all, like most of its predecessors *An American Dilemma* has a special social role. And while we do not quarrel with it on these grounds necessarily, let us see it clearly for what it is. Its positive contribution is certainly greater at this time than those negative elements— hence its uncritical reception. The time element is important. For this period of democratic resurgence created by the war, *An American Dilemma* justifies the desire of many groups to see a more democratic approach to the Negro. The military phase of the war will not, however, last forever. It is then that this study might be used for less democratic purposes. Fortunately its facts are to an extent neutral. This is a cue for liberal intellectuals to get busy to see that *An American Dilemma* does not become an instrument of an American tragedy.

—Unpublished. Written in 1944 for *The Antioch Review*.

RALPH ELLISON is an Oklahoman who was trained as a musician at Tuskegee Institute from 1933 to 1936, at which time a visit to New York and a meeting with Richard Wright led to his first attempts at fiction. Since 1939 his reviews, short stories, articles and criticism have appeared in national magazines and anthologies. He is the winner of a Rosenwald Fellowship and, following the publication of his first novel, *Invisible Man*, the National Book Award and the Russwurm Award. From 1955 to 1957 he was a fellow of the American Academy in Rome. After he returned from Europe he taught at Bard College and in the fall of 1961 served as an Alexander White Visiting Professor at the University of Chicago. He was in 1962–1964 Visiting Professor of Writing at Rutgers University. During 1964 he delivered the Gertrude Clark Whittall Lecture at the Library of Congress and the Ewing Lectures at the University of California. He was appointed to the American Institute of Arts and Letters in 1964. He was a charter member of the National Council on the Arts and Humanities and is a trustee of the John F. Kennedy Center for the Performing Arts, The New School for Social Research, Bennington College, the Educational Broadcasting Corporation, and the Museum of the City of New York.

Since 1970, Mr. Ellison has been Albert Schweitzer Professor in the Humanities at New York University.

VINTAGE CRITICISM,
LITERATURE, MUSIC, AND ART

VINTAGE POLITICAL SCIENCE
AND SOCIAL CRITICISM

VINTAGE HISTORY—AMERICAN